D1479475

PROPERTY
AND
LANDSCAPE

PROPERTY AND LANDSCAPE

A Social History of Land Ownership and the English Countryside

---

TOM WILLIAMSON
AND LIZ BELLAMY

George Philip

British Library Cataloguing in Publication Data

Williamson, Tom, *1955–*
Property and landscape: a social history of land ownership and the English countryside.
1. Landscape—England—History 2. Land tenure—England—History
719'.0942GF551
I. Title II. Bellamy, Liz
ISBN 0-540-01125-8

First published by George Philip, 27A Floral Street, London WC2E 9DP

Printed in Great Britain by
Butler & Tanner Ltd, Frome and London

TITLE-PAGE ILLUSTRATION **Stowe, Buckinghamshire**

Acknowledgements

Many thanks to Michael Aston, Steve Daniels, Richard Muir and Christopher Taylor for reading and commenting on an early draft of this book. Thanks also to friends and colleagues in Cambridge, Norwich and elsewhere for help, advice and inspiration, and in particular to: John Barrell, Steve Bassett, Alan Carter, David Dymond, Andrew Fleming, Stephen Heath, Oliver Rackham, Norman Scarfe, A. Hassell Smith, Keith Snell, Peter Warner and Richard Wilson.

We are grateful to John Harris, Brian Horne, Richard Muir and Ben Taylor for supplying photographs, to Helen John for her editorial assistance, and last but not least to Lydia Greeves for her thoughtful if sometimes provocative editing.

Illustration Acknowledgements

The Animal and Grassland Research Institute pages 210–11; *BBC Hulton Picture Library* page 101; *The Bodleian Library, Oxford* page 44 (Ms.C17:49 (257)); *Janet and Colin Bord* page 194 (left); *The British Library* pages 33, 142; *Cambridge University Collection of Air Photographs* pages 24–5, 34–5, 38, 39, 46–7, 92, 118; *Richard Harris* page 117; *Brian Horne* pages 7, 9, 14, 15, 27, 81, 84, 85, 104, 126, 134–5, 137, 141, 148–9 (above), 152–3, 167, 168, 171 (below), 173, 177, 184, 194–5 (right), 207, 218, 226–7; *A. F. Kersting* title page, pages 133, 146; *Richard Muir* pages 11, 12, 48–9, 55, 56, 57, 58, 62–3, 64, 67, 82, 89, 95, 97, 106–7, 109, 113, 129, 140, 156, 171 (above), 178, 189, 190, 214–15, 216–17; *The National Gallery* page 147; *Royal Commission on the Historical Monuments of England* pages 52–3, 69 (below), 160–1, 182; *Sheffield City Libraries* page 155; *Edwin Smith* page 183; *Ben Taylor* pages 69 (above), 77, 120, 165, 187, 199; *The University of Reading Institute of Agricultural History and Museum of English Rural Life* pages 98–9, 222–3.

The authors are also grateful to the Journal of Historical Geography for permission to reproduce the maps on pages 18 and 19.

Contents

Introduction

'GOD MADE THE COUNTRY, and man made the town,' wrote William Cowper in 1783, in his lengthy poem *The Task*, and the sentiment has been echoed by many subsequent writers.[1] People have always liked to see the countryside as natural, and as a pleasing contrast to the corruption of urban society. Yet there is a certain irony in the circumstances surrounding Cowper's composition of this line. *The Task* was written between 1783 and 1784, when Cowper was living in the village of Olney in north Buckinghamshire. Around this time, the rural Midlands was being radically changed by parliamentary enclosure. In hundreds of parishes, including Olney itself, the ancient pattern of vast, unhedged open fields was being replaced by a network of straight hedges, straight roads and rectangular fields.[2]

As Cowper would have been well aware, this change, like the process which created open fields almost a thousand years before, had nothing to do with God. It was a consequence of changes in human society, the economic structure and patterns of landholding. Man has made the country as well as the town, and the rural environment, with its local and regional variations, has been shaped by all the different communities that have lived within it.

As people went about their business, providing themselves with food and shelter, they inevitably left an impression on their surroundings. But the nature of this impression was determined by more complex factors than the simple need to satisfy material requirements. The way in which wealth was distributed in society, the relationship between the various classes, and the changing demands of the national economy all influenced the appearance of the countryside. The present landscape is the product of the activities of innumerable different communities over thousands of years. Its varied fabric and features pose a host of questions about the nature of societies of the past.

The grassy parklands around Wimpole Hall in Cambridgeshire, for example, are covered in low, wave-like earthworks, created by the ploughs of medieval farmers. This corrugated sward is not only a reminder of the agricultural methods of the past, but gives us clues to the

ABOVE RIGHT **Wimpole Hall, Cambridgeshire**
The parkland surrounding the hall was landscaped by Lancelot 'Capability' Brown in the eighteenth century. The low ridges in the grass show that this was once arable land.

BELOW RIGHT **St Andrew's Church, Wimpole, Cambridgeshire**
When the owners of Wimpole Hall extended their park, they removed the old village of Wimpole. This was eventually replaced by New Wimpole, several miles away. But the parish church was left isolated in the park, beside the hall, and in 1748 it was largely demolished and rebuilt in order to give it a more fashionable appearance.

lives of the villagers who worked the land. Each of these long thin ridges belonged to an individual farmer, and the massed ranks of these earthworks reveal how extensively the strips of all the villagers were intermingled. Why was there this seemingly inconvenient disposition of holdings? How was the open-field system of agriculture organized, and why was this system practised in Wimpole, but not in the region of broadly similar soils less than 20 miles to the south?

Next to the house, in the midst of the park, stands Wimpole parish church, but there are no other obvious signs of a village to house the people who once worked in the open fields. Where did they go, the farmers who furrowed the land, and why were their arable strips turned into a pleasure ground for the élite? What inspired the informal style of parkland, with its wide, grassy vistas dotted with clumps of trees?

Some of the questions posed by landscapes such as these may be answered by the use of written sources. In particular, it is often possible to use documents to discover something about the lives of the landed rich — about people such as the Yorkes and Hardwickes, whose great seventeenth- and eighteenth-century tombs crowd Wimpole church, or about their medieval predecessors, the Uffords, whose dynastic connections are proudly displayed on the windows of the north chapel. We can read books and poems that were written by the landed classes. We can look through their deeds and accounts. We can even learn something about those of a less elevated status in life, through studying documents such as manorial court rolls or poor law records. But in all these different written sources there is always much that is left out, and there is much that orthodox history cannot tell us about the relationship between rural communities and the land.

The North Chapel, St Andrew's Church, Wimpole, Cambridgeshire
The medieval stained glass displays the dynastic connections of the Ufford family, for many years the owners of Wimpole Hall. The body of the church is crowded with the tombs of the subsequent owners, the Chicheleys and the Yorkes.

This book will try to fill in some of the gaps in the historical record, by reading the social

document that lies in the landscape. In the changing pattern of fields and settlements, the changing styles of parks and gardens, and in the changing architecture and organization of great houses, cottages and farmhouses, we can learn much that cannot be discerned from other sources. For the way in which communities arranged their environment often reflected the unconscious assumptions and beliefs that underlay their social organization. The fabric of the landscape gives a particular insight into the communities that have lived and worked within it, and above all it embodies a history of power in the land.

ONE

An Old Country

GENERATIONS OF CHILDREN in English schools have been taught about the open-field system of medieval England — about how people lived in villages surrounded by common fields, and worked their lands under communal controls in a system of rotation. But this simplified picture ignores the very varied nature of the medieval landscape. It is easy to forget that the nucleated village, with houses grouped in a compact settlement, was not found all over England, and that the open-field system was used in different ways in different parts of the country. The landscape of the early Middle Ages varied strikingly from region to region, and this basic regional pattern had a profound effect on the subsequent development of the countryside.

The medieval landscape can be very loosely classified into 'upland', 'woodland' and 'champion' countryside. Such a tripartite division suppresses the multiplicity of local and regional differences in our infinitely varied environment, but it embodies fundamental contrasts that existed in the medieval period. The upland landscapes are the most easily defined and probably the least contentious of these three categories. In areas like the Pennines the soils, topography and climate ensured that only a small proportion of the land was suitable for arable cultivation. As a result population levels tended to be low, settlement was scattered, and various forms of pastoral activity were of considerable importance. There were also areas of arable, but these were markedly dissimilar to the great open fields which characterized the Midland plain. They were small, and although they were divided into strips, these were held by only a limited number of farmers. These arable fields were surrounded by extensive areas of rough, moorland grazing, usually grazed in common by the beasts of many farmers.

Elsewhere in England, however, the regional variations cannot be explained on the basis of topography or geology. We are using the terms 'woodland' and 'champion' to describe the two main variants, although in a way these are rather controversial labels. They were first used only in the sixteenth century, and therefore described landscapes rather different from those of the early Middle Ages. Yet the contrast between the areas that were to be woodland in the sixteenth century and those that were to carry champion landscapes was already evident at the time of Domesday. It may have been less clear than it was to become, and may have been manifested in rather different ways, but it was there all the same.

Champion regions were those in which agriculture was organized in the classic open-field system. The settlement pattern was one of nucleated villages, and the arable land was held in numerous small strips. These strips, usually less than an acre in size, were grouped together in bundles known as shotts or furlongs. Furlongs were similarly arranged in two, three or four huge fields, and, as neither strips nor furlongs were hedged, the resultant landscape tended to be rather bleak and featureless. Villages were often isolated amidst vast, open plains of agricultural land.

Each farmer's strips were scattered across the fields of a village, so that he had to abide by the communal pattern of rotation. All the land within a furlong would be planted with the same crop, and every year one of the huge fields would lie fallow and provide grazing for all the village animals. This system was only workable because the strips were so extensively intermingled, thus ensuring that each farmer always had some fallow land and some land under crops.

The strips within the open fields normally had a slightly sinuous profile, often taking the form of a reversed 'S'. This was a result of the unwieldiness of the medieval ploughing tackle, since the ploughman had to approach the end of a strip at a slight angle in order to be able to turn his team. In many parts of the country it is still possible to trace this characteristic curve, for where the open fields were put down to grass on enclosure, and have not subsequently been ploughed up, the outlines of the strips have been preserved as the earthworks now known as

Thornthwaite, near Harrogate, North Yorkshire
This landscape is typical of the upland areas of England, with farmsteads of many different ages and origins scattered across the countryside.

Wadenhoe, Northamptonshire
These wave-like earthworks, known as 'ridge and furrow', represent the old ploughlands of an open field. Formerly to be seen all over the Midlands, they nowadays survive only in areas which have been under grass since this form of ploughing was abandoned.

'ridge and furrow'. These often consist of quite substantial banks, which were deliberately built up to by open-field farmers, primarily to facilitate drainage. In parts of the Midlands field after field is still rippled with snaking ridges.

As well as establishing the systems of rotation, the medieval village communities enforced the regulations controlling the exploitation of common grazing. This 'waste' was a vital component of the open-field agricultural system. The beasts it supported provided milk, wool and meat, the manure to put on arable crops, and the motive power to pull the ploughs. Village communities also managed meadow lands which were cropped for hay. Located in the dampest land, these water meadows were of great importance to a village economy because hay was essential for keeping animals alive through the winter when the grass did not grow. The open-field community therefore operated an integrated system of mixed farming, but its primary purpose was to maximize the production of arable crops. The majority of land in any open-field village was given over to arable, and the pasture was used to feed the animals essential to this system of cultivation.[1]

Many parts of lowland England carried a champion landscape in the medieval period and practised some variation on this basic pattern of open-field agriculture. But there were many areas which did not. In the sixteenth century these became known as 'woodland' landscapes and were strikingly different from those of the champion regions. Woodland landscapes were only partly farmed with communal open fields and communal wastes, and did not have the bare, open plains of the champion areas. Rather, they were characterized by small hedged fields. Although the woodland regions were often more densely wooded than the champion, it was the hedges which gave them their generally 'woody' appearance and their name.

In the sixteenth century there were still some

open fields in many woodland areas, but these were fast disappearing to be replaced by small hedged fields. Furthermore, woodland open fields were markedly different from those found in champion country at that time. Whereas champion villages had only a few very large open fields, the woodland parishes tended to have numerous small ones. These made up what historians have called an 'irregular open-field system', similar to that found in the uplands, with small open fields containing the strips of a handful of farmers.

Woodland farmers tended to work land which, whether in common fields or closes, was not sited very far from their farmsteads. This was only possible because the pattern of settlement was more dispersed in the woodland than the champion regions. Villages were rather strung out, and there were usually large numbers of subsidiary settlements, small hamlets and isolated farms. As the sixteenth-century writer William Harrison noted:

> It is so, that our soile being divided into champaine ground and woodland, the houses of the first lie uniformelie builded in everie town togither, with streets and lanes; whereas in the woodland countries . . . they stand scattered abroad, each one dwelling in the midst of his owne occupieng.[2]

Even in the medieval period, woodland areas were noticeably different from champion regions. Woodland settlement patterns were more dispersed, and the arrangement of fields revealed that agriculture could not have been organized on a thoroughly communal basis. In some areas the arable land was largely in irregular open fields, but in others it appears even in the early Middle Ages to have been largely in individually worked closes. In all these woodland landscapes, however, the landholding units were relatively discrete.

This ensured that from the early Middle Ages woodland landscapes evolved in very different ways from those of the champion, so that even today there are marked contrasts between the two. Champion regions are still characterized by nucleated villages, with the houses closely clustering around the church or village green. In contrast, the settlement pattern of woodland regions still contains many isolated houses, and hamlets scattered amidst the fields.

Communal systems of agriculture within the champion regions were so strong that these areas were not enclosed for a long time. While the open fields of woodland areas were being formed into hedged closes from the medieval period onwards, it was not until the seventeenth and eighteenth centuries that enclosure took place in the majority of champion lands. Thus the woodland landscape of the present is evidently the product of a long and gradual process of enclosure. In contrast, the champion landscape has usually been redrawn in the relatively recent past.

In the woodland regions there are many old hedges, which generally contain a rich variety of species including maple, hazel, dogwood, wayfaring tree, spindle, oak, ash and elm. The more recent hedges of the champion regions are far less species-rich, and often primarily consist of the hawthorn with which they were first set. The old hedges of the woodland regions are sinuous and there is an ancient feel to the oddly shaped fields and to the network of winding roads and lanes. In contrast, the field patterns of many former champion lands are evidently modern. They are characterized by straight roads and rectilinear boundaries drawn up when they were enclosed. As a result, they are sometimes referred to as areas of 'planned countryside', in contrast to the 'ancient countryside' of woodland regions.[3]

In many parts of the country these different landscapes intersect, demonstrating the contrasting nature and appearance of the two. This can be appreciated, for example, on an afternoon's drive along the minor roads and byways of Essex and Cambridgeshire, in the area between Harlow and Cambridge. Setting out from Harlow you will come across a network of small winding lanes, many of which,

despite the depredations of modern agriculture, are still bounded by thick hedges rich in species. Innumerable road junctions crop up along these lanes marked by signposts to small hamlets such as Levels Green, Mallows Green, Maggot End and Pond Street, and you will often come across the hamlets themselves, the houses grouped around a road junction or a small green. Here and there are isolated farmsteads, their buildings often ancient and sometimes moated. Their distant origins may be indicated in strange and archaic names, like Curtles Manor, Butlers Hill and Rumballs Farm. Villages occur every now and again in this landscape, but they tend to be amorphous and loosely strung out along the roads and lanes.

Contrasting landscapes
Two lanes, at Elmdon in Essex (LEFT) and Ickleton in Cambridgeshire (BELOW), provide a striking illustration of the present differences between woodland and former champion areas. One is ancient and sinuous, bounded by high hedge banks; the other runs dead straight for as far as the eye can see. Yet these two lanes are only three miles apart.

As you go north, however, the landscape undergoes a change that is often quite dramatic. Beyond the villages of Chrishall, Elmdon and Great Chesterford, the roads become straighter and fewer and the fields are bounded only by spindly hedges. Settlements are no longer spread through the landscape, but take the form of large villages, such as Ickleton, Hinxton and Thriplow. Here the houses are closely clustered together, but between these settlements the landscape is virtually empty, the only sign of human habitation being the occasional farmhouse dating from the eighteenth or nineteenth century.

Although such contrasts can be discerned in many parts of the country, where woodland and champion landscapes lie cheek by jowl, it is not with such local patterns of landscape that this book is primarily concerned. Our preoccupation will not be with the minutiae of the distribution of woodland and champion, but with the basic patterns into which these landscapes fall, and with the way in which they dominate certain regions.

Woodland or ancient landscapes predominate in the west of England, in Herefordshire, Shropshire, Cheshire and Devon, and in

parts of neighbouring counties, but they also characterize the south and east — Surrey, Sussex, Kent, Hertfordshire, Essex, the borders of London, much of Hampshire and Berkshire, the Chiltern areas of Oxfordshire and Buckinghamshire and much of East Anglia. This is a distribution which has no correspondence with any aspect of the natural environment. It seems to have no direct relationship with rainfall, soils, drainage or topography. So what underlies the difference between woodland and champion, and what explains their curious distribution?

These are very teasing questions, and ones to which no convincing answers have so far been proposed. Some historians suggest that woodland landscapes occur in areas which were extensively cleared and settled in the late Saxon period, several centuries after those which carried a champion landscape. But while some woodland areas were certainly settled late, there seems no reason to believe that this was generally the case. On the contrary, it is becoming increasingly clear that woodland and champion areas alike were extensively cleared and settled at a very much earlier period than this theory would suggest, and new evidence indicates that most of the English landscape was being farmed by the end of the Iron Age.

Much new evidence has been produced by the laborious technique of fieldwalking. This involves the careful and systematic examination of ploughsoil for the scatters of pottery and sometimes rubble which mark the sites of early settlements. Since the 1960s such research has tended to suggest that Roman settlements were far from limited to the light and easily-worked soils where they were formerly believed to have been concentrated. Romano-British hamlets and farmsteads have been found right across the country, even on the heaviest and most inhospitable clay soils.[4] A few gaps have been discovered, but these probably represent areas of woodland and grazing exploited by large numbers of farmers. Extravagant claims have

The distribution of woodland and champion countrysides in medieval England
The distribution was extremely complex and most regions contained a mixture of landscapes. Moreover, some areas—such as parts of Norfolk—displayed features characteristic of both types of countryside. The map represents the basic regional distribution, and suppresses the multiplicity of minor local variations in the landscape of medieval England.

recently been made for the size of the Romano-British population. Although we would not suggest that it was as high as the six million which has been proposed, it seems likely that at least three million people were inhabiting and exploiting the Roman province of Britannia.

The Roman landscape was as densely settled, as intensively farmed and probably less wooded than that of early medieval England. Moreover, late prehistoric and Roman communities were able to bring about considerable alterations in the appearance of the landscape. They not only created huge defensive structures, such as Maiden Castle in Dorset, but, from at least the Bronze Age, they also organized large tracts of the country into systems of planned fields. It is still possible to detect traces of these early field systems in marginal areas of the country, where earthworks and sometimes dilapidated walls still survive, and they are sometimes revealed by aerial photography in lowland regions. Some of these systems are really huge, with fields laid out through the subdivision of vast parallel axes. On Dartmoor, for example, some field systems cover an area of at least 7000 acres, suggesting that the landscape had been shaped long before the arrival of the Saxons and used in ways that are not explicable in purely economic terms.

In the post-Roman period the population of England seems to have dropped considerably, leading to some settlement desertion and woodland regeneration, especially on the heavier clays. There is, however, no evidence that vast areas of the country reverted to untamed forest, or that these changes affected what were to be woodland areas any more than what were to be the champion regions. Recent research in the woodland region of northwest Essex has shown that the dispersed pattern of Romano-British settlement was largely maintained into the Middle Ages, with desertion and recolonization occurring only on the heaviest soils. Indeed, much of the ancient settlement pattern has survived to the present day. Many of the hamlets and isolated farmsteads that characterize the modern commuter landscape around Saffron Walden stand on or close to the sites of their Roman, or even Iron Age, predecessors.[5]

Over the past few years some archaeologists have identified substantial areas of the present woodland landscape which appear to have been largely laid out in the Roman or pre-Roman period. This conclusion is derived from the technique of 'topographic analysis', a method which involves the examination of the overall organization of the landscape. It attempts to identify the earliest surviving features in any area by determining the relative ages of routes and field boundaries.

When a modern motorway is carved through the countryside its designers pay scant attention to the previous layout of the landscape. It cuts through field boundaries and minor trackways at any and every angle, and irregularly shaped pieces of land are frequently produced. Many of the smaller and more ridiculously impractical fields are gradually removed as farmers rationalize their field boundaries, but even so the pattern of the landscape indicates the relatively recent origins of the road.

The discovery that the M25 has very modern origins is not, of course, of earth-shattering significance, but what is really exciting is that in certain woodland areas Roman roads seem to behave much like the motorways.[6] They reveal a charlatan disregard for the field boundaries and minor roads which are depicted on the earliest available maps, cutting through them at odd angles in just the same way as twentieth-century motorways cut through eighteenth-century fields. This suggests that field patterns in such areas must have been established before the construction of the Roman road. Indeed, studies in Kent, Essex, Suffolk and Norfolk suggest that not only the basic framework but much of the fine detail of these landscapes is Roman or even Iron Age. At Yaxley in Suffolk, for example, the relationship between the Roman Pye Road and the system of fields through which it runs leaves little doubt that the road was constructed *after* the fields had been set out.

Some Roman roads run through fields which do not merely lie at random, but are arranged into patterns which indicate that they must at some stage have been carefully planned and painstakingly laid out. Many of these field systems are very extensive, and much larger than those which have survived as earthworks on moorland and downland. In some areas, such as that around Dickleburgh in south Norfolk, remnants of the field system can still be discerned on modern maps. By ignoring all the features that are medieval or modern, an extensive grid of fields is revealed, based on subdivisions of a series of long parallel axes similar to those identified on Dartmoor.

Elsewhere there are similar field systems which appear to be Roman because their axes run parallel to roads of Roman date. One example is the field system that lies in the area between Bungay and Halesworth in north Suffolk. It is located on heavy, poorly drained soils, and consists of a vast system of parallel lanes and field boundaries extending over more than 6000 acres. Such landscapes serve to

Yaxley, Suffolk
The Tithe Award Map of 1839 shows the course of the Roman Pye Road in the south of the parish. It is clear from the disposition of the boundaries that some of these fields were laid out *before* the road, and must therefore be of early Roman or prehistoric date. In many woodland areas the pattern of boundaries and roads is very old indeed.

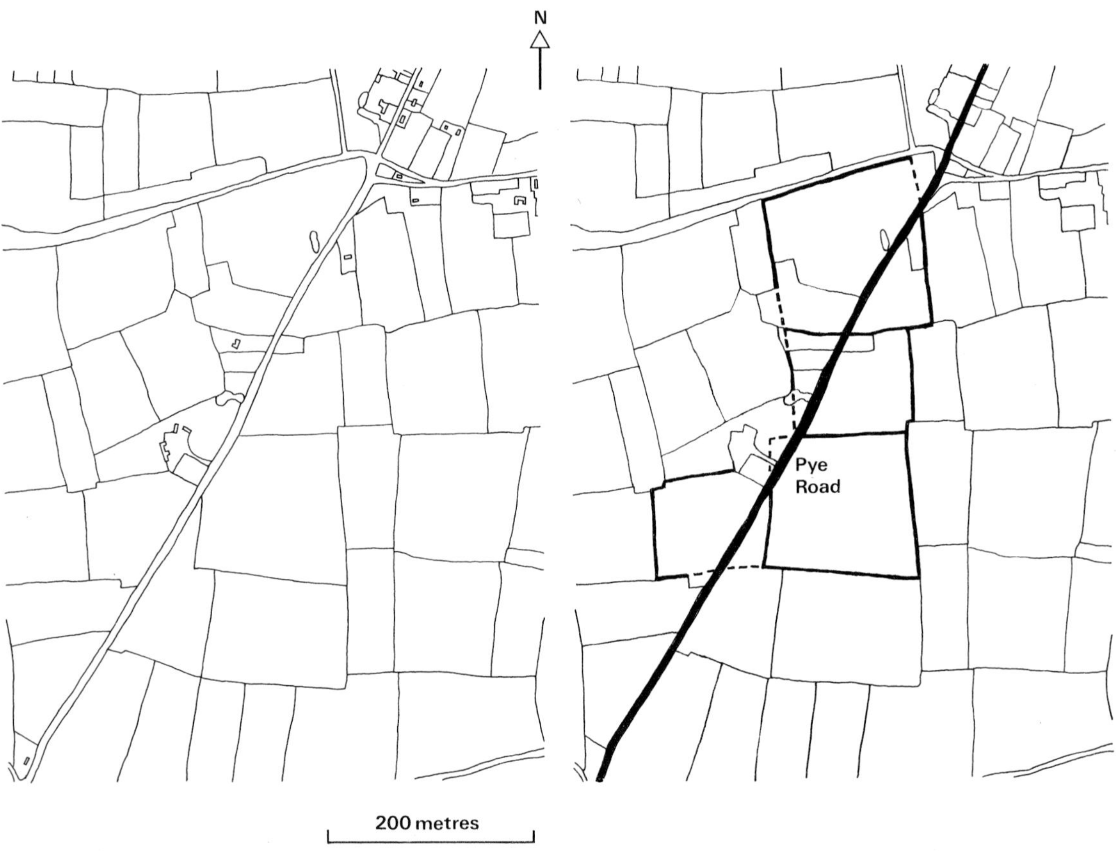

An Iron Age field system in south Norfolk
Not all the fields in woodland regions were created through the gradual expansion of cultivation. In some areas there are traces of vast planned landscapes of prehistoric date. In the area between Tivetshall St Mary and Scole in south Norfolk the Roman Pye Road cuts through a landscape of sinuous, roughly parallel lanes and boundaries, probably of Iron Age date. This landscape is revealed when medieval and later features are removed from the earliest available maps of the area.

confirm that England was well-populated and thoroughly exploited in the Iron Age and Roman periods, but their survival also indicates that there was no substantial regeneration of woodland in the post-Roman centuries. Although most of these early landscapes contain gaps, suggesting that some areas subsequently went out of cultivation, it is clear that woodland regeneration cannot have occurred to any marked extent. Had it done so, the pattern of field boundaries would very soon have been lost.

Far from being the products of late clearance, many woodland landscapes appear to be the result of a gradual process of evolution. They have developed from a Roman landscape and pattern of settlement. Champion landscapes, in contrast, seem to have had a more chequered history. These areas carried a dispersed settlement pattern like that of the woodland at the end of the Roman period. At some point after this they must have undergone a process of settlement nucleation, when the cultivated land was reorganized into a system of large open fields. But when did this dramatic change occur?

A number of archaeologists, including Colin Hayfield, Glen Foard and David Hall, have carried out fieldwalking surveys which have thrown considerable light on this problem.[7] Their studies in various champion areas have shown that the earliest Saxon sites perpetuated the dispersed pattern of settlement of Roman and earlier periods, particularly on lighter soils. Nucleated villages, which characterize champion regions, were not introduced at the time of Saxon settlement but developed some time afterwards, and it seems their evolution took place in different ways at different times in different areas. In some places they may have developed as early as the ninth century, but did not emerge until the eleventh century in others. In some regions villages resulted from the gradual fusion of neighbouring hamlets, so that they had a rather ragged, irregular form, based around a number of centres. Elsewhere, nucleated villages grew out of the expansion of individual hamlets, accompanied by the desertion of outlying settlements.

In many places these changes coincided with a rather dramatic alteration in the appearance of the land, for the landholding structure of many champion areas seems to have undergone a total reorganization in the late Saxon period. Village land was laid out in open fields of a very peculiar form. The strips and furlongs were not like those of the ordinary open-field village but were incredibly long, sometimes as much as a mile in length, and they often ran all the way from the settlement to the edge of arable lands.[8]

Later in the medieval period, most of these long furlongs were subdivided to form more orthodox furlongs. In a few places, however, such as parts of Holderness and the Yorkshire Wolds, such subdivision never came about. Long furlongs were still being used in the eighteenth and nineteenth centuries, when these areas came to be enclosed.[9]

Elsewhere, the open-field landscape seems to have developed gradually. In some areas, for example, the boundaries of furlongs appear to overlie the ditches of earlier fields. At Duxford in Cambridgeshire, a 'headland' (a low ridge that had lain between two open-field furlongs) was found to have grown up on top of a ditch which contained sherds of Romano-British pottery. Such evidence suggests that in some areas the open fields may in part have come into existence as a result of the fragmentation of a much more ancient pattern of fields.

From the ninth century champion regions thus began to lose the dispersed settlement pattern which they had had for centuries, and nucleated villages surrounded by open fields began to develop. In woodland areas the history of the landscape was rather different. While villages became more common in the course of the Saxon period, the settlement pattern remained basically dispersed. Instead of developing a system of extensively intermingled holdings, each farmer continued to occupy a relatively discrete holding.

Although historians can discover the various processes by which the landscape was re-organized in the champion regions, it is difficult to determine why these changes came about. This question has been hotly debated in historical circles and numerous theories have so far been proposed. One of the most interesting and plausible relates the development of the open-field system to changes that were taking place in the population of Saxon England, and in the organization of estates.[10]

By the end of the Saxon period, England was divided up into tenurial units called manors. These were local estates under the control of a lord, who had the rights to certain labour dues and rents from the peasantry who lived on the estate land, and who were, in varying degrees, subject to his authority. In the early Saxon period, however, while there may have been some parts of the country where this tenurial system existed, the majority of land in England was held by farmers who owed their duties directly to one of the tribal kings. Many of these farmers were probably of freer status than the villeins, cottars and bordars of Norman England, and the land on which they lived was organized into large territories which are sometimes called 'multiple estates' by modern scholars.[11] These may have been prehistoric in origin, and their continuity into the early medieval period may indicate the survival of an essentially tribal society beneath the veneer of Roman civilization. The communities of farmers which such estates contained not only had to provide goods for their own subsistence needs, but were also obliged to produce a particular surplus commodity which could be sent to the estate centre. In addition, such farmers had to carry out certain customary duties, such as repairing the buildings at the centre of the estate.

It may have been the agricultural specialization fostered by multiple estates which has led to many of the place-names which are common today. Shepton, for example, was the *tun* or settlement which specialized in the rearing of sheep; Chiswick was the cheese farm, and Barton was the settlement where barley was grown. Other place-names appear to suggest that at some time in the past the settlements to which they refer were not seen as independent entities but as parts of a larger whole. The many Ea(s)tons, Westons, Nortons and Suttons in the landscape seem to have been regarded as lying east, west, north and south of places of greater importance. These places may have been the administrative headquarters of very extensive early estates.

Settlements within each of these ancient estates were all subordinate to the estate centre, and they may have co-operated with one another in a number of ways. In particular, they may have combined in the seasonal exploitation of large tracts of common grazing and woodland, which were usually located at a distance from many of the hamlets.

Although ultimately the property of tribal kings, such estates seem to have been often granted for limited periods to members of the tribal nobility, many of whom were members of the king's family. They were administered by a separate class of men, the *thanes*. As time passed, however, and the population rose, the estates began to fragment and went out of the hands of the royal families. This process began after the conversion to Christianity in the seventh century, when the tribal kings had to donate portions of land to the Church. A number of these gifts are recorded in the earliest surviving land charters, and the documents reveal that many of the estates were very extensive. In the late seventh century, for example, Caedwalla, the King of Wessex, granted an estate at Farnham in Surrey for the support of a monastery. This included lands stretching five miles to the south of the estate centre, and four miles to the east, 'with everything belonging to them, fields, woods, meadows, pastures, fisheries, rivers, springs'.

As extensive estates of this kind fragmented during the eighth and ninth centuries, the grants of land described in the charters became increasingly smaller. Also, as the kingdoms of England became larger and more sophisticated, culminating in the unification of England under Alfred, estates, or pieces of them, fell into the hands of laymen. These privately-owned lands were more likely to be split through grants, sale and inheritance than the royal estates, so the size of the average landholding unit continued to decline. Indeed, many parcels of land probably passed into the hands of the thanes who had formerly administered them.

In place of large economic units embracing a multitude of inter-dependent settlements there arose a number of much smaller and self-sufficient estates. Farmers ceased to owe their dues and duties to a relatively distant noble or king. They had their own local lord who was able to oversee their actions, and who collected the surplus produce of their holdings. Meanwhile, the Church required the payment of its tithe, and in the tenth century the Crown introduced a land-tax, known as the geld. The cumulative impact of these burdens was too much for many farmers, who became increasingly dependent on their local lords, and eventually surrendered their freedom. It has therefore been argued that the fission of extensive early Saxon estates was associated with a decline in the status of peasants who had formerly been considered free.

This process of fission, and the growth in population with which it was associated, may well have encouraged the emergence of champion landscapes in many parts of the country. There would inevitably have been considerable disruption to the economic organization of communities in Saxon England, as they became part of small, self-sufficient tenurial units rather than of large territories of interdependent settlements. This may have created a situation in which considerable benefits could be gained from the reorganization of landholding and the creation of a regular open-field system. In particular, the tenurial changes may have accentuated the growing shortage of grazing. As territories were broken up, many communities would have been deprived of areas customarily used for grazing, because in the ancient estates these were often sited at some distance from many of the farmsteads by which they were exploited. The reorganization of the landscape in champion regions may have been partly initiated as a response to this grazing shortage, and a number of historians have created a very convincing model to explain how the expansion of agriculture and the resultant paucity of pasture could have led to the emergence of the open-field system.

The expansion of population in the late Saxon period produced an ever-growing demand for food, and this led many villages to convert their waste into arable fields. As each patch of land was cleared it had to be split between all the farmers who had formerly had rights to the land as waste. The resultant holdings took the form of long thin strips of arable land because these were peculiarly suitable to being ploughed by a heavy plough pulled by a team of oxen. Large areas could be ploughed without having to go to the trouble of turning the oxen round.

Fragmentation of holdings was encouraged by the way that farms were inherited in the Saxon period. When a number of sons took over their father's holding, they did not each take control of a unified block of land. In order to make sure that the division of land was as fair as possible, each son would be given a number of strips distributed throughout the holding. They would thus all have a bit of good and a bit of bad, a bit of distant and a bit of accessible land.

The increase in arable cultivation led to a decline in the amount of land available for grazing, aggravating the loss of pasture which many villages suffered as a result of the fission of the multiple estate. The stubble that was left after the harvest and the weeds growing on the fallows therefore became important sources of grazing for the villagers' livestock. In a system of unhedged and intermingled strips such grazing would clearly have been difficult to organize on any kind of individualistic basis. If the farmers had all planted, reaped and laid their lands fallow in accordance with different cycles, some of the strips would have been used for grazing while others carried standing crops. This would have been disastrous, for it would have been difficult to keep the animals within the bounds of the unfenced lands of their owners, and to prevent them from causing serious damage to the crops in the neighbouring holdings.

The development of a communal system of agriculture, in which everyone planted, harvested, and put their beasts out together in a standard pattern of rotation, may have seemed the only sensible solution to the problem of organizing agriculture within a multitude of strips. Such a communal system of farming must have necessitated a reorganization of landholding, since communal agriculture could only work where the farmers had strips that were evenly scattered over the land of the village. There are, however, various other reasons why such a reorganization may have seemed desirable. In particular, the increasingly heavy exactions imposed on the farming communities as smaller territorial units emerged would have created a considerable incentive for the institution of an egalitarian distribution of land. Whether paid to the Church, the lord, or the Crown, these exactions were based on the size of the landholding units, and not on their quality or profitability. Farmers may therefore have combined to ensure that every landholder had an equal share of productive and unproductive land, so that no-one was peculiarly penalized.

A number of historians have suggested that the reorganization of landholdings could only happen in villages that were under the thumbs of powerful local lords. Such authoritarian figures would have been able to impose the reallocation of land over the heads of dissenting farmers, creating not only open-field agricultural systems but also the associated nucleated villages. The emergence of champion landscapes would therefore have been doubly dependent on the fragmentation of ancient, extensive estates, since their disintegration led both to a shortage of pasture and to the emergence of a multiplicity of strong minor lords.

Adherents of this authoritarian model have cited the 'long furlong' landscapes as evidence. They have suggested that such landscapes could only have been introduced as a result of seignorial planning, imposed on the communities from above. Yet although the creation of champion landscapes may have involved emergent lords, we believe that it is not necessary to presuppose the interference of such powerful figures to explain the reorganization of land and agriculture in many villages. This may equally well have been carried out by the communities — that is, by all the farmers who held and worked the land. There is no reason to believe that these people were inherently incapable of the co-operative endeavour necessary to replan the landscape.

This explanation of the origins of champion landscape does not, of course, explain why settlement nucleation and the evolution of open fields did not take place to any great extent in areas of the south, east and west of England. It is sometimes suggested that in the Saxon period these areas had lower population levels than the regions which were to develop a champion landscape, and so they failed to experience the critical shortage of pasture that encouraged the reorganization of settlements and fields elsewhere. This may have been true of a few places in what were to be the woodland regions, but it cannot be taken as a general explanation of why these areas did not develop in the same way as the champion regions.

The theory is not supported, for example, by any of the information that we have about levels of population in early medieval England. Domesday Book gives no indication that woodland regions were more sparsely settled and less thoroughly exploited than other parts

of the country in the eleventh century. Indeed, even though the statistics of the survey should be treated with caution, it would seem that several woodland areas (such as south Norfolk and central Suffolk) were amongst the most populous and intensively cultivated.

Other historians have suggested that Saxon lords were relatively weak in woodland regions so that communities lacked the incentive or mechanisms for reorganizing the landscape. Yet this theory also has problems. Domesday Book indicates that there were considerable regional variations in the strength of lordship in England in the eleventh century, but there is no general correlation between areas in which lordship was strong at the time of Domesday, and areas which were organized into a champion landscape in the Saxon period. Domesday represents a fairly straightforward division of the country into the east, where lordship was relatively weak, and the west, where it was relatively strong. This suggests either that the power of the lords was not instrumental in the introduction of the champion landscapes, or that, if it was, the creation of these landscapes was followed by a complete alteration in the distribution of the power of the lords.

The origins of the woodland and champion dichotomy are clearly buried very deep in the past, and may be impossible to recover. However, there is some slight, tantalizing evidence to suggest that these variations in the landscape may have their origins in the period following the end of Roman rule in Britain. They may be related to variations in the way in which the Anglo-Saxon settlers took power in England, and in the extent to which they disrupted the social and economic organization of the communities into which they moved.

Luppitt, Devon
With its scattered settlement pattern, its ancient winding hedges, and its small irregularly shaped fields, this landscape is typical of the woodland or ancient countryside areas of England.

Much of our knowledge about the earliest Anglo-Saxon settlers comes from their graves. Unlike the majority of the indigenous population, the first Saxons were pagan and buried their dead with a range of weapons or ornaments. Some of these burials involved cremated remains, often in pottery urns, while others were inhumations. It has been suggested that the latter burial practice was the result of Roman influence, for most people living within the Roman Empire were Christian and did not practise cremation. This influence could either have been absorbed by the Anglo-Saxons from the indigenous inhabitants of Britain, or it could have been picked up in their tribal homelands before they emigrated. Some Saxon settlers had dwelt close to, or may even have lived within, the frontiers of Imperial Rome.

Distinctive Saxon cemeteries have been discovered in many parts of England, but they are by no means omnipresent. There are none in the woodland area of the west, which was not densely settled by tribal groups in the fifth and sixth centuries, but was subject to political conquest in the seventh century, when the Saxons were gradually being converted to Christianity. Furthermore, although numerous Saxon cemeteries have been found in woodland regions of the southeast, these are concentrated in certain specific areas. Many occur, for example, in clusters along the coast, often in the vicinity of the great Saxon Shore Forts. Between the clusters are large tracts of land where no cemeteries have been found. In contrast, Saxon burials seem to be more widely and evenly spread in areas later dominated by champion landscapes. Moreover, the graves that occur in woodland regions are almost all inhumations, whereas those in the champion are both cremations and inhumations.

There are also certain place-names which have a regional distribution, and may give us some clue to the sort of impact that the Saxons had in different parts of the country. The Anglo-Saxons managed to change almost all the place-names of England, with only a handful surviving from Roman Britain. In addition to this handful, however, there are various Saxon place-names which incorporate words which have been derived from Latin. The Latin *vicus* meaning a small settlement was combined with the Saxon *ham* to give *wicham*, an element of numerous place-names.[12] Adoptions of this kind, as well as the few Latin names that have survived, suggest that there must have been a period of peaceful coexistence, and of cultural interchange, between the Saxon settlers and the indigenous inhabitants. These significant place-names are clustered in woodland areas of the south and east.

Together with the evidence of the cemeteries, these place-names suggest that Saxon settlement in the south and east of England was rather less catastrophic than it was in the Midlands and northeast. In the southeast the newcomers seem to have achieved dominance without bringing about a radical disruption of the existing social order. This was also the case, in a rather different way, in the west of England, where indigenous élites were only gradually replaced in the seventh and eighth centuries through a process of political conquest. It was these areas, where the Anglo-Saxons rose to power without a radical disruption of the existing economic and tenurial systems, that failed to develop nucleated villages and open fields on the classic model. By contrast, in areas which were to develop champion landscapes the Saxons seem to have brought about a much greater disruption of the status quo.

Although there seems some reason to relate the evolution of woodland and champion landscapes to regional variations in the impact of Saxon settlement, we can really only speculate on the mechanism which led these regions to develop in different ways. Perhaps the Anglo-Saxons who moved into the champion areas came as aggressive invaders, who created an economic base for themselves by seizing parcels of land. This served to disrupt established systems of economic organization within ancient tribal estates, as many relatively small and independent units emerged. While still owing goods and services to a distant royal estate centre, these communities became increasingly dependent on their own local resources as they ceased to be bound by economic ties to a wide range of settlements within a large territorial unit. Moreover, the disintegration of extensive tribal territories may have encouraged the emergence of an intermediate level of local administrators, responsible for collecting the king's dues.

Once communities lost their links with distant tracts of land formerly exploited as woodland and pasture, they began to develop more localized and intensive systems of agriculture and to co-operate with the settlements in their immediate vicinity. With the decline in extensive systems of communal exploitation, tribal grazing areas were freed for colonization by neighbouring communities or their thanes.

The arrival of the Saxons in what were to be the champion regions may thus have brought about a dramatic alteration in their social and economic organization. A network of interdependent communities was disrupted by the emergence of a multiplicity of small and independent land units. These tenurial changes cut many communities off from the lands which they had traditionally used for grazing while, at the same time, farmers may have been forced to expand their arable cultivation in order to meet the extra exactions imposed by increasingly powerful local administrators. It was these areas, therefore, that were the first to experience the economic pressures produced by rising population and the increasingly hierarchical structure of society, and this led to the emergence of nucleated villages and regular open-field systems.

In the woodland regions, however, where the impact of Saxon settlement was far less disruptive, the pattern of tenurial development was rather different. In these areas the social and cultural dominance of the Anglo-Saxon settlers was not associated with the radical disruption of existing patterns of territorial organization. Communities kept up their economic links with one another, and traditional shared grazing lands were maintained for many centuries after the arrival of the settlers. These tracts of woodland and pasture were only gradually settled and cleared as the population

View from Coploe Hill, Ickleton, Cambridgeshire
This landscape of rectangular fields and straight hawthorn hedges epitomizes the geometric rigidity of the 'planned countryside' of the former champion regions, where open fields and commons were enclosed relatively recently.

rose. This explains why the dispersed pattern of settlement in some woodland areas is very ancient, whereas in others it is the result of 'assarting' (land clearance) in the late Saxon and early medieval periods.

An increasing population ensured that woodland areas were eventually afflicted with a shortage of pasture, but this occurred rather later than in what were to be the champion areas. Furthermore, large territories, with their numerous interdependent settlements, survived much longer here than in the champion. Woodland farmers did not, therefore, build up the close links with their neighbours which would have been the basis for developing a communal system of agriculture in response to economic pressures. Fields often fragmented into strips as the population rose, but farming remained individualistic, and the pattern of landholding and settlement did not undergo a radical reorganization. Unimpeded by the constraints of communal agriculture, woodland farmers were able to devise alternative farming strategies to deal with the crisis that beset them. Moreover, as the economy developed in the twelfth century, many farmers moved into the expanding service sector and into non-agricultural industries. As future chapters will show, this early distinction between woodland and champion regions ensured that their future development took place along radically divergent lines.

This model of the origins of the distribution of woodland and champion landscapes is only a very tentative hypothesis, to add to the many others which have been proposed. Perhaps all that we can say about this fundamental pattern in the landscape is that its origins lie very deep in the past. It is one of the tantalizing mysteries of landscape history and may always remain a subject for conjecture rather than certainty.

TWO

The Early Middle Ages: A Customary Landscape

'THE THRONE STANDS ON these three supports: those who work, those who fight, and those who pray', wrote Abbot Aelfric of Eynsham, two generations before the Norman Conquest. Many books on the history of landscape have stressed the role of the fighters, the barons and knights of medieval England, in shaping the countryside. These nobles are usually seen as ruthless autocrats dominating society through the often tyrannical suppression of 'those who work'. In turn, the peasantry is represented as little more than a group of serfs, without rights or property and wholly subject to their manorial lord. In this chapter we suggest that this image of medieval society is fundamentally flawed. The appearance of the medieval countryside was to a large extent determined by those who worked rather than by those who fought. It was the communities of farmers who formed the agricultural environment in the Middle Ages, laying out hedges and walls, and establishing a network of tracks and footpaths through the landscape. It was they who expanded the frontiers of woodland and waste, and combined in the drainage of great tracts of marshland.

In the early Middle Ages society was not based around simple concepts of individual ownership. Farmers had certain rights to the land which they worked, but they were also bound by obligations to their lord. Similarly, lords had a right to profit from their tenants' payments, but in turn they had to make various renders to the king, and in many cases to great landed magnates to whom they owed allegiance. In medieval England, land was part of the network of personal relationships and obligations which held people together in a complex hierarchy.

Many duties and obligations were incorporated into the 'feudal system', which defined the relationships between the various landed classes. Introduced by the Normans, this increased the rigidity of social stratification in a society which was already highly hierarchical. The Saxon lordly élite was maintained by the labours of the peasantry and many of the lesser lords, or 'thanes', were in turn obliged to render allegiance and services to great nobles, the 'ealdormen'.

Under the feudal system the king distributed land to major landholders, or 'tenants-in-chief'. No cash transactions were involved, as the system was theoretically based on the provision of certain services in exchange for the use of land. These services were primarily military, ensuring that the king could raise a strong, experienced and well-equipped army at short notice.

In return for their lands or 'fiefs', tenants-in-chief periodically had to attend the king with a number of fully-equipped knights. In the early years after the Conquest they kept the requisite number of knights within their household, ready at a moment's notice to rush to arms. But, as *King Lear* indicates, such knights tended to be troublesome and disruptive and so, instead of having them about the house, tenants-in-chief began to grant them pieces of land, known as 'knight's fees', in return for their military services.

Most knights did more than just fight for their feudal superiors. They were bound to them, owing loyalty and allegiance, and they performed a variety of personal services. They gave advice and help (sometimes financial) and generally made themselves useful. The feudal system also involved the payment of various dues and duties by inferiors to superiors on occasions such as marriages or deaths. Feudalism was therefore not just a system of landholding, but a complete social and economic structure determining everyday details in the lives of the landed classes.

In the centuries following the Conquest feudalism became increasingly complex as new classes developed, and as alterations were made in the terms by which land was held. In particular there was a gradual change in the nature of the knight's fee.[1] Around the time of Domesday knights were usually granted land only for the duration of their lives. On their deaths their fees automatically reverted to the lord. Thus Abbot Gilbert Crispin granted to William Bayard, 'a certain berewick of the vill of Westminster called Tottenham to accommodate him and to hold for his life for the service of one knight .... on the condition that after his death it will remain free and quit to our church.' Not long after Domesday, however, knights began to gain hereditary rights over their estates and, even though they did not 'own' them, they were able to will them to their descendants, much as tenant farmers of the present day are able to pass on their holdings from father to son.

As the military rationale of the feudal system waned, knights began to take on the role of landholders. From the time of William I, the King's army was increasingly dependent not on the feudal system of personal service, but on paid mercenaries. Knights were frequently able to avoid military obligations by the payment of 'scutage', or shield money. Many knights and barons continued to play an important part in national defence, but they began to do so professionally, rather than in return for the use of their land.

As time passed, many knights became fighting figures in theory alone, and their fees were increasingly treated as if they were private property. They were inherited, exchanged in contracts of marriage, and, above all, freely bought and sold in an active land market. In consequence, instead of working a holding granted by a single lord, and owing obligations to him alone, a knight might hold land from many barons, between whom his service and loyalty would have to be divided. For example, when Haimo Dapifer received a grant of land from St Augustine's priory in Canterbury in 1120 he promised to give 'counsel, aid and succour to the church, to the abbot and his successors . . . against all the barons *except those whose vassal he will have become*' [our italics].[2]

As lands began to be divided and sold it became extremely difficult to determine from whom military services could be expected. In 1230 William Kentwell, a minor tenant-in-chief who held most of his land in Suffolk, confessed that he had lost control of seven of his fees and did not know who held them. Similarly, many tenants were theoretically responsible for the provision of a small fraction of a knight. The knights gradually consolidated their economic position, so that by the thirteenth century many were landowners of considerable local importance. Moreover, as society became more peaceful in the late twelfth and thirteenth centuries, the business of estate management became more complex and more profitable, and hence increasingly professional. Estate managers and all sorts of officials, lawyers and administrators thrived in this environment and formed a flourishing middle class keen to become holders as well as managers of land.

Middling landholders became an increasingly diverse class, so that by the fourteenth century they were divided into a number of categories. Some were styled knights, some esquires and others were simply called gents. These labels indicated differences in status and wealth, ranging from those who held several manors to those who had only one. These middling men were clearly distinct from the most powerful sector of society, the one hundred or more great magnates who held vast estates administered by small armies of officials. This élite was made up of abbots and bishops as well as lay barons.

As the feudal system developed, these great barons no longer gained the allegiance of their inferiors with grants of land, but maintained their influence through access to extensive political power and patronage. Since increasingly large numbers of administrators and minor functionaries were needed on royal and baronial estates, this patronage was of real importance. The route to personal aggrandizement for a knight or an esquire often lay through a post in a baronial establishment as an escheator, steward, bailiff, receiver, chamberlain or whatever.

Great magnates could also influence the appointment of members of the House of Commons, a position which was in itself seen as a step towards further and, most importantly, royal patronage. An act of 1429 limited the franchise to those with property worth 40 shillings a year, so that the electorate was small with many constituencies dominated by a great magnate. Thus Thomas Hungerford, the steward of the Black Prince and John of Gaunt, was returned as Member of Parliament for Wiltshire eleven times, and for Somerset four times. Moreover in 1377 the influence of Gaunt gained him further promotion when he became Speaker of the House of Commons.[3]

The expanding royal administration was another source of patronage in the fourteenth and fifteenth centuries. Great magnates could use their influence with the king to get their supporters appointed to crown offices, such as that of sheriff or coroner. The extent of their influence largely depended on the size of the armed following they could command.

Armed strength was also important at a local level, where it could be used to protect the interests of a baron's family and supporters in times of dynastic rivalry and gang warfare. In particular, these bodies of men could intimidate law courts and prevent the administration of impartial justice. In 1439, for example, Lord Fanhope burst into Bedford town hall, accompanied by fifty armed men, and broke up a meeting of the justices. Events such as these were fairly common in the turbulent years of the fifteenth century.

These bodies of armed men were partly composed of a lord's permanent household. This consisted of the younger sons of knights or members of the gentry, and of elder sons waiting to take over their father's estate. These men not only fought when necessary, but helped their lord to administer his estate, and acted as servants at meals and on public occasions. A magnate could also call on the military support of lesser knights, members of the gentry or prosperous yeomen, who wore his symbol or badge, regularly received a small payment of money, and had the promise of his support and protection.

Thus, as medieval society evolved, the ties of lordship and personal service continued to be important, but they became increasingly divorced from the possession of land. Service began to be given in return for patronage and cash payment, rather than as a condition of tenure. Nevertheless, some aspects of the old system survived. Feudal lords kept an interest in the lands which their forefathers had granted out, and in particular they maintained the right of wardship. This meant that a lord automatically became the guardian of an estate where the heir was under age. Yet in effect the fiefs and fees of barons and knights increasingly came to be treated more or less as private property.

While the knights and barons usually kept a proportion of land in their own hands, or leased it out to a third party, the greater part of their estates was customary land held and worked by peasant farmers. The lord's rights in this land were largely confined to the dues and duties owed by the peasants by whom it was worked. A characteristic of medieval England was that the profits of agriculture were taken out of the hands of peasants and spread throughout society by means of a complex system of extortion based on the obligations that were owed by inferiors to superiors. This manorial system formed the basis of the relationship between landlords and tenants.

Like the feudal system, the manorial system was not static, but adapted to changes in society. Moreover, it was not uniform but followed a complex pattern of regional variations. Much of our knowledge of this pattern comes from its eleventh-century form as recorded in Domesday Book. Completed in 1086, this represents a comprehensive survey of English property in the period immediately after the Norman Conquest. Yet the varied pattern of estates depicted in Domesday Book was already well established by the time the Normans invaded. King William's survey shows the landholding system which the new élite took over from the English.

Domesday Book describes a landscape divided up into basic tenurial units known as 'manors'. Each was under the control of a manorial lord who drew an income from the renders of the peasants who lived within it. Domesday classifies these peasants in various ways, although the French terms of the survey probably conceal a more complex system of social divisions. There were freemen, sokemen, villeins, bordars, cottars and slaves. Different combinations of these groups are found in the entries for different Domesday manors and, as is clear from later documents, each of them had a particular set of obligations to their lord.

The Luttrell Psalter
The medieval landscape was, above all, the creation of the farmers and labourers who worked the land. The Luttrell Psalter from the mid fourteenth century depicts several farming scenes. (ABOVE RIGHT) A horse-drawn harrow is followed by a boy who is scaring away birds; (BELOW RIGHT) harvesting — the most critical and busiest time in the farming year.

Freemen and sokemen were defined as free, while villeins, bordars and cottars can best be described as 'semi-free' and were subject to certain constraints. These semi-free tenants were particularly dependent on their manorial lords. For instance, they were not allowed to grind their own grain, but were obliged to take it to the lord's mill. They had to pay a fine when they inherited their farm, and on occasions like the marriage of their daughters. Above all, they had to render labour services to their lord. For as well as the land that was occupied by tenant farmers, most manors contained an area of land 'in demesne'. This was a kind of home farm and was held directly by the lord, to produce both goods and profits for the estate. The demesne was supposed to be worked by the semi-free tenants, but in some cases tenants were able to get this labour service commuted into a cash payment.

The villeins were the most substantial farmers of the semi-free tenants. Often quite wealthy, their name seems to have originally meant something like 'villager'. Bordars and cottars were lesser men, smallholders and part-time labourers. Below these classes were the unfree, the *servi* or slaves. Their numbers were fast declining in the late eleventh century, and it was not long before they disappeared altogether, becoming bordars and cottars as they received small quantities of land.

Freemen and sokemen had to pay dues and rents to their lords, but as free tenants they were not usually subject to labour services. This did not mean, however, that they were necessarily wealthier than the semi-free tenants, for the

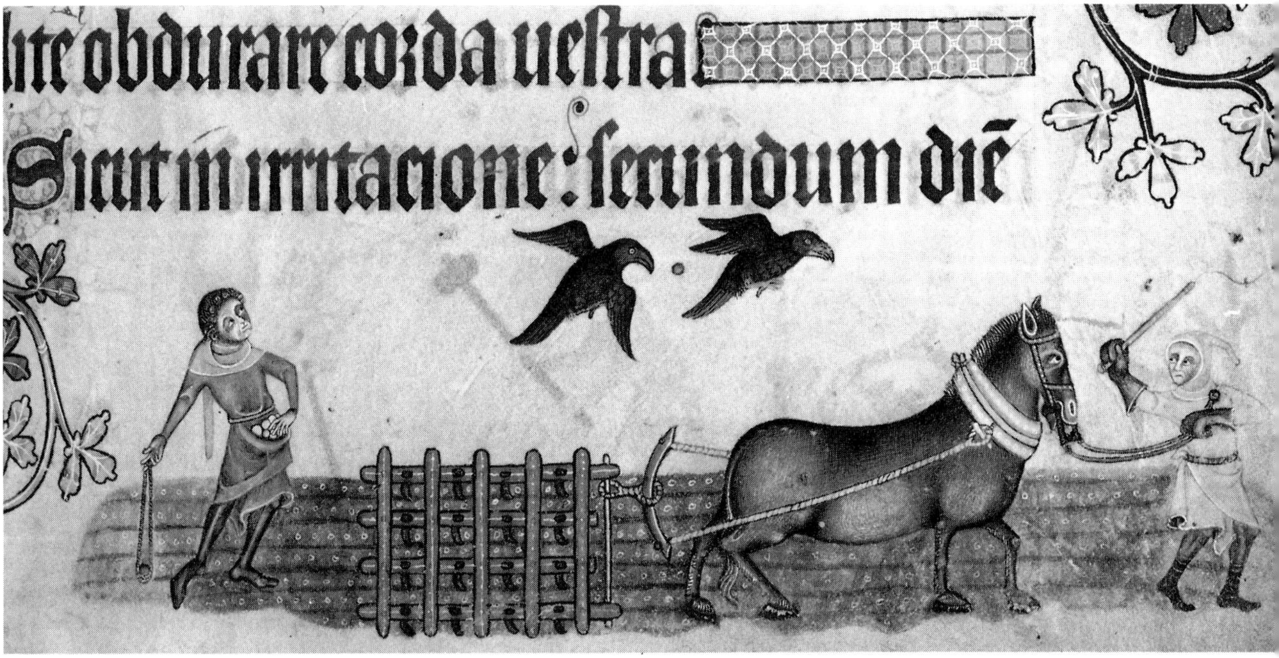
lite obdurare corda uestra
Sicut in irritacione: secundum die

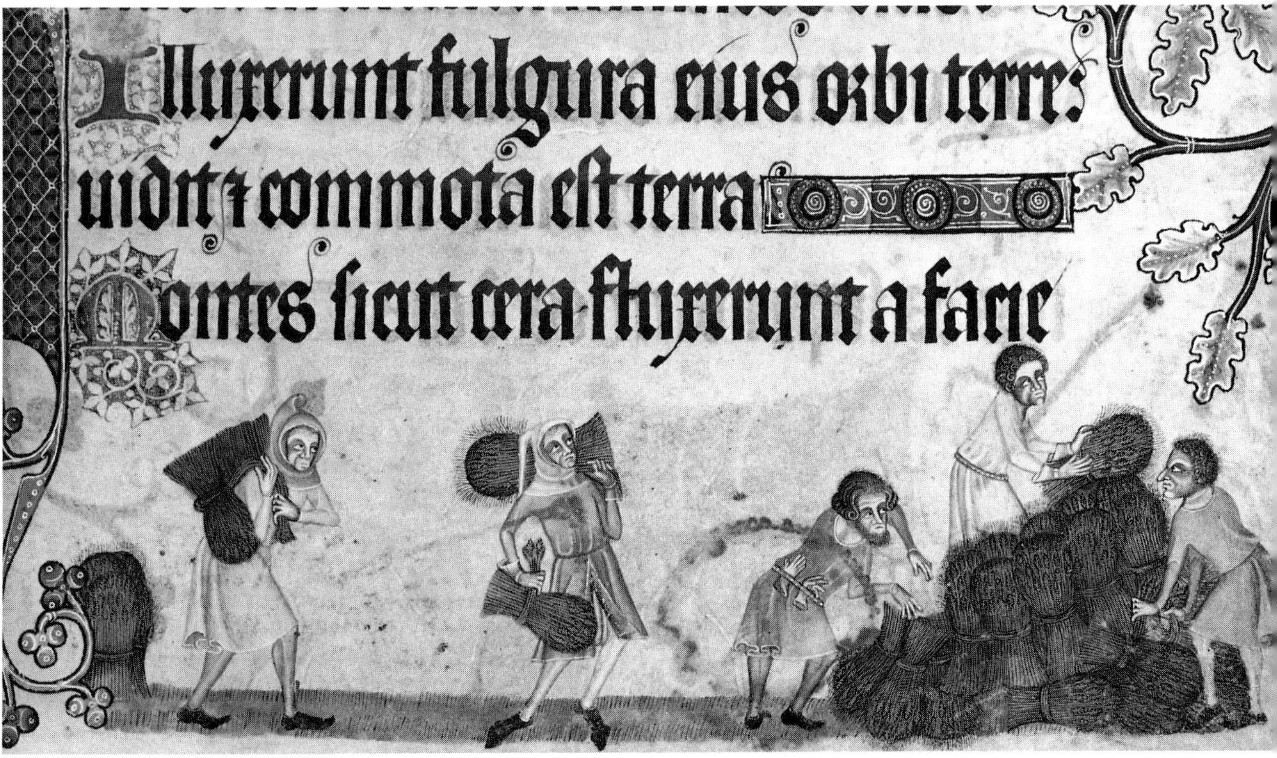
Illuxerunt fulgura eius orbi terre:
uidit et commota est terra
Montes sicut cera fluxerunt a facie

distinction between the two groups was tenurial rather than economic. Many villeins were richer and worked larger holdings than the neighbouring freemen, particularly in parts of the south and east. In contrast, the freemen were frequently struggling smallholders, eking out a living on a tiny parcel of ground.

Apart from payments made to the lords, farmers also had to render various taxes and services to the state. These were not imposed through the manorial structure, but through a separate system of extortion based on an administrative unit called the 'vill'. Each vill was made up of a number of holdings, and the farmers within it had to carry out duties delegated by central government, as well as pay the onerous land-tax known as the geld.

At the time of Domesday the size of manors and vills varied from place to place, but there were also regional contrasts in the kind of communities which they contained, and in the way in which they related to one another. For just as the soils and the topography of England differed from region to region, so too did the social structure of the villages, and the relationship between the lords and the farmers.

In some vills farmers held their land from a single powerful lord, but in others they were the tenants of two, three or even more. The population of some vills was largely made up of villeins, and the demesne land which utilized their labour was correspondingly large. Elsewhere, the majority of farmers were freemen and so the vills tended to contain little land in demesne. But in some places the manors were entirely composed of demesne land, and were farmed by hired labour, smallholders and slaves.

The composition of vills varied considerably on a local basis, but on the whole it followed a broad, regional pattern.[4] In some areas manors quite frequently corresponded to the kind of ideal manor-form which is often described in textbooks on medieval history. This was a manor with extensive demesne lands, in which the majority of the tenants were semi-free and the area of which was exactly conterminous with the administrative unit of the vill. Such manors, though scattered all over the country, were a particular feature of the counties of the central and southern Midlands — Wiltshire, Berkshire, Oxfordshire, Gloucestershire, Buckinghamshire, Northamptonshire and Leicester-

shire. Even here, however, the manors were not invariably of the classic mould. Some vills encompassed more than one manor, and there were also a number of huge manors which embraced several vills. None the less, the coincidence of manor and vill was common enough to be considered the norm in this part of the country.

Swaffham Prior, Cambridgeshire
Where the land of a vill fell in more than one manor, this occasionally led to the division of the vill into two parishes. Swaffham Prior, where two medieval churches stand side by side in a single churchyard, is one of several examples in the east of England.

Elsewhere in England such classic manors were far less common. In the west and southwest, for example, many manors still contained large numbers of slaves in the eleventh century, despite the decline of this class in the years immediately after the Conquest. In Kent manors were frequently fragmented and composed of numerous scattered blocks of land. But it was in eastern England that there were the most striking departures from the classic manorial norm. In the northeast, in much of Yorkshire, Lincolnshire, Nottinghamshire, Derbyshire and Leicestershire, there were some classic manors, but there were also large numbers of freemen, some of whom lived in vills with no demesne land at all, and owed their duties to a distant manorial hall. In East Anglia, Cambridgeshire and parts of Essex, there were also a lot of freemen, but in these areas there was no clear relationship between the pattern of manors and that of vills. The vills were usually divided between numerous manors, and both the east and the northeast seem to have had relatively weak lords. This may have been the result of Danish settlement here in the ninth and tenth centuries.

Some historians have suggested that the numerous freemen and sokemen who characterize Domesday entries for the north and east were the direct descendants of demobbed Danish soldiers. These warriors eventually gave up raiding, and, in the words of the Anglo-Saxon chronicles, 'engaged in ploughing and making a living for themselves'. Other historians believe that the impact of the Danes was rather more indirect. Their settlement may have retarded the development towards manorialism and lordship which continued uninterrupted in those parts of the west which were less affected by the invaders. Whatever produced the distinction between the free east and the unfree west, it is clear that this dichotomy was superimposed on the more ancient social variations underlying the division of the country into woodland and champion regions.

In the centuries after Domesday some manors divided, others combined, and there were alterations in the composition of the various classes of tenant. In the northeast, in particular, many of the free population were downgraded to the ranks of the semi-free, although slaves were gradually being emancipated in all parts of the country at this time. But these developments did not drastically alter the broad regional variations in the form of the Domesday manor. Above all, the coincidence of manors and vills continued to be a feature of the central and southern Midlands, while East Anglia was characterized by vills which were divided between a multiplicity of manors.

Regional variations in the lords' power over the farming population were not directly manifested in the landscape for the lords did not attempt to interfere in the day-to-day management of the countryside. Both they and the state confined the exertion of their power to the serious business of extorting money or labour from the peasants, rather than in becoming involved in the processes by which the money was created or the labour force maintained.

Not all historians of the landscape agree with this view. Some writers see medieval English knights and barons as men interested in the practicalities of agriculture, rather than as primarily political figures, content to live off wealth produced by humble tenants. To support this view some people cite the evidence for a considerable amount of planning in the medieval landscape. The open fields, in particular those with long furlongs, seem to have been laid out in accordance with a prearranged plan, but in addition there were many places where the fields appear to have been replanned later in the Middle Ages. It has been suggested that both these phases of landscape organization could only have been brought about by the unilateral action of a powerful lord. Others believe that the explanation is not quite so simple.

In many communities the later reorganization of field systems was based on a change from a two-field system, associated with a two-course rotation, to a three-field system and a three-course pattern of rotation. Such a transition made the land more productive since it ensured that less was left fallow each year, but it also required a considerable reallocation of strips. Elsewhere, open fields were reorganized following the creation of more arable lands by the clearance of some village waste.

The resultant landscapes were often made up of strips arranged in a highly regular pattern and distributed amongst the villagers in accordance with a careful plan. The strips of any one farmer would always be bordered by those of the same two neighbours. Thus in the village of Steeple Claydon in Buckinghamshire, the land of Thomas de Hampton was always next to that of Henry de Kaam. As a result of this system, there was no one farmer who held land that was significantly better than that of the rest.[5]

In some places the strips within the open fields were allocated so as to correspond to the pattern of houses within a village. The house plots or 'tofts' lay on either side of a single street. Taking this as a notional circle, each villager held a strip within each furlong that corresponded to the position of his house on the street. This arrangement was always based on the assumption that the circle of houses and strips would be read clockwise.

In such villages, therefore, all the strips of y would be bordered on the left by those of x and on the right by those of z; similarly x would have a house on the left and z one on the right of y. Thus when Robert de Tolebu granted a carucate of his demesne land in the village of Yarm in Cleveland to the canons of Guisborough Priory, he defined the carucate in question as:

> That one which lies nearer the land of Robert de Lestria, with half my meadow which lies next to the meadow of the same Robert, and with a toft that is next to the toft of the same Robert.[6]

The clockwise arrangement of plots and strips within these villages was derived from the apparent behaviour of the sun, which seems to move clockwise in the northern hemisphere. This standard way of reading the order of the strips ensured that it was always possible for the villagers to describe the relative position of strips within the open fields. The holdings in the south and east of each furlong were said to lie 'towards the sun', whereas those in the north and west were regarded as lying 'towards the shade'. This way of ordering fields has been described as 'sun division' by modern scholars, and may be Scandinavian in origin.

This egalitarian system of distribution helped to ensure that peasants could meet the manorial and other exactions which were imposed on them. These were rated on customary units which were partly based on arable acreage but which also represented shares in the other resources exploited by the community. These units varied from vill to vill, but were the same within any single vill. In the north they were usually called 'bovates' or 'oxgangs', and were about 10 to 15 acres, and in the south they were 'virgates' or 'yardlands',[7] usually equivalent to about 20 to 30 acres. In the eleventh and twelfth centuries a villein farmer usually held one yardland or two oxgangs.

In close-knit English medieval communities the organization of the tax system would have provided considerable pressure to ensure that the arable land farmed by each person was of equal quality as well as quantity. The careful replanning of field systems may therefore represent attempts to achieve a more equitable distribution of land. This was in the interests of the farming community as well as the manorial lords and both probably had a hand in the replanning. Sometimes lords may have acted unilaterally in reordering the landscape, but it seems likely that on many occasions their influence was more indirect, as the peasants responded to financial pressures imposed from above.

Some idea of what went on in these communal replannings is revealed in a docu-

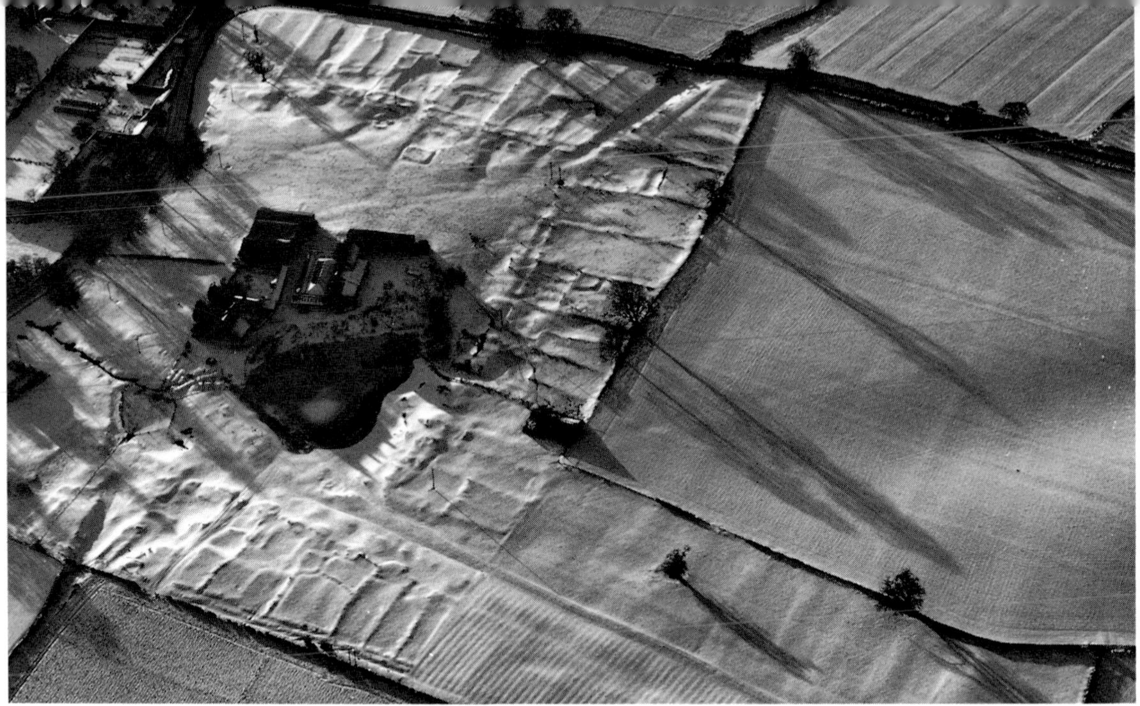

ment describing the reallocation of land at Segenhoe in Bedfordshire in the 1160s, which had been necessitated by the unjust seizure of property during the anarchy of Stephen's reign (1135–54), and the expansion of arable cultivation. The redistribution took place in the courts of the two lords in the village where, in the presence of six old men, 'knights, freemen and others . . . surrendered their lands under the supervision of the old men and by the measure of the perch, to be divided as if they were newly-won land, assigning to each a reasonable share'.[8] Such a system of administration hardly tallies with the model of a landscape dominated by arbitrary autocratic lords.

It is in the planning of medieval villages, rather than their fields, that the hand of the tyrannical lord has been most frequently discerned. No doubt some villages were reorganized with the active intervention of their manorial lord, but once again the degree of organization and initiative that existed in the medieval communities should not be underestimated. There are a great many planned medieval villages in the north of England, often with houses set around a rectangular village green. This pattern can clearly be seen in deserted medieval villages such as Walworth in County Durham, where the arrangement of the original houses has not been disrupted by subsequent development. It is also still discernible in many villages which are still standing; for example, Milburn in Cumbria and Appleton le Moors in North Yorkshire.[9]

Many of these northern settlements seem to have been planned in the years after 1100, following the devastation and virtual depopulation of this region between 1069 and

ABOVE **Walworth, County Durham**
The planning which determined the form of some medieval villages can be seen most clearly where the settlement has subsequently been deserted and the property boundaries preserved as earthworks. This modern farmstead is sited in the middle of a square village green, and the neat pattern of medieval tofts and crofts is picked out by a light cover of snow.

RIGHT **Appleton-le-Moors, North Yorkshire**
The regular layout of this village indicates that it was originally planned, probably in the late eleventh or early twelfth century. It may well have been laid out during the recolonization which followed William I's 'harrying of the North'.

1071, as a result of William the Conqueror's scorched-earth policy to deal with Scandinavian invaders and the northern rebels against his regime. Domesday Book graphically records the consequences, with entry after entry for the northern sections simply stating '*wasta est*', 'it is waste'.

The majority of planned villages in the north must be seen in the context of the special circumstances of this razed and depopulated landscape. Recent research has suggested that, although some of the villages built in this area provided housing for indigenous inhabitants, the majority were intended to attract new tenants from the less productive areas of the Pennine foothills and the Dales. They may not, therefore, reflect the dominance of an arbitrary lord, reordering settlements and communities at whim, but may have been more like a medieval equivalent of Milton Keynes. They were built by great magnates, and in particular ecclesiastical institutions, to encourage the settlement and development of an area suitable for economic expansion.

The rigidly formal plan of these villages may have sprung from the complex system of taxation and exactions imposed on the medieval peasants. Often the frontages of house plots are precisely in proportion to the size of the holdings to which they were attached. Thus at Thornton-le-Beans, Hemingbrough and Upper Poppleton in North Yorkshire, the frontages correspond with the holdings in a ratio of two perches for every bovate held.[10] Such regular plans left the inhabitants in no doubt about how much they owed in manorial dues and taxes, but they may also have had another function. People seem to have been tempted to take up holdings in planned villages by the offer of favourable rents, and in some cases grants of free tenure. The fact that the extent of the exactions the tenants would have to pay was represented in the village plans may have served as a guarantee on the part of the lord that the basis for assessing rents and payments would not be changed in the future.

Planned settlements seem to have been much rarer outside these devastated northern areas. The advantages accruing from a formal structure were not usually sufficient to stimulate the reorganization of existing villages, but nevertheless there are examples of planned medieval settlements in the south. Some, such as Newton Bromswold in Northamptonshire and Isle Abbots in Somerset, were planned throughout, and others, such as Quainton in Buckinghamshire and Okeford Fitzpaine in Dorset, had planned sections. On the whole, however, it seems that villages were only given an orderly form when they were being rebuilt or relocated anyway.

Like the redistribution of arable land, the impetus for the introduction of formal village plans may have come as much from the community as from the manorial lord. Either way, the involvement of the lords in this aspect of village administration reflects the nature of their interest in the land beyond their demesnes. The lords were primarily concerned with the exaction of taxation, manorial rents and labour services, and village planning helped to simplify this process considerably. It was therefore probably seen to be in the interest of landlord and tenants alike since it helped to minimize manorial disputes.

The lords' interest in farming revenues did not, however, extend to a concern with the practical details of agriculture. One indication of this may be the nature of the estates that were held by the medieval landed magnates. At the time of Domesday the estates of most major landholders were not made up of compact blocks of land, but were widely scattered across the country. The Count of Mortain, for example, held land of the king in twenty different counties, and this was the rule rather than the exception. Even within counties the landholdings of various lords were usually extensively intermingled.

This apparently inconvenient disposition of holdings may have been caused by the way in which land was transferred from the Saxon to the Norman élite. Domesday suggests that each Norman tenant-in-chief held an estate made up of the lands of a large number of small Saxon landlords. The estate of Robert de Busli, for example, had been previously held by eighty individuals, so that it was extensively fragmented.[11] Yet it may be that Domesday is misleading in this as in so many other respects. The holders of the lands taken over by Robert de Busli may all have been the feudal dependants of a single, powerful Saxon noble. Following the Conquest, Robert may have been merely taking the place of this Saxon overlord, rather than having to accumulate his numerous scattered lands piecemeal.

Even the most diligent medieval baron would have found it difficult to become closely involved in the agricultural exploitation of his far-flung lands, but it seems that most of them did not want to do any such thing. The estates of major landholders were not only scattered when first taken over; they stayed scattered for many centuries.

Local knights may have been more directly involved in farming their demesnes, but in most cases demesne land made up only a small proportion of each vill. Most of the land was in the hands of small peasant producers, and these farmers tended to adhere to local time-honoured methods. Indeed it is the medieval villagers' adherence to tradition which makes these communities so important in understanding the medieval landscape. Most farmers tilled the land and established patterns of rotation, seeding densities and so on, not at the behest of their manorial lord, but in the way that these things had always been done in that particular part of the country.

Even the lord's demesne was usually farmed by the customary local methods and in champion regions this was often unavoidable since the strips of the demesne were frequently intermingled with those of the rest of the village. Moreover, the reeve who ran the demesne was usually a local villein elected by the community. He was brought up in local ways and practices and so too were the villeins and wage labourers who worked the lord's land.[12] These people would have been extremely wary of any attempt to depart from the tried and true, and there is no evidence that a lord would have been sufficiently interested in agriculture to try to force them to do so. A number of agricultural treatises were published in the medieval period, of which the most famous is probably the tract written by Walter of Henley. These works make relatively little mention of the practicalities of arable cultivation, which was the main business of the medieval village, but tend to concentrate on the details of agricultural administration, and to some extent on stock-breeding. Their main purpose was often to offer advice on how lords could stop manorial officials cheating.

Further evidence that medieval lords did not exert firm control over agricultural methods on their lands can be found in the lack of standardized practices within the great estates. Manorial records show, for example, that Battle Abbey employed much lower seeding densities on its manors in Berkshire, Wiltshire and Oxfordshire than it did on those in Kent and Surrey.[13] What we know of medieval farming suggests that it was local farmers who introduced such agricultural innovations as there were.

Conversely, medieval villagers were able to exert a certain amount of influence over the way that they were treated by their lords. A thirteenth-century villein was theoretically tied to the manor of his birth. He could be sold by one lord to another, arrested and imprisoned without trial and was generally devoid of rights of self-determination. However, although individual villeins may have been subjected to this arbitrary and tyrannical treatment, it rarely happened to entire communities. In practice the power of the lords was limited by their financial dependence on the peasant community. The lords could not afford to antagonize the farmers of the villages, because arbitrary or unpopular action on their part could lead to disputes, non-cooperation, legal actions, or even a rent strike. Some historians have suggested that disputes between lords and their tenants occurred as often in medieval society as industrial disputes do today.[14]

This may be an overstatement, for then as now many people were prepared to accept extreme inequalities of power and wealth as part of the natural order of things. None the less disputes were certainly more common than one might expect, and in the Middle Ages as today they were frequently stimulated by attempts to overturn a customary way of doing things. Trouble could arise, for example, when the lords sought to introduce any reduction in the rights and benefits of the community. Thus in 1291:

> All the villeins of the township of Broughton . . . went away from the great harvest boon, leaving their work from noon till night . . . giving the malicious and false cause that they did not have their loaves as large as they were accustomed formerly and ought to have them.[15]

Such disputes could involve individuals as well as groups of tenants. In 1288, for example, in the village of Shillington in Bedfordshire, the son of Hugh Walter lay at the head of a strip at harvest and impeded the work of the lord. This was presumably an early form of passive resistance, for which the protester received a fine of 6d at the manorial court. On other occasions entire communities became embroiled in disputes. In 1282 the whole of the vill of Abbots Langley in Hertfordshire was fined 18 shillings by the manorial court, for failing to come to the Abbot's harvest with thirty-six sickles. Moreover, many of the communities engaging in such acts of defiance seem to have been highly organized. When villeins of Newington in Oxfordshire, for example, were in dispute with their lord in 1300, they not only refused to carry out their mowing service, but also appear to have set up a fighting fund to which they each contributed 4d. Led by their reeve, the villeins of Stoughton in Leicestershire raised the money to hire a lawyer to represent them in the royal courts against attempts on the part of their lord to increase labour services.

Some disputes ran for years, like that between the abbots of Halesowen in the West Midlands and their tenants. This continued on and off from 1243 to 1327, and involved numerous proceedings in the royal courts, royal inquests and a petition to the king as well as more violent confrontations. In 1278 the Bishop of Worcester ordered the excommunication of all those who had physically attacked the abbot and his monks at Beoley. The following year, jurors were asked at the manorial court:

> To tell the truth about all those, whether they are men or women, who withdrew themselves from the lord's land with their chattels, where they are and who they are and where their chattels are.[16]

Incidents of tenants running away from their holdings, as well as other forms of direct action, proliferated in the fourteenth and fifteenth centuries, but even before this they were probably not particularly uncommon. Strong medieval communities could circumscribe the actions of their lords. Although the lord maintained certain rights over customary land, such as the right to any minerals within it, it was custom and the community, rather than lords and the feudal system, which were the principal instruments in shaping the countryside. The lot of the medieval peasant may not have been particularly enviable, but material deprivation was not necessarily accompanied by a lack of any power of self-determination.

The customs of the medieval village were usually defined by the manorial court. This dealt with minor criminal and civil offences, determined the means by which land could be sold or inherited, dictated agricultural practices, and set the number of days to be worked and the amounts of money to be paid by tenants. It settled the balance of power in the community by establishing both the status of tenants, and the relationship between the tenants and the lord.

The court was not simply an instrument of feudal oppression. It was also a system of self-regulation run by the community. The court was presided over by the steward, who was the lord's representative, but the jury was made up of villeins. They not only judged the facts of each case, but articulated the customs of the manor on which their judgements were based. Since manorial courts were partially controlled by the peasant community, their regulations tended to reflect particular local conditions; their records reveal immense regional variations in the customs of medieval England.[17]

The extent of these variations is recognized in the *Rectitudines Singularum Personarum*, a fascinating late Saxon tract on estate management: 'The estate law is fixed on each estate; at some places . . . it is heavier, at some . . . lighter, because not all customs about estates are alike.' Seven centuries later a seventeenth-century manorial steward expressed the same concept: 'Customs . . . of this nation are so various and differing in themselves as that a man might almost say that there are as many several customs as manors or lordships in a country, yea, and almost as many as there are townships or hamlets in a manor.'[18]

Despite this diversity in the details of manorial custom, certain broad, regional patterns emerge. These embody the differences between the various types of community in the medieval landscape, and in particular the contrast between the communities of the woodland and those of the champion. Regional variations relating to the means by which land could change hands clearly bring out these distinctions.

Generally speaking, free tenants practised partible inheritance — that is, they could divide their holdings between all their sons on their death — and they were usually also free to buy and sell land. Villeins, on the other hand, were not free to do what they liked with their holdings, but had to adhere to the customs relating to the transfer of land which were dictated by the manorial court.

In champion regions the majority of villeins had to practise 'primogeniture' in the twelfth and thirteenth centuries, and pass their holdings undivided to their eldest sons, but in woodland and upland manors partible inheritance was sometimes practised.[19] This did not always lead to the fragmentation of landholding units, for when a number of sons took over their father's farm in the twelfth and thirteenth centuries they would often run it together as a single unit.[20] More important, however, were the variations between the woodland and champion areas in the customs relating to the alienation of land. In woodland areas villeins were often free to alienate — to dispose of their land by gift or sale. A fine had to be paid to the manorial lord, but otherwise the market in villein land was virtually unrestrained, particularly in the southeast. Thus the manorial courts in these areas tended to serve more or less like conveyancing clerks, recording numerous land transactions. This freedom to alienate villein land was also a feature of many champion areas, particularly in the east, where the manorial structure was complicated and the power of the lords over their customary tenants was weak. But in the champion areas of the south and central Midlands, where manors were most frequently coincident with vills, the market in villein land was often very restricted.

Differences in the size of villein farms in the twelfth and thirteenth centuries underlined these local variations in the system of landholding. In many champion villages, especially those held by a single lord, the majority of farmers held the same amount of land. This was originally a virgate, but as time passed and the population grew, the standard landholding unit became half a virgate in many places. These close-knit communities were bound by a joint interest in preserving the tenurial status quo, and would not have welcomed the disruption of the landholding system which the proliferation of small uneconomic holdings would have caused. There would probably also have been some hostility towards anyone who attempted to

Open field, Aston Rowant, Oxfordshire
A nineteenth-century map gives some impression of the disposition of property in an open field, although by this time the amalgamation and consolidation of strips had considerably simplified the medieval pattern of landholding.

accumulate an especially large holding. Some historians have therefore suggested that in areas where the villagers lived and worked together, and in particular where they were all subject to a single manorial lord, the belief was shared that holdings should pass undivided from father to son.[21]

This was not the case in all champion villages, however. In the eastern areas where there were many free tenants and a confused manorial structure, there was often extensive alienation of land, so that the holdings varied considerably in size. But it was in the woodland regions that there were the greatest deviations from the classic champion village. These areas probably never had the kind of close-knit communities which had an interest in maintaining a relatively equal distribution of land. Land was freely bought and sold, divided and recombined, even in areas like Hertfordshire and central Essex where manorialism was strong. Woodland landscapes were therefore characterized by a wide disparity in the size of holdings, and often by a multiplicity of smallholdings, produced by the fragmentation, alienation and division of land. The fact that Domesday reveals a large number of small tenants in woodland areas suggests this was the case from a very early period.

The way in which land was held in the medieval village and the restrictions on its inheritance can therefore be directly related to the social structure of the communities concerned. The farmers who lived together in heavily manorialized champion villages formed very different communities from those scattered amidst the woodland landscape. These differences are revealed in other customs and by-laws besides those relating to the sale and inheritance of land. The co-operative system of agriculture in champion areas ensured that custom dictated a whole range of day to day activities. In the woodland areas, on the other hand, where agriculture was rather more individualistic, there were not so many customary controls.

However, although farming in the champion was organized through a host of communal regulations, individuals lived off the produce of their own lands and farming was not in any way communistic. Crops were not harvested in common and then distributed amongst the people. The customs and by-laws of the champion villages suggest a society that was both democratic and restrictive. Rules were developed by the community for the good of the community, and the rights of the individual were invariably subservient to what was seen as the common good — or, at least, as the good of the most prosperous and influential villagers. Mobility was severely limited, particularly at harvest time, for it was only by ensuring that the labour force was at its maximum strength that a village could safeguard the all-important harvest. In many villages, able-bodied workers faced a fine if they did not turn up to work at the harvest, or if they went away to work in another, better paid, area. A fifteenth-century by-law for the village of Burwell in Cambridgeshire stated: 'It is ordered at this court as well as by the lord as by the whole homage that no-one shall leave town for gain who is able to earn a penny a day and food under pain of 20d.'[22]

The by-laws of many medieval villages hardly give an impression of a community characterized by outstanding honesty. Innumerable regulations were instituted to prevent theft, and particular efforts were made to stem the theft of crops from the fields at harvest time. Many by-laws were intended to restrict the movement of the village population after dark. As another fifteenth-century by-law for Burwell stipulated, 'no-one henceforth through the whole of the autumn shall cart any grain away from the field at night nor shall he transport it in any other way neither in the evening nor in the morning while it is still night under pain each of paying the lord 40d without mitigation'.[23]

In woodland regions the organization of agriculture was far more flexible and usually allowed farmers a certain amount of individual choice. Although many woodland regions, such as areas of Essex, the Chiltern Hills and the Thames Valley, contained some land in open fields of a kind, the common rotations imposed on these fields were seldom instituted in the hedged closes that were individually held. Moreover, where all the land was in such closes, as in central Essex, or where common rotations were not imposed on the strip fields, as in Kent, the activities of the farmers were even more unrestrained. The agricultural role of the manorial courts in these areas was limited to such matters as controlling the exploitation of common wastes, and co-operation between tenants tended to take the form of ad hoc agreements between two or three neighbours, rather than an adherence to precedents sanctioned by the whole community.

In the light of these differences it is not surprising that the replanning of fields and villages is a feature of champion rather than woodland areas. In the close-knit champion communities, where the farmers all lived together and worked co-operatively, there was an emphasis on fairness that was not to be found amongst the more individualistic farmers of the woodland regions. In woodland areas the evidence for the existence of planned field systems is rare, and that for the planning of villages non-existent, an indication of the importance of local communities in the planning of the medieval countryside.

The appearance of the medieval landscape embodied the differences between the communities that lived and worked within it. Champion villages were made up of closely clustered farmsteads, a pattern which reflected the communal attitudes of the farmers. The villages were clearly separated from each other, often standing isolated amidst the bare, bleak landscape of open fields. Just like the lives of the inhabitants, individual holdings lay intermingled, the unfenced strips often divided by no more than a furrow. Beyond the arable lay the waste, for the common use of the villagers and therefore also unfenced. The bareness of the champion landscape, its lack of hedges and clearly defined boundaries, was not merely a consequence of agricultural considerations; it embodied the villagers' attitude to property. It was a landscape in which individual property rights were subordinated to rights and interests defined by the community.

In woodland areas, and to some extent in the uplands, individual property was more clearly defined. The dispersed settlement pattern of scattered farmsteads and hamlets indicated the less cohesive nature of the communities. The lives and holdings of the farmers were not thoroughly intermingled, and farming practices tended to be fairly individualistic. Yet even in these areas the waste remained unfenced, and was open to all who had a claim on it.

The striking visual differences between the landscapes of the woodland and champion regions indicate the variations that existed in the social composition of medieval England. In

Padbury, Buckinghamshire
The interlocking strips of the open fields are preserved in the landscape as ridge and furrow, giving some idea of the complexity of the pattern of property in the medieval champion regions. The straight field boundaries which cut across the earthworks were created after the enclosure of the parish of Padbury in 1795.

some areas the population was individualistic from a very early period, and relatively unrestrained by social controls, while elsewhere the villagers had a long tradition of co-operative endeavour and accepted extensive communal restrictions on individual rights. Of course, there was no sharp or simple dichotomy between the two types of community, or between the landscapes with which they are associated. There were a whole host of local and regional variations. But in almost every case it was the community rather than merely the landed élite who moulded the agricultural environment of the early Middle Ages.

There is, however, one significant exception to this otherwise general rule. There was one group of landowners who wanted to change the landscape despite communal controls. These revolutionary landholders were the religious institutions, which became increasingly involved in land ownership and management and often controlled vast estates.

By the time of Domesday the monastic institutions were already well-endowed. In 1066 about sixty Benedictine foundations, many of great antiquity, possessed around 15 per cent of the land of England. The Conquest led to some loss of ground, for the monasteries had to fulfil their military obligations by endowing knights with land, and some of the Normans seem to have seized monastic lands which had been leased to Saxon laymen. In the twelfth century, however, these losses were more than made up by a wave of donations to existing monasteries and the foundation of numerous new ones. The Cistercians, the Tironensians, the Grandmontines, the Savigniacs, the Carthusians and others established many new houses, as a wave of religious enthusiasm swept through the knights and

Rievaulx Abbey, North Yorkshire
These imposing ruins give a striking impression of how the monastic institutions must have dominated the countryside around them.

barons of medieval England. By the early fourteenth century there were around 700 abbeys and monasteries, which held almost 25 per cent of the land of England.[24]

There were various reasons why the medieval nobles chose to endow or found religious houses. Genuine piety and religious fervour, and a respect for the Christian work of the various orders were probably amongst the motives, but another incentive must have been the prominence given to important benefactors in the oft-repeated prayers of the community which, according to medieval theology, would do much to assist their subject to salvation. Advantages for life in this world may well have been of as much importance as the rewards to be received in the next. The founders of monasteries and their heirs could claim hospitality for their household as they travelled the country and they sometimes retained the right to nominate candidates to fill vacancies in the ecclesiastical hierarchy of the house concerned. Plate and treasure could be stored in the monastery, horses and hounds kept in its stables, and nunneries provided a useful sanctuary for unmarried daughters. Indeed, in the eighteenth century, when there was believed to be a surplus of women, various forthright Englishmen advocated the endowment of protestant nunneries in which the excess female population could be stored. Medieval monasteries provided careers for the younger sons of their benefactors, and like the nunneries provided a place where the lord's dependants could be pensioned off. Furthermore, nunneries often provided a refuge for aristocratic widows. These women either became members of the community, or merely lived as permanent boarders.

Such arrangements were not always entirely satisfactory, however, for grand widows occasionally disrupted convents with their aristocratic peccadiloes. The tranquillity of the nunnery of Langley in Leicestershire was rudely disturbed in 1440 by the arrival of Eleanor, Lady Audley as a boarder. The abbess was forced to complain about:

> her great abundance of dogs, insomuch that whenever she comes to church there follow her twelve dogs, who make a great uproar in church, hindering them in their psalmody, and the nuns thereby are made terrified.[25]

Towards the end of the twelfth century there was a decline in the rate at which monastic institutions were being founded. By this time all the great families were attached to a religious house and newer orders had to build up their estates from the donations of less wealthy men. The friars, who were not established until the thirteenth century, drew most of their support from the rich burgesses of the growing towns. By the fourteenth century general disillusionment with the monastic institutions caused a considerable reduction in lay generosity.

Even after they had ceased to be the recipients of regular and substantial gifts of land, the monasteries continued to expand through astute purchases of land and the careful management of their estates. As permanent institutions, monasteries were immune from many of the problems which afflicted the great lay estates. They were not subject to dynastic accidents, such as the failure of lines, and were less susceptible than lay landowners to the confiscation of their estates through political disasters, or the loss of royal favour. None the less, monasteries could suffer in the short-term through the appointment of bad or incompetent abbots. This was the case with the monastery of Bury St Edmunds in Suffolk, when it was under the control of Abbot Hugh from 1157 to 1180. As Jocelin of Brakelond wrote:

> Discipline and religion and all things pertaining to the rule were zealously observed within the cloister: but outside all things were badly handled, and every man did, not what he ought, but what he would, since his lord was simple and growing old. . . . The woods were destroyed, and the houses of the manors threatened to fall into ruin, and day by day things went from bad to worse.[26]

In 1279 an investigation by the Cluniacs into their priory at Wenlock found the prior John of Thefford guilty of downright fraud. Apparently a 'ruthless and discontented man', he had alienated much of the priory's property, and had run up debts of 1880 marks. Yet John was not prepared to accept such accusations lying down, and when confronted with the evidence 'in his own papers and documents' he 'appeared, of course, very much astonished'. On the whole, however, the monasteries were astutely managed, and took advantage of their position as permanent institutions to extend their estates.[27]

From the twelfth century the monasteries encountered increasing hostility, not only from ordinary people, but also from the court and great magnates. In 1279 the statute *de Viris Religiosis* was passed — now better known as the Statute of Mortmain. In theory this forbade all grants of land to the Church, although its effect (and probably its aim) was to ensure that such grants were controlled, and that the Crown was able to get a share of the action. In order to give any land to a monastery a series of licences had to be obtained, not only from the king, but also from all the various layers of the feudal hierarchy with a stake in the land in question. Under Edward I a further attempt was made to weaken the power of the monasteries with the passing of the Statute of Westminster in 1285. This declared that the heirs of founders of monastic institutions could take back any land or income which the monastery had alienated or misused.

However, the greatest animosity towards monastic institutions probably came from the lower classes of medieval society. Unlike many lay lords, monastic institutions involved themselves directly in agriculture, and were tenacious in upholding their rights. These were never allowed to lapse with the passing of time, for the monasteries kept scrupulously efficient records. The interventionist style of monastic landlords often brought about violent confrontations with their tenants as, for example, the armed assaults on the abbeys of St Albans, Abingdon and Bury St Edmunds in 1327. But despite declining popularity and dwindling numbers, the monasteries were not afflicted by any radical attacks on their power and wealth until the sixteenth century, and they were unaffected by the Lollards' radical proposals that they should be disendowed.

The great wealth of the monasteries and their capacity for long-term planning made it possible for them to become more closely involved than great lay estates in the details of agricultural production, and to carry out various schemes of improvement and capital-intensive farming, especially in the thirteenth century when agricultural prices were high. Benedictine houses, for example, were involved in various large-scale drainage projects, in particular the abbeys of Glastonbury and Muchelney in the Somerset Levels, and Spalding and Crowland in the Fens. Many of the drainage ditches and field boundaries now to be seen in these areas are the product of monastic activities. As Matthew Paris wrote of the Fens:

> Concerning this marsh a wonder has happened in our time: for in the years past, beyond living memory, these places were accessible neither for man nor for beast, affording only deep mud with sedge and reeds. . . . This is now changed into delightful meadows and also arable ground. What therefore does not produce corn or hay brings forth abundant sedge, turf and other fuel, very useful to the inhabitants of the region.[28]

The extent of monastic involvement in agriculture is indicated by the size and quality of their agricultural buildings, a number of which have survived to the present day (unlike the more modest structures of early medieval laymen). At Temple Cressing in Essex, for example, there are two barns, the Wheat Barn and the Barley Barn, which were built by the Knights Templar in the thirteenth century. The immense size of these buildings, as well as their proven durability, gives some indication of the investment which this order put into the agricultural exploitation of its lands. These great barns were not, however, purely for the storage of the produce of the ecclesiastical estates. In part they were intended to house the corn which the monasteries collected as tithes

Temple Cressing, Essex
As its name suggests, Cressing was a manor of the Knights Templar. Huge barns such as this indicate the extent to which the monastic orders, as permanent institutions, were involved in long-term investment.

from the surrounding peasant farmers.

The Cistercian order was particularly endowed with the entrepreneurial spirit. Its houses were sited in remote locations, away from the temptations of secular life, and often occupied large tracts of poor quality and marginal land. Through investment, management and specialization, particularly in the production of wool, such land could be made extremely profitable.

As the estates of priories and abbeys were farmed by 'lay brothers' rather than by the labour services of a hidebound peasantry, they were not bound by local customs and were free to innovate and experiment. The usually small and weak communities who had occupied these mainly upland areas were often removed to make way for new farming methods. The gaunt Cistercian abbeys of the north of England, Fountains, Bylands and Meaux, are a graphic reminder of the power and wealth of this order. They still dominate the landscape, but in the Middle Ages this dominance was actual as well as visual. The establishment of these three abbeys alone may have caused the destruction of as many as fifty settlements.

None the less, even in the case of these powerful religious orders, the extent of their disruption of the tenurial status quo must not be overestimated. The destruction of villages was not necessarily brought about by the arbitrary action of a barbarous monastic tyrant. Some settlements, such as Old Byland, were relocated. In others the inhabitants were gradually bought out. The process was hardly benevolent, but it was nothing in comparison with the clearances that were to come.

Monastic institutions were exceptional not because of the extent of their power and wealth but because they used their power to intervene directly in the established patterns of land use. They stood alone amongst the early medieval élite in trying to alter the basic fabric of the landscape, and to impose innovations and specializations over the heads of the local communities. 'Those who worked' were primarily responsible for the creation of the medieval landscape, but 'those who prayed' also made a vital contribution. Those who fought, on the other hand, the lay landowners, displayed the extent of their power and wealth through individual features in the landscape rather than in its overall structure.

THREE

Power in the Land

ONE OF THE MOST powerful symbols of the Middle Ages is the great stone castle. More than any other feature, it confirms the conventional images of medieval society. With their martial exteriors and austere interiors castles inevitably suggest that life for their inhabitants was an unpleasant combination of occasional danger and constant discomfort. Such images may, however, be rather misleading. They not only exaggerate the importance of the castle in normal medieval society, but also emphasize its military role at the expense of civilian functions. Castles were more than merely defended strongholds. They also served as administrative centres, and as symbols of power and prestige. In this chapter we will look at the impact of castles and other status symbols on the appearance of the medieval landscape.

The Normans introduced castles as we know them into the English landscape. There had been some defended residences before the Conquest, as well as more extensive constructions known as 'burhs'. Some of these were simply protected enclosures to which the neighbourhood could retreat in times of trouble, while others were heavily fortified towns, such as Wallingford in Oxfordshire. This was formerly a Saxon burh, and it is still possible to see the remains of the extensive ramparts on its outskirts.

But Norman castles were very different from these municipal fortifications. They were much smaller and were used by more limited groups of people. In the decades after the Conquest they were built all over the country to help consolidate the power of the new élite. Some were constructed by the king, some by tenants-in-chief, and in the troubled regions of the Welsh borderlands some were built by quite minor local lords. Each private castle owner had to get a licence from the Crown, although in the anarchy of Stephen's reign many 'adulterine' or unlicensed castles appeared.[1]

Although several thousand castles were built in England in the century following the Norman Conquest, this does not mean that the landscape was dominated by numerous large and imposing structures. Castles that attract tourists today are by no means typical of the structures that were put up in the eleventh and twelfth centuries. Some castles had huge mottes, like those at Thetford in Norfolk and Clifford's Hill in Northamptonshire, and the mottes of the most important castles were eventually topped by formidable stone towers or keeps, like the Tower of London or Hedingham Castle in Essex. But the vast majority of early castles only consisted of a small stockade or a wooden watch-tower on top of a fairly small and uninspiring mound. Indeed, some of these even lacked the defended enclosures, or baileys, which usually surrounded the motte, or were attached to it.

Great awe-inspiring castles, symbolizing the power of the early medieval nobility, were never a very common feature of the English

Berkhamsted Castle, Hertfordshire
The keep has gone but the massive eleventh-century motte still survives. The flint wall around the bailey replaced defences of earth and timber in the middle decades of the twelfth century, when the castle was held by Thomas Becket in his capacity as Chancellor.

landscape. This was largely because, as castles became more complex and sophisticated, resembling our image of what a castle should be, there was a drastic decline in the number built.

A sequence of changes in the form of larger castles, culminating in the evolution of concentric castles, began in the twelfth century. Round keeps like that at Conisbrough, South Yorkshire, began to replace earlier square ones, while various attempts were made to strengthen the defences around the enclosure at the foot of the motte. Substantial walls were built, with towers dispersed along them at intervals, and in the thirteenth century a series of improvements were made to the gateway. As a result a substantial and fortified gateway had become the most important part of the castle by the fourteenth century. These stylistic developments were largely a response to changes in military technology, but in part they were caused by the changing practical and aesthetic demands of the baronial élite. At a time when status was indivisible from strength, the medieval castle was not only a display of might, but also a symbol of wealth and power, indicating the authority and importance of the inhabitants.

The more complex the castle, the greater the expense involved. The simple motte-and-bailey

castles of the early years could be constructed in a matter of days, like those built by William I at Dover in 1066 and at York in 1069, each of which was put up in little more than a week. In contrast the elaborate castle which Henry II built at Orford, with stone keep and rectangular internal towers, was constructed over eight years, from 1165 to 1173, and cost £1400. To put this sum in perspective, this was at a time when members of the gentry could live comfortably on ten to twenty pounds a year, and when only seven of the great magnates of England had an annual income of more than £400. Thus as time passed only the king and the most powerful and wealthy could afford to construct castles and fewer and fewer were built. After 1154 it is unlikely that there were ever very many more than 200 in England.[2]

Although the ownership of true castles became increasingly exclusive, many homes of

BELOW **Laxton, Nottinghamshire**
The majority of early medieval mottes were nowhere near the size of that at Berkhamsted (page 55). Most, like this diminutive mound at Laxton, were fairly minor features, topped with a wooden watchtower or stockade.

LEFT **Orford Castle, Suffolk: the keep**
Built by Henry II between 1165 and 1173, Orford Castle cost the huge sum of £1400 and utilized all the latest developments in military design.

minor lords, as well as lesser residences of the great magnates, began to have a fortified appearance. In the north of England, pele towers and bastles — small, strongly-defended stone towers — testify to the insecurity engendered by Scottish raids in the fourteenth and fifteenth centuries. In most parts of England, however, manor houses were adorned with turrets and battlements that had little connection with practical defence. A good example of this type of building is Greys Court in the Oxfordshire village of Rotherfield Greys, now owned by The National Trust. The fourteenth-century manor house was surrounded by a low wall, punctuated by four small towers of flint and early brick. Two of these towers are still standing, along with part of another, and there is a large square tower located within the walls.

It is clear that these fortifications were constructed primarily for the sake of aesthetic display rather than as serious defences, and in the later Middle Ages even the great baronial

Greys Court, Rotherfield Greys, Oxfordshire
Despite their impressive appearance, the fourteenth-century fortifications of the manor house at Rotherfield Greys were probably intended more for display, as an ostentatious expression of prestige, than for any serious military purpose.

residences began to be built along similar lines. The construction of new castles came to an end in the course of the fourteenth century, and many of the grand old defensive structures ceased to be adapted and maintained. None the less, many of the residences of the baronial élite continued to have a semblance of martial strength. Tattershall Castle in Lincolnshire, for example, which was built between 1430 and 1450, has battlements and a wide moat. These could only have served as decorative features giving the building an appearance of strength, for the large windows and unguarded entrance of the castle would have made it virtually indefensible.

Despite their prominence in twentieth-century images of the past, the castle was far less conspicuous in the medieval landscape than the buildings of the monastic institutions. Like castles these structures were a reflection of power, and their appearance served to emphasize the wealth and status of the order concerned. The different styles of architecture employed in these monastic buildings can give us some indication of the fortunes and preoccupations of their builders. For example, the prominence of Norman romanesque architecture in many monastic buildings shows the number of these institutions that were founded or rebuilt in the eleventh and twelfth centuries when this style was current. Many examples of this style of architecture can still be seen. It was often used in additions to Benedictine houses, and as many of these also served as cathedrals, they tended to survive the Dissolution better than buildings of other orders. Thus in cathedrals such as Durham and Gloucester it is possible still to appreciate the grandeur of romanesque monastic architecture, with its characteristic round arches, thick walls and simple, heavy vaulting.

In the last quarter of the twelfth century the Early English style was introduced. This was the first phase of what is now known as gothic, and featured pointed arches but relatively simple tracery. It was pioneered at various Cistercian houses, such as Fountains and Kirkstall, which were founded at this time, but it was also used throughout the thirteenth century in extensions, new buildings or reconstructions for existing institutions, often financed with the wealth generated by the exploitation of monastic estates. At Peterborough, for example, the impressive west front of what is now the cathedral was constructed in the early thirteenth century, using profits derived from the drainage and improvement of the Fens.

On the other hand, by no means all building projects were funded by the revenues from monastic estates. Most monastic orders had various strings to their bow, and in particular they were astute in exploiting the pilgrim industry. Like the tourists of today, medieval pilgrims provided a considerable source of income, and the wealth of a monastery could be greatly enhanced by the discovery of a relic which would draw the crowds. Thus the priory at Canterbury Cathedral was extensively rebuilt after the fire of 1174, largely on the proceeds of the cult of the martyred Thomas Becket. It may be no coincidence that the 'discovery' of the bodies of King Arthur and Queen Guinevere by the monks of Glastonbury came soon after the disastrous fire of 1184.

In the late thirteenth century Early English was superseded by the more sophisticated Decorated style of gothic architecture, characterized by complex window tracery. This tended to be used in extensions to monasteries which were paid for by wealthy families who had founded the house or had close associations with it. There was a considerable increase in this kind of building in the late thirteenth century, for in 1274 the doctrine of purgatory had been officially recognized. By endowing a chapel, and paying for masses to be said, an individual could ease the passage of his or her soul through the pains of purgatory, to the eternal bliss and peace of heaven.

At the same time, monastic buildings were increasingly used to display the elaborate tombs and heraldic symbols of the landed families who were associated with them. The great gatehouse of Butley Priory in Suffolk is adorned with the arms of many important benefactors, and from the late thirteenth century many monasteries became, in effect, 'tomb churches', filled with the memorials of a particular landed family. One of the most magnificent collections of medieval monuments is to be found in the abbey church at Tewkesbury in Gloucestershire. In the fourteenth century the east end of this church was extensively rebuilt, at the expense of the de Clare family and their successors the Despencers. They financed a whole series of chapels, and many of these are filled with large and lavish dynastic tombs.

Later chapels in this collection were built in the Perpendicular style, the final and most elaborate form of gothic architecture. These buildings are characteristically light, airy boxes — tall and wide, with large, ornate windows. Although examples of Perpendicular architecture are common in parish churches, they are much rarer in monastic buildings. By the time this style became popular, by the middle of the fourteenth century, there were few large-scale monastic building programmes. But surviving Perpendicular features provide an insight into the priorities of the monks at that date, for many of them were designed to improve standards of comfort within the monasteries. At Lacock Abbey in Wiltshire, for example, glazed cloisters were introduced in the fifteenth century, and this period also saw the construction of a new refectory (or dining room) at Cleeve in Somerset. Many building schemes of the later Middle Ages extended or improved the accommodation of the priors and abbots. Abbot's lodgings were added to Muchelney Abbey in Somerset in the early sixteenth century, and at the end of the fifteenth century Richard Singer built new lodgings and a guesthouse at Much Wenlock Priory in Shropshire. Such features indicate the laxity and hedonism of late medieval monks, and represent a striking departure from the austerity of the early orders.

Improvements in domestic accommodation coincided with various attempts to strengthen the defences of monasteries. Impressive castellated gatehouses were built in various places, such as Thornton Abbey in Humberside or St Osyth's Priory in Essex. Some of these were primarily for show, to give the institutions a semblance of strength, but some, such as that at the abbey of Bury St Edmunds, had a genuine defensive function. This gatehouse was completed in 1346, as a response to the riots of 1327, and included arrowslits and a portcullis. Such architectural developments suggest that monastic institutions were well aware of the hostility that was developing towards them.

The imposing ruins of Glastonbury or Tintern give us an impression of the way that medieval monasteries must have dominated the surrounding landscape, but it is difficult to appreciate just how many monastic landmarks there were in the Middle Ages. The majority disappeared at the Reformation, and were replaced by, or incorporated into, country houses, or demolished so their stone could be reused. Indeed, the prevalence of medieval monasteries in the upland areas of England is not purely a consequence of their original distribution. The ruins of Bylands, Fountains and Rievaulx still stand largely because there was less pressure on building stone in sparsely populated and rocky areas of upland Yorkshire than in the lowland regions of the country.

Within the landscape of medieval England, however, the most widespread embodiments of wealth and status were not monastic institutions but the houses of the secular élite. These ranged from great baronial residences, which were only used from time to time, to the manorial halls of lesser figures such as knights and local gentry which were more or less continually occupied. The great landed magnates of the twelfth and thirteenth centuries had a peripatetic existence, travelling with an immense retinue around the far-flung lands of their estates, and staying for limited periods at each of their numerous residences. The houses of these great men were not only numerous, but large, for each had to accommodate the lord and all his servants and retainers. The homes of lesser figures were less spectacular, for such men did not have the vast households that accompanied the most powerful barons.

The homes of the medieval landed élite were larger, better built and clearly of higher status than those of the rest of the population, but the lords did not display their exclusivity by divorcing themselves from the rest of the community. From the houses of the greatest magnates to those of minor knights, medieval manor houses were almost invariably sited within villages, surrounded by the homes of the other inhabitants. Status was displayed to the neighbourhood, rather than to other members of a national élite. The medieval manorial hall was the product of a very different society from that which produced the eighteenth-century country house, separated from the labouring community by an insulating landscape park.

In all larger medieval houses the most important room was the great hall, an airy space, open to the roof, and warmed by a large fire. Those which belonged to great barons were often vast, like the cavernous hall which can still be seen at Penshurst Place in Kent. This was built in 1341, and covers a ground area of 62 by 39 feet. When the lord was in residence these halls were used for a host of elaborate ceremonies. The lord would dine in the hall, surrounded by his household, and often there would be huge feasts attended by hoards of feudal inferiors and dependants. At all such occasions the wealth, the power and the benevolence of the lord would be conspicuously displayed. One particularly gargantuan blow-out was the great feast held in September 1465 at Carwood Castle, near York, to celebrate the enthronement of George Neville as Archbishop of York. Around 2500 people attended, and 113 oxen, 6 wild bulls, 1000 sheep, 2000 pigs, 2000 chickens, 4000 venison pasties and 12 porpoises were consumed.[3]

In the manorial halls of the lesser gentry a small-scale version of such ceremonies probably took place. The gentry also dined in the hall amidst their household, enacting formal rituals throughout their meal. Feasts were held on occasions such as Christmas and Easter, to which members of the local community would be invited, and in many places this practice was maintained by the local gentry into the sixteenth century or later.[4] In many villages the hall also served as a place where the manorial court met. As a result these courts were commonly referred to as 'hallmotes', that is, moots or assemblies that met in the hall.

The status of the lord, and his exclusivity, was constantly brought home to the community, even on festive occasions. The lord was seated at the upper end of the hall on a dais, which raised him above everyone else. The most finished surfaces, the 'upper faces' of the hall timbers, were invariably turned towards the dais end. Although in most cases these timbers could not possibly have been visible from the floor of the hall, the anticipated position of the lord none the less determined how the frames should be set when the hall was constructed.[5]

The function of the hall, as a setting for meetings and ceremonies, ensured that it was the interior rather than the exterior of the building which received the most lavish decoration. In a society in which status and authority were established on the basis of personal relationships, external appearances were of limited importance. Thus in the details of their construction, as much as in their plan and location, the residences of the landed élite reflected the nature of the culture that created them. They were clearly the product of a society which was strongly hierarchical, but in which authority was expressed directly and personally. Nevertheless, even in the medieval period there were signs that these social attitudes were starting to change. From the fourteenth century the great barons began to dine and entertain in the more exclusive environment of their private chamber, rather than in the almost public space of the hall, although this practice did not become common amongst the lesser manorial lords until the fifteenth and sixteenth centuries. Moreover, in the thirteenth and fourteenth centuries, local lords began to build their homes on the fringes of a village, rather than in the centre.[6] At the same time, a number of manor houses and the homes of wealthy farmers began to be constructed with moats. These would have served a variety of functions, providing a water supply, a source of fresh fish, a security system and a repository for sewage. But above all, they seem to have been status symbols, imitating the moats of great defended houses and castles, and separating their owners from the rest of the local community.

Manorial halls were noticeably different from the dwellings of humbler villagers. They were larger, and more substantial, but even these buildings would normally have paled into insignificance in comparison with the parish churches. With their tall towers churches were by far the most striking features in the landscape of much of medieval England, and their grandeur and number represented the importance of the religious establishment in medieval society. They are still impressive today, and must have been much more so in the Middle Ages, when their durable stonework formed a marked contrast to the flimsy hovels of peasant parishioners.[7]

The earliest churches were minsters, missionary establishments which served the spiritual needs of a wide area. One example is the

Foxearth, Essex
A moat such as this would have served many functions in the medieval period — as a supply of water, a source of fish, a system of waste disposal, and a protective boundary against intruders. But the primary function of such features was probably to confer status on their owners, whether manorial lords or aspiring freemen. The house in the centre of the moat was built in the fifteenth century, but the moat is probably two centuries older.

church at Brixworth in Northamptonshire, now the largest surviving Anglo-Saxon church in the country. Minsters were usually built in settlements at the centres of great Anglo-Saxon estates, particularly those under the control of the Church or Crown. It was only after these had fragmented, and local territorial units evolved, that churches came to be built elsewhere. As time went on, local lords began to pay for churches to be built, either to serve as private oratories, or to cater for the spiritual needs of their tenants. It is for this reason that the boundaries of present-day parishes often follow the Saxon estate boundaries described in early charters. Moreover, as it was usually the manorial lords who endowed churches, paid for their construction and donated the land on which they stood, churches were usually sited next to the manorial hall. In woodland areas the church and hall often stand together, separated from the scattered farms and hamlets of the parish.

Saxon lords were involved in church construction for many reasons, but probably the most important one was the fact that the possession of a church was a symbol of lordly status. In addition, in the late Saxon period lords were recognized as the owners of the churches which they had built. The Norfolk lady Siflaed, who died in the early eleventh century, referred in her will to 'my' church at Marlingford, and to 'my' priest Wulfmaer. As tithes and other revenues derived from a church could be used for the lord's private purposes, as well as for the maintenance of the priest and fabric, ownership gave the lord a direct financial incentive for church building.

Following the Norman Conquest, manorial

lords continued to be responsible for the construction, extension or alteration of churches. As the new Norman élite took control of the old Saxon manors, they often began extensive rebuilding programmes in the churches which they came to own. This usually involved the introduction of the more refined architectural styles which they brought with them from the continent. In Norman churches such as that in the village of Stewkley in Buckinghamshire, it is still possible to appreciate something of the impact that buildings in the new style must have had on the inhabitants of the surrounding countryside.

The role of manorial lords in the construction and maintenance of early medieval churches has been revealed in excavations at the deserted village of Wharram Percy in the Yorkshire Wolds. An impressive new manor house was built here in the second half of the twelfth century, and it is clear that the team of masons who constructed this stone building were simultaneously working on various alterations to the church. They rebuilt the east end of the apse, and added a new aisle. This suggests that the lord of the manor — probably a new arrival — was attempting to display his power and authority by an impressive and extensive building programme.

From the twelfth century, however, the ecclesiastical hierarchy and the monasteries began to take control of the parish churches, as a climate of religious fervour induced manorial lords to donate their churches to bishops or monastic houses. As the ecclesiastical organization was regularized, many private churches appear to have gone out of use altogether. The building which has been recently excavated at Raunds in Northamptonshire, for example, was converted into a manor house. Although many lords maintained the right to appoint priests and to take a share of the tithes, by the end of the twelfth century the privately-owned church had disappeared. At this time around 25 per cent of the churches were in the hands of religious institutions, and the rest were under the control of the bishops.

As churches passed out of the direct control of manorial lords, they ceased to be purely manifestations of their status and piety. The subsequent alterations that were made in the fabric of the church, the repeated building and rebuilding, were sometimes carried out through donations from wealth individuals, but sometimes through the co-operative action of the community as a whole. It was generally the parish that was responsible for the maintenance of the church building, apart from the chancel. This was the responsibility of the incumbent, or of the lay or ecclesiastical patron who took the tithes and appointed the incumbent. The lord would have made an important contribution to any general church-building programme, but evidence suggests that much of the money for such projects was raised by the rest of the villagers, including those who were relatively poor.

The fourteenth-century Black Book of Swaffham in Norfolk lists the names of 123 benefactors of the church, and of 52 people who had promised sums of money to help to repair the tower. These sums ranged from 2d to 6s 8d and the very poor no doubt contributed the only thing that they could to the renovation of this communal building: their labour.[8]

The community got together the money to maintain the church and its equipment through fund-raising events similar to those held by church bodies today. Parishioners often organized plays, for example, which toured neighbouring villages. Such communal ventures were, inevitably, the occasional cause of disputes within the village. There was considerable upheaval in the village of Pulloxhill in

Stewkley, Buckinghamshire
Dating from the mid twelfth century, Stewkley is a rare example of a Norman parish church which has been very little altered. It was probably built to proclaim the power of the local landowner over the surrounding countryside as much as to the glory of God.

Bedfordshire in the late thirteenth century, when church funds were embezzled. John Russell had raised £4 by putting on a play, but this sum, as the churchwardens complained at Chancery:

> the seyd Churchewardens oftyn tymes hathe requeryd of the seyd John to use of the seyd Church accordyng to his promyse, and that to do the seyd John at all times hathe denyde and yet denythe, to the grete hynderyng of reparacyon of the seyd Churche and of other ornamentes of the same.[9]

In addition to such activities, in some villages some of the fines levied by the manorial courts had to be donated to the church. Thus a fifteenth-century by-law for the village of Broughton in Northamptonshire stated that:

> it is ordered by the common consent of the lord and his tenants that no inhabitant shall call any of his neighbours who dwell there whoreson . . . or cuckold on pain of 4d of which one half to the fabric of the church and the other to the lord of the fee.[10]

Since the church was usually the only communal building in the medieval village, communities tended to measure status by the splendour of their pile. Parish would vie with parish in fervid architectural rivalry. Indeed, many of the contracts for church-building drawn up in the Middle Ages cited the churches of neighbouring villages as models. When, for example, the inhabitants of Walberswick in Suffolk engaged masons to build a new church tower in 1425, they stated that it should be similar to the tower at Tunstall, and that it should have a west door and windows 'as good as' those of the tower of Halesworth.

Wealthy individuals often made gifts in the form of impressive features added to the fabric of the church, such as doors, windows, towers, roofs and occasionally additional side chapels. The small heads of lay figures that are sometimes carved on medieval church porches, for example, may represent important benefactors. By the thirteenth century, a period for which documentation is relatively abundant, individuals rarely paid for a church to be totally rebuilt. None the less, it did happen from time to time, especially in the later Middle Ages. These churches were usually constructed both to serve a parish and to provide a chantry chapel in which clerks were employed to say prayers for the souls of the founders. At Ewelme in Oxfordshire, for example, the Duke and Duchess of Suffolk rebuilt the parish church (except the tower) in the fifteenth century, in the fashionable perpendicular style. The resultant building is light, airy and impressive, but it is also unusual in that the main structure dates from a single period. Most parish churches have no such definable origin, but have gradually reached their present form over the centuries. In a pot-pourri of architectural styles, it is usually possible to recognize elements from many different periods.

The fact that the cost of church maintenance was borne by the local community helps to explain why the size of a church was not closely related to the population of the parish which it served. Rather it was the wealth of the parish that was revealed in the size of the church. The church fulfilled many purposes besides those which were strictly religious. Parish possessions were stored there and it was used for meetings, as well as social gatherings such as 'church ales'.

As the medieval period progressed, the church began to be filled with objects which overtly indicted the wealth and status of particular families. Heraldic symbols of wealthy dynasties were displayed on tombs, and also on stained-glass windows. In Wimpole church in Cambridgeshire, for example, a fourteenth-century window displays the coats of arms of all the families that were allied to the Ufford line. At the same time tombs increased in size and prominence, as substantial free-standing structures replaced the less conspicuous slabs or brasses which had been the usual form of funerary monument up to the fourteenth century. Within the church at Ewelme, for example, is the free-standing tomb of Alice de la

St Mary's Church, Ewelme, Oxfordshire
With the exception of the tower, which dates from the fourteenth century, the church was entirely rebuilt by the Earl and Countess of Suffolk in the 1430s.

Pole, daughter of the Duke and Duchess of Suffolk. Her stone effigy lies within a massive ornamental framework, decorated with the heraldic devices of the de la Pole family and its numerous connections. Beneath the effigy, dimly discernible through low arches, is a *memento mori*, the carved figure of a decaying corpse. The tomb provides a grisly reminder of the transience of mortal life, but it also commemorates the church's founders and indicates their wealth. Elsewhere, wealthy families paid for chantry chapels to be built within, or added to, their parish churches, and these were often decorated with the family's heraldic symbols.

Yet at the same time as churches were becoming filled with such dynastic symbols, they were also increasingly dominated by religious images and icons. Wall paintings proliferated in the thirteenth and fourteenth centuries, and statues of saints and subsidiary altars appeared in the aisles. At least from the mid thirteenth century, the nave and chancel were separated by a brightly painted rood screen, surmounted by the great crucifix known as the rood. This marked the division between the space belonging to the parish and the area which was the responsibility of the priest, and it also gave a particular prominence to the mystery of the mass, and thus increased the impact of the ritual and ceremony which formed the major part of the villagers' religious experience. Amidst all this religious iconography the elements of secular display would have been comparatively inconspicuous. The medieval parish church embodied the status of the community as much as that of individual families within it, but also represented the importance of the church within that community.

The Church was an international organization which had considerable influence over the lives of the medieval population, but it was somewhat divorced from the institutions of lay power. Despite the links between Church and State at both local and national level, the medieval church had a moral authority and a system of organization relatively independent of the secular world. None the less, the way in which the relationship between parishioners and God was expressed within the medieval church mirrored the structure of authority within the community and the secular link between peasant and lord.

Nowadays it is difficult to get an impression of how the interior of a church must have looked in the Middle Ages, because modern churches, unlike those of the medieval period, are usually full of seats. From time to time, however, it is possible to find a redundant church from which the seating has been removed, and which has something of the spaciousness and atmosphere of a medieval building. Such churches bear a remarkable similarity to the manorial halls of the Middle Ages and in particular to the large halls of the early medieval period, like that built towards the end of the twelfth century at Oakham Castle in Leicestershire. A hall and a church nave are both cavernous stone-built chambers and both are aisled, a visual similarity enforced by certain parallels in the way these spaces were used.

Manorial halls had developed a fairly standardized plan by the thirteenth century in which the central part of the building was open to the roof, but there was a two-storey section at each end of the hall. At the lower end, divided from the hall by a through passage, there were service rooms, the buttery and pantry, in which food was stored. Above these were rooms which provided accommodation. At the other end of the hall, the upper end, there was a private parlour, into which the lord could retire. Above this was the chamber, a kind of private bed-sitting room.

In many ways the medieval church follows this same basic plan. Entering the church from the south door would be like entering a manorial hall through the 'screens passage' — the passage between the hall and the lower end. To the left, in the place occupied by service rooms in the manorial hall, there was usually a tower and 'non-liturgical' space, used as a general storage area for all the common possessions of the parish. On the right, instead of the hall, lay the nave, at the far end of which stood the rood screen and rood. These two great symbols signified the earthly face of God and they were located in the same position as the secular lord sitting on his raised dais in the manorial hall. Beyond the rood screen lay the chancel or private space of the priest, bringing to mind the private parlour of a manorial lord. The congregation therefore stood in front of the great crucifix of the rood in the same position as peasants faced their manorial lord.

The activities of the lord within his private parlour were concealed from the villagers, and so, to some extent, were the activities of the incumbent in his chancel. The parishioners could therefore feel towards their religious master the same combination of familiarity and respect that the peasants felt towards their secular one. Their religious and secular loyalties were neatly reinforced. Indeed it is striking that

Didlington, Norfolk
Where seats have been removed from parish churches the visitor can get some idea of what church interiors must have looked like in the Middle Ages. The airy spaciousness highlights the similarities between the layout of the church and that of an aisled open hall.

Oakham Castle, Leicestershire
The great aisled hall is the only surviving remnant of Oakham Castle. Built around 1180, it resembles a towerless church.

in many of the vernacular religious writings of the medieval period, and in particular in the work of mystics such as Julian of Norwich, the appeal was towards the loving and approachable figure of Christ, rather than to a less accessible God. It was only as the face to face communities of the Middle Ages began to break down that a distant and authoritarian God began to replace a paternalistic Christ as the subject of religious devotion.

The architecture of the two principal buildings in the medieval village, the church and the manorial hall, was very much a product of the society which created them. The relationship between the villager and his local and heavenly lords was direct and personal, but involved formalized rituals which would have inspired awe and deference. The spatial organization of the landscape was not used to display status or the distance between social classes, for the social, political and economic structure of the state, as well as its philosophy, emphasized the links between interest groups and classes, rather than their divorcedness. From the peasant at the bottom to the king at the top, people were bound together by ties of personal loyalty and obligation. In addition there was little scope for divisive conspicuous display in the working landscape, at a time when the majority of land was under the control of the peasant farmers.

Only in the deer park did medieval lords make a distinctive contribution to the overall framework of the landscape. These were areas of rough pasture dotted with trees, interspersed with clumps of woodland, and bounded by a pale, usually a substantial bank topped by a fence or wall. The park provided the lord with some grazing for cattle and horses, with a source of wood, timber and venison, but above all with pleasure, the thrill of the chase.[11]

Nowadays it is difficult to find a park which still resembles its medieval form, as most have been extensively restyled and altered. None the less there are a few, such as Moccas Park in Hereford & Worcester, where many of the original features can still be seen. Here the deer still browse under ancient pollards, and the park is still encircled with a traditional cleft oak pale. The great majority of medieval deer parks were either absorbed into later landscape parks, became woods, or were converted into agricultural land. In the latter case the characteristic sub-rectangular outline of the park can often still be discerned, fossilized in the hedge lines of the present day, while names such as Park Farm and Park Field often indicate the former presence of a deer park.

Before the Norman Conquest there were already a few parks in England, and Domesday records thirty-three of them in 1086. They seem to have spread only gradually through the twelfth century, but between 1200 and 1350 they proliferated, no doubt reflecting the affluence of the landed classes of England in this period. By the early fourteenth century, when they were at their densest, there may have been on average as many as one park for every 10,000 acres of land.[12]

Parks were not cheap to create or to maintain. In particular, the pales were very costly, especially in the larger parks. In the early fourteenth century the average circumference of the parks was around $1\frac{1}{4}$ miles, but parks with boundaries of $2\frac{1}{2}$, $3\frac{3}{4}$ or 5 miles were not unusual, and some were $7\frac{1}{2}$ miles or more. There was also the expense of stocking the park. The principal inhabitants were fallow deer which had been introduced by the Normans, and these had to be fed in winter, and provided with sheds for shelter. A keeper had to be employed to maintain both the park and the herds, and to protect them from poachers. But perhaps the most important consideration was that they took up land which could be more profitably deployed. Although they could provide some timber and grazing, the intensive exploitation of these resources was not compatible with the keeping of deer. The innumerable medieval parks therefore represented the 'conspicuous wastage' of the great magnates.

Deer parks could only be created by

obtaining a royal licence, and this was in itself a mark of distinction. Having made a fortune in trade, aspiring medieval families acquired parks as a symbol of their new nobility. The de la Pole family were Hull merchants who became Dukes of Suffolk, and as well as building the church at Ewelme, they demonstrated their aristocratic status in the fifteenth century by constructing numerous deer parks on their estates.

Deer parks clearly conferred status on their owners, and their exclusivity was confirmed not only by their cost, but also by their privacy. Unlike most features in the medieval landscape, deer parks were private; the village community was kept strictly beyond the pale. As such they served as forerunners of the landscape parks that were to become such an important feature of the eighteenth-century English countryside. There the similarity ends, however, for although deer parks were a luxury, they were also essentially functional. They did not represent any attempt to mould the landscape for aesthetic reasons, and they did not indicate that medieval lords had even the slightest interest in the appearance of the countryside.

Most parks lay at some distance from their manorial hall, although some ran up to the rear of halls that were sited amongst other dwellings. It was only rarely that medieval halls were actually isolated within the parks. The moated sites which can often be found within deer parks were usually homes for the rangers who managed the parks, or temporary accommodation for the lord and his retinue, rather than the lord's permanent residence. None the less, these medieval equivalents of holiday homes were often quite luxurious. The hunting lodge at Higham Ferrers in Northamptonshire, for example, included a hall, a chamber, a chapel, a kitchen, a brew-house and a bake-house.[13]

Even though deer parks did not fulfil the social and aesthetic functions of subsequent status landscapes, they were still exceptional in the medieval countryside. They were created by a single powerful individual, and used for recreation and the display of status at a time when the rest of the landscape was being exploited for agriculture and was largely organized by the local communities.

FOUR

Crisis in the Countryside

SCRATCHED HIGH ON THE NORTH WALL of the massive church tower at Ashwell in Hertfordshire is a simple message: 'the first plague was in 1349.' Further down is a more plaintive piece of graffiti, written, like the first, in dog-Latin: '1350, wretched, wild, distracted. The dregs of the people alone survive to tell the tale.' These crudely etched words give some impression of the despair and confusion created in the mid fourteenth century by the ravages of the 'Great Pestilence', the Black Death. Coming after a period of crop failure, animal disease, and climatic deterioration, this plague produced a catastrophic population decline, and wrought radical changes in the economy, the landscape and the pattern of landholding in England.

Before the reverses of the fourteenth century, the economy of medieval England was expanding rapidly, and between Domesday and the beginning of the fourteenth century the population seems to have more than doubled. From around $2\frac{1}{4}$ million, it rose to 5 or even 6 million, bringing an increased demand for food and land, and a surplus of labour. In the later Middle Ages, from the Black Death to the fifteenth century, things were very different; the population was relatively low, land was abundant and labour was scarce.

Many books on landscape history have stressed the importance of the initial expansionary phase, emphasizing the connection between the rise in population and the extension of arable cultivation. Yet the process by which open waste and grazing was converted into arable land was by no means simple and straightforward. It did not merely involve the clearance of unused and unclaimed land, but was part of a general change in the pattern of the ownership and management of land. The impact that population growth had on the landscape, like that of its dramatic decline, was often quite subtle, complex and indirect.

Even in its early expansionary phase, the economy of medieval England was not based purely on subsistence production, with people primarily concerned to grow food for their families. It was a market economy, and the majority of the peasantry laboured on the land to make money as well as to satisfy their hunger. Population growth was thus not immediately followed by the 'natural' disaster of famine, but by a period of rapid inflation. As demand for food rose and outstripped supply, prices also rose, further stimulating the production of agricultural goods. Lords and peasants alike were keen to cash in on rising prices, and tried hard to maximize the yields from their land. Only by doing so could they protect the value of their income and maintain their standard of living in an inflationary age.

From the late twelfth century the manorial lords became increasingly involved in the farming of their demesne land. They resumed control of those lands which had been leased out in the previous century, and at the same time increased the exactions on their villeins. Heavier labour services were introduced, and such services were often reimposed in cases where they had previously been commuted to cash payments. At the same time, significant changes were taking place in the legal status of villeins. They were increasingly regarded as totally unfree, so that they were unable to bring cases against their lords in the royal courts. Any dispute had to be settled within the manorial court, from which villeins had no recourse to any higher authority. Thus they were prevented from contesting the increasingly onerous burdens placed on them.

As the population and labour force grew, wages declined. At the same time, land and rents became more expensive, as demand for land increased. As the lords flourished on the profits of agriculture, the position of many peasants and labourers appears to have got worse. Those peasants who possessed a substantial amount of land were well placed to reap the profits of the inflationary economy, but many of their landless fellows were impoverished by the high price of food. On the other hand by no means all peasants and labourers in the twelfth and thirteenth centuries were primarily involved in agriculture. In the complex economy of medieval England there was a great proliferation of cottage industries, services and trades. The poll tax returns and other documents give us some idea of the range of rural occupations that were practised in the fourteenth century and amongst those mentioned are smiths, carpenters, rope-makers, thatchers, pedlars, spinners, weavers, dyers, fullers, shoemakers, tailors, butchers, bakers, glaziers, lime-burners, inn-keepers, glovers, hosiers and skinners. Indeed, those living primarily off the produce of an agricultural holding were a minority in many areas.

In view of this complex and broadly-based economy, with an active market in land and the percolation of cash through the whole of society, some historians have suggested it is inappropriate to describe the lower classes of medieval England as a peasantry in any meaningful sense. It is certainly true that the diverse lower classes of this period could not be compared to the peasantry of Eastern Europe in the eighteenth and nineteenth centuries. They have few classic peasant traits, such as close ties with the ancestral landholding, a strong and extended family structure, or a primarily subsistence-based agriculture. They were not a homogeneous agricultural class, and it is clear that the economic pressures of the twelfth and thirteenth centuries served to accentuate the variations in their wealth and social status. The benefit of some was the ruin of others, and as the population increased, the 'peasantry' (for want of a better word) lost what homogeneity it had formerly possessed.[1]

Some have gone so far as to suggest that thirteenth-century tenant farmers, far from being downtrodden peasants, were competitive and egocentric figures, with an outlook comparable to anyone living in a modern Western capitalist society. In our opinion, however, this conclusion should be treated with considerable caution. It underestimates the strength of community in medieval society, the way it functioned and also the extent to which communities varied from region to region. In other words, it takes no account of the social variations which underlay the diverse landscapes of England. This is an important omission, for different areas reacted in rather different ways to the economic pressures of the twelfth and thirteenth centuries.

The polarization of the peasantry which resulted from economic upheaval did not occur equally across the whole country. In a few woodland areas a drastic reduction in the size of all holdings was produced by the limited restrictions on the division or alienation of land, the individualistic agricultural methods and the phenomenal growth in population. In parts of thirteenth-century Norfolk the average holding was a mere five acres. Such widespread reductions in landholding units were, however, uncommon, and in most woodland areas there was a much greater degree of polarization.

The systems of landholding in the woodland regions generally ensured both the prosperity of some tenants, the medieval kulaks, and the indigence of others, whose holdings had disintegrated. At Redgrave, in Suffolk, for example, over half the tenants in the thirteenth century had holdings of no more than two acres, while the wealthier peasants held 50 or even 100 acres. At the same time, a local market encouraged many of the landless to become involved in manufacture and trade. In both these respects Redgrave typified the kind of communities that inhabited the woodland regions, particularly in the southeast of England.[2] Likewise those parts of the eastern champion which were characterized at the time of Domesday by a wide range of landholding units continued to display this pattern into the thirteenth century. But in the majority of the champion areas, where land was traditionally held in standardized open-field units, the peasantry did not polarize into landed and landless to anything like the same extent. In the central and southern champion lands in particular, where manorial control was stringent, there was often comparatively little fragmentation of customary holdings.[3]

There were also considerable variations between woodland and champion regions in the way in which the status of the labouring population was changing. Even though villein tenures had been declared unfree, the proportion of the rural population who were of free status was increasing, but this process did not occur to the same extent in all parts of the country.[4] In most woodland areas, especially in the southeast, there was a marked rise in the proportion of tenants who were holding by free tenures. But in the champion areas of the east, which had traditionally been free, it was the unfree classes which became more prominent, as many of the free tenants had their status downgraded. This was a significant change in the free east/unfree west division which is clearly discernible in Domesday.

It is not clear why this change took place, and in particular why there was an increase in the number of free tenures in the woodland areas. Some people in the woodland parts of the southeast who were classified as free in the thirteenth century may have been regarded as unfree at the time of Domesday. They may have been able to get their status upgraded when local villein tenures were regularized, because of the extent of their economic power. The flourishing markets of London and the demand created by East Anglian textile workers ensured that farmers thrived in counties such as Hertfordshire, Middlesex and Essex. They may have been in a position to assert the free nature of their tenures, at a time when similar tenures elsewhere were being classified as unfree.

But free tenures also increased in the twelfth and thirteenth centuries in the woodland areas of the west, which were far from the industrial centres of the southeast. In these areas it may have been the ability to alienate their land which made it possible for the more successful farmers to claim free status. Freedom to buy and sell was a particular feature of the villein tenures in woodland areas. For example, the local customary tenure of Kent, known as *gavelkind*, which involved partible inheritance, was officially recognized as a free tenure in the thirteenth century. As the *Lex Kantiae* states, 'All the persons of Kentishmen should be free, as much as the other free persons of England. . . . They should be allowed to give and sell their lands and their tenements without asking leave of their lords.'[5]

As well as these general alterations in the status of certain forms of tenure, it was also possible for individuals to buy their freedom from their manorial lord, and thereby escape from the social stigma of villeinage. Like the general emancipations, these individual upgradings were more common in the woodland areas than in the champion. The peasantry of woodland areas showed the widest variations in wealth and status and it was in these areas that the most prosperous and upwardly mobile villeins emerged.

There were some areas which did not carry a woodland landscape where the number of free tenures increased in the twelfth and thirteenth centuries. This was so, for example, in the Fenland, a part of the country which cannot be easily accommodated in the neat division between woodland and champion. Here there was an abundance of marshland available for reclamation, and this supported the growing free and fiercely independent population which was a feature of the region both during and after the Middle Ages. None the less, it was primarily in the woodland regions that significant increases in the proportion of free tenures took place, and it was these regions, rather than the east of England, which began to be characterized by communities of free peasants.

The expansion of cultivation in the early Middle Ages took place in the context of this complex pattern of landholding. Many writers on the medieval landscape describe this process of 'assarting' as if it involved the clearance of an unused wilderness. Yet from Saxon times assarting is really more accurately described as a change of land use. The waste which fell under the plough in the Middle Ages was land in which numerous people had rights, and which was an important source of fuel and building materials as well as grazing.[6]

In the early Saxon period wastes were very extensive, while rights to them were loosely defined, and held by large numbers of people. Sherwood Forest, for instance, was once as the name implies the wood of the entire shire of Nottingham. Such 'intercommoning' was often maintained long into the post-medieval period. The inhabitants of twenty-two parishes still enjoy full common rights on Dartmoor, while the holders of land in the rest of the county (apart from Totnes and Barnstaple) still have more limited rights of pasture. These rights were quite widely exploited in the nineteenth century, and in summer cattle were brought from considerable distances by train to graze on the moor. But in most places, as time passed and waste dwindled, the rights to its use came to be strictly defined and confined to much smaller groups of people. Where a large number of villages had formerly shared in the use of a waste, the land was increasingly apportioned between them. These partitions were often encouraged by disagreements between interested communities over the management of waste.

For instance, the Bishop of Bath and Wells, the Dean and Chapter of Wells, and the Abbots of Glastonbury and their tenants were all involved in a great dispute over the grazing of the Brue Valley in the Somerset Levels. In this area disputes over wasteland were traditionally acrimonious, and this one was far from being conducted with ecclesiastical restraint. Ditches and marker stones were destroyed, animals were killed and maimed, buildings were pulled down, there was open brawling, and the combustible peat was fired: passions for waste ran high in the Brue Valley.

Even where the waste was recognized as indisputably belonging to a particular village, there were frequent quarrels within the community over how the land should be used. Sometimes areas of common grazing were enclosed by individuals for their sole use, to the exclusion of the rights of the rest of the community. At Doningsby in Yorkshire more than a hundred men were accused in the mid-thirteenth century of letting their animals trample the corn of the lord of the manor. They answered the charge by declaring that the land should never have been enclosed, and that they had common rights upon it.[7]

Yet it was not usually the lords of the manor who carried out the conversion of common wastes into arable land. They encouraged and no doubt benefited from this process, for it raised their rents and the value of their estates. But it tended to be tenants rather than their landlords who were responsible for individual enclosures, with the notable exception of monastic and other ecclesiastical landowners, who instituted various capital intensive schemes for the reclamation of wastes. On many occasions too, whole communities rather than individuals made a joint decision to cultivate tracts of their common grazing, dividing the arable lands between those who had formerly had common rights.

The extent to which the commons were removed varied from place to place and there were also striking regional variations in the means by which the majority of this land was cleared. In some areas most of the wastes were formed into enclosures owned by individuals; in others communal clearances most frequently occurred.

The wastes survived well in upland areas where the population was low and the commons of little use as arable. This is evident today, for the most extensive areas of common land are in the rugged landscapes of the north and west. Before the widespread enclosure of the commons in the eighteenth and nineteenth centuries, however, there was not such a close relationship between the distribution of commons and regional variations in soils and topography. The commons tended to be on the poorest soils within each area, but they were not confined to the poor land nationwide. Nor was their survival in the medieval period closely related to population density. Norfolk, for example, was the most densely populated area of medieval England, yet vast tracts of common survived in the county. Even in the nineteenth century 143,346 acres remained.[8] This suggests that the distribution of commons may have been influenced by social and economic factors as well as by demography and geology, and landscape evidence suggests that the extent to which the communities of the twelfth and thirteenth centuries were cohesive and community spirited was particularly important.

In champion areas, where villages were accustomed to act together, the communities seem to have been able to limit unilateral enclosures and to combine together in projects of communal clearance. A collective decision could be made to plough up the common pasture, producing arable strips which were divided between those who had formerly had rights to the use of the land. Even where small areas of waste were enclosed by individuals, the community normally ensured that these could be used for common grazing when they lay fallow. Moreover, such enclosures often quickly fragmented into strips when the land was divided on sale or inheritance, and were incorporated into the system of open fields.

The assarting carried out by champion communities in the eleventh, twelfth and thirteenth centuries therefore tended to produce additional arable furlongs around the perimeter of the open fields. In some places such clearance led to fields becoming so extensive that they could not be efficiently farmed, and in these circumstances a daughter settlement was sometimes established, on the outskirts of the lands of the village.

In woodland areas the communities were much less accustomed to working together and there were much greater variations in the size of the holdings. Wastes were often not seen as areas to be used by the community as a whole, the farmers frequently exploiting only those parts which were closest to their farmstead. Thus if one wealthy farmer attempted to appropriate an area of grazing, with the backing of the local lord, he would usually be opposed only by the handful of farmers accustomed to using it. Unilateral assarts of this kind were often not just endorsed but openly encouraged by manorial lords, who offered grants of free status to wealthy tenants prepared to carry them out. At the same time there was also considerable small-scale assarting by poorer people.

Despite the unilateral enclosure of woodland wastes, in general common grazing survived better here than it did in the champion regions. Woodland communities did not have a strong common interest, since there were wide differences in wealth and status. It was therefore more difficult for these disparate communities

Central Norfolk in 1797
Thousands of acres of commons still survived in Norfolk at the end of the eighteenth century. Most were subsequently removed by parliamentary enclosure. William Faden's map shows clearly the distinctive shape of the commons, with their irregular curving outline, and the characteristic scattering of farms and cottages around their periphery.

to co-operate in the clearance of large tracts of waste in which substantial numbers of farmers had rights than it was for the more homogeneous champion villages, which had a tradition of communal endeavour. In addition, woodland areas often contained large numbers of small-holders or part-time farmers, who depended on common rights for their survival.

By the twelfth century many communities which had extensive waste had developed specialized industries based on this land which were sufficiently important to provide an added incentive for the wastes to be preserved. In the low-lying marshes of east Norfolk, for example, the extraction of peat for fuel became a major medieval industry. This specialized activity has left a very distinctive mark on the landscape; the flooded remains of the deep pits dug to extract the peat are now known as the Norfolk Broads.

From the middle decades of the thirteenth century there was an important change in the legal tenets surrounding enclosure with the passing of the Statute of Merton in 1236. This statute was an attempt to limit disputes over the enclosure of common land, by empowering lords to enclose manorial waste provided they left sufficient pasture for the requirements of their free tenants — in other words, it enshrined the rights of free tenants in national law. But it also marked a significant decline in the independence of the villeins, for it made no provision for compensation in cases where they lost their customary rights. The Statute of Merton was the first attempt to impose a national definition of property which would overrule local customary systems, and was thus the first time that national law was concerned with the question of the distribution of power in the land.

Before the passing of this act, free tenants seem to have been able to oppose any unilateral enclosure of the waste by appealing to the royal courts. After 1236, however, it was legally recognized that the lord of the manor was the ultimate owner of the commons — as, indeed, is usually the case today, although in many cases the manorial rights have been purchased by local authorities. The Greater London Council, until its sad demise, was the owner of Hampstead Heath, since the Metropolitan Board of Works had purchased the manorial rights in the late nineteenth century.

The Statute of Merton appears to have had a profound effect on the landscape in some areas. June Sheppard's study of the Yorkshire village of Wheldrake has demonstrated the striking difference between the way in which assarting was carried out before and after the act. Before 1236 newly cleared land tended to be absorbed into the open fields, since all the villagers shared common rights on this land when it was not under crops. After 1236, however, cleared land tended to be formed into individually owned fields, so that the arable open fields came to be surrounded by a ring of small hedged closes.[9] Nevertheless, although the rights of villeins were not sanctioned by the royal courts once the Statute of Merton had been passed, the continuing strength and importance of local communities and local customs ensured that their rights to common grazing did not immediately disappear. Even in the fourteenth century there were still instances of wastes cleared by communities rather than by individuals which were formed into open-field strips that were divided between the villagers. For example, a charter of 1308, recording a grant of land in Harlestone in Northamptonshire, refers to 'all that portion of heath when, by the agreement of the community of the vill, it will be broken up'.[10]

The effects of the Statute of Merton were, in fact, complex, for it did not invariably encourage the erosion of wastes. In areas where the majority of the population were farmers with free tenure, the provisions of the statute ensured that commons survived well. The statute stipulated that sufficient pasture had to be left for the needs of free tenants, so where these were in a majority the opportunities for assarting were limited. The prior of West Acre in Norfolk, for example, was given a royal licence to enclose two acres of common in the village, but only on condition that he provided an equivalent area of land elsewhere.[11] Commons tended to survive in woodland areas, but it was in those parts where free tenures were most dense that they were eroded least. The number of free tenants may well be the reason why the commons of Norfolk survived so well.

In some areas the clearance of commons and woods was limited not merely by local tenurial and geological conditions, but by national law. These were the areas which were denominated *forest*. The term forest did not mean that they were covered in trees, for 'forest' has only come to refer exclusively to dense woodland in the last hundred years. In the Middle Ages forests were areas which were subject to forest laws, aimed at encouraging deer to breed in order to provide game for royal hunts. The distribution of royal forests is still not fully understood. Most of the very densely wooded areas of the country, such as the Weald of Kent, were never subject to forest law. Conversely, many areas that became forest, such as Dartmoor, had lost much of their woodland at an early date, and others, such as the forests of Huntingdon or Rockingham, were relatively well-wooded pockets within the otherwise fairly treeless champion Midlands.[12]

The forests in lowland England usually contained some enclosed woodland, often owned by the Crown, but also cultivated fields and settlements. Those villages in the champion Midlands which lay within royal forests often appear to have been no different from ordinary champion settlements. For example, one of the earliest maps in England depicts the village of Boarstall, in Bernwood Forest in Buckinghamshire, showing it as a normal nucleated village, surrounded by traditional arable open fields. Elsewhere forests displayed the irregular field systems and scattered settlement characteristic of woodland regions.

But many details of the lives of the inhabitants of these areas were determined by forest law, which was devised to give the deer of the forest as much protection as possible. For example, all large dogs in forest areas had to be 'lawed' — that is, have their fore-claws removed so that they were lamed — to stop them harassing the deer. There were also controls on the clearance of woods and wastes, to ensure that there was scrubland available within which deer could breed. This law was not rigidly enforced throughout forest areas, and many farmers were able to get away with clearing some waste, providing they were prepared to pay a substantial fine to the Crown for the privilege. Nevertheless, both woodland and common waste tended to survive better in the areas under forest law than they did in non-forest areas with comparable soils and topography.

The commons were the most important component of the medieval forest, and by the end of the Middle Ages the term 'forest' had begun to be used to refer specifically to these wastes, rather than to the whole area that was under the control of forest laws. In many cases the Crown was the owner of the soil of the commons, and also of the standing timber growing upon it, but in areas of forest as elsewhere the amount of timber gradually declined in the course of the Middle Ages because many forest communities had rights to it. In 1251 villagers in the royal forest of Geddington in Northamptonshire had the right to: common pasture for all animals except pigs and goats; large timbers for house repairs, walling and ploughs; 'a reasonable livery of branches against Christmas for burning', and any dry wood lying on the ground that they could gather 'with their hands without using any sharp weapons'. It was inevitable that in areas where rights such as these existed many commons were gradually reduced to almost treeless tracts of rough pasture.[13]

Not all the common waste that was taken into individual enclosure in the eleventh, twelfth and thirteenth centuries was turned over to cultivation at this time. The increase in population had precipitated not merely a demand for food, but a crisis in natural resources of all kinds. In particular, there was a serious shortage of wood.

Although manorial lords were rarely directly involved in the clearance of wastes for arable, in many areas they sought to enclose common wastes in order to create woods. Unlike the commons, the woods of medieval England were almost invariably the private property of the manorial lord. The villagers often maintained some rights within these woods, such as the right to collect a certain amount of firewood or material for house and fence repairs, but these rights were usually quite stringently limited. In particular, grazing within woods was banned so that livestock did not destroy young trees.

Coppices in particular could only survive if livestock was excluded. Coppicing was the usual system of wood management, with most trees cut down to a stump or stool every five to ten years, so that they produced a regular crop of long, thin poles. The poles were ideal for firewood and other domestic uses, but they could only be produced in woods which were not grazed, and where the villagers were denied the right to help themselves to wood. Coppiced woods were protected by substantial earthwork banks which excluded livestock and emphasized that they were under private control.

Many medieval woods have survived to the present day, but most have not been coppiced for generations. Bradfield Woods in Suffolk, however, is an exception in that it is an area of woodland which has been continually coppiced from at least 1252.[14] Nowadays it is a nature reserve, and it gives the visitor a very good idea of what the majority of English woods must have been like. There are few fully grown trees, and as a result the depths of the wood are strangely light and airy.

Where woods were not in private hands, and the rights to their exploitation were widely shared, they were gradually destroyed in the course of the Middle Ages and turned into open common grazing. Woods inevitably survived best in the woodland regions, where a considerable amount of land was held in individually owned enclosures. Deer parks are also a feature of these parts of the country, because unilateral enclosures could be carried out more easily here than in champion regions.

Nowadays, many commons are covered in woodland, but this would hardly ever have been the case in the Middle Ages. Some of the more extensive medieval commons contained substantial numbers of trees, particularly in the royal forests where the timber was protected by special regulations, but in most areas the trees that can now be seen have only grown up as the land became less intensively grazed. In the Chiltern Hills, for example, many commons have become wooded only in the last 150 years. In earlier times they would have been made up of rough pasture with small amounts of scrub, and a few pollarded trees on the larger commons.

In contrast to coppiced trees pollards were cut at the top rather than the base of the trunk, so that the poles sprouted a couple of yards

RIGHT **Bradfield Woods, Suffolk**
In the medieval period most woods were coppiced in order to produce a regular crop of long, relatively thin 'poles'. Far from being dark and shady, the typical wood would have been light and airy for the most part, and large timber trees would have been rare. Here at Bradfield coppicing has continued without interruption since before 1252. Wood management of this kind was only feasible where community rights in the wood were limited: if the land had been subject to common grazing, the regeneration of the coppice stools would have been prevented.

BELOW **Pollarded trees in Hatfield Forest, Essex**
The trees on the left of the picture have been pollarded fairly recently, those in the centre not for very many years. This kind of scene would have been found in many parts of medieval England, for most of the larger commons (especially those within royal forests) as well as the majority of deer parks consisted of this characteristic mixture of rough grassland, pollarded trees, and small amounts of scrub.

above the ground. This meant that they were out of the reach of grazing animals, and could survive in the hostile environment of common land. Although trees in deer parks and hedgerows were pollarded, it was a form of tree management peculiarly associated with areas in which rights to the land were extensively shared. Indeed, in typical medieval fashion, there was often a division of the rights to individual trees, with the manorial lord taking the timber, and the tenants having the use of the poles. Pollarding was particularly practised on commons within forests, and ancient pollards are still managed in Hatfield Forest in Essex, now a country park.

The survival of commons and woods in the woodland areas and their erosion in the champion accentuated the already existing contrasts between these two types of landscape. In the course of the twelfth and thirteenth centuries the open-field landscapes of the champion became increasingly reduced to unrelieved arable plains, whereas in the woodland regions the woods, commons and deer parks gave the countryside considerable diversity. These differences in land use were echoed in the settlement patterns of the two regions.

Despite the establishment of a few subsidiary hamlets in the champion regions, the extension of arable agriculture in the twelfth and thirteenth centuries did little to disrupt the traditional pattern of nucleated villages except in certain forest areas. Even where small areas of waste had been enclosed 'in severalty' (i.e. by a single individual), the farmstead was seldom moved to the holding. These new enclosures tended to be located on the outskirts of the open fields at a distance both from the village and the rest of the tenants' holdings. Champion villages did expand, but they usually remained locked in their ever-growing open fields. In many cases new homes were built on the edge of the existing settlement where men gradually acquired blocks of land that were big enough for them to build a house. Expansion of this kind appears to have been particularly common in the eastern champion areas, where there were more free tenants, where manorial control was relatively weak, and where there was much buying and selling of land. In many Cambridgeshire villages, such as Burwell, Grantchester and Cottenham, the pattern of property boundaries still preserves the distinctive contours of open-field strips. In contrast, in the more strongly manorialized communities of the central and southern champion areas, there were more stringent restrictions on the buying, selling and consolidation of open-field strips, and there was also less proliferation of holdings since there were fewer free tenants and primogeniture was strictly enforced. As a result these villages do not seem to have spread out over their open fields to quite the same extent as the villages of the eastern champion regions, and the growth of the population was often accommodated by the subdivision of existing house plots in the village.

The pattern of settlement in the woodland areas was much more flexible and fluid. In the course of the late Saxon period settlements were gradually established in the large tracts of ancient common woodland and grazing which had survived in these regions from the days of the extensive tribal estates, and this process of colonization continued into the twelfth and thirteenth centuries. In the Forest of Arden, for example, there was widespread clearance of scrub and woodland by free settlers in the thirteenth century. This produced a pattern of scattered farmsteads, most of which proclaimed the newly-won status of their owners by being endowed with moats.[15]

Even in woodland areas which had long been

Burnham Beeches, Buckinghamshire
The existence of this old pollarded beech within an area now occupied by woodland shows that this land was formerly grazed by animals. The area was once open common land. Only as the intensity of grazing declined in the last two centuries has it come to be covered with trees.

settled and cleared, there was far more mobility in the settlement pattern than in the champion regions. Tenants had more choice over where to live, because land could be freely bought and sold, and there were many more parcels of land which were of sufficient size to carry cottages or farmsteads. In many places, particularly in East Anglia, the landscape of today shows evidence of the settlement mobility of the past. Many churches stand isolated from the villages to which they belong. As the archaeologist Peter Wade Martins has shown, these churches were originally the focus of settlement, for small scatters of Saxon and early medieval pottery have been found around them. In the twelfth and thirteenth centuries, however, the houses were all resited at a distance from the church around an area of common grazing.

Indeed there were even some peculiarly active villages which moved more than once. The village of Longham in Norfolk, for example, was originally centred around the church, but in the early medieval period the houses shifted to Southall Green. In the late medieval period the settlement moved again to the edges of the nearby Kirtling Common, where most of the village is today.[16]

Roe Green, Sandon, Hertfordshire
Hamlets like this, with houses and farmsteads loosely scattered around an area of common land, could be found in many woodland areas in the medieval period. They usually resulted from the migration of farms to the margins of pockets of common land in the twelfth and thirteenth centuries, as areas of grazing dwindled under the impact of a rapidly rising population. Nowadays this characteristic settlement form can be difficult to identify, for the central common has usually been enclosed and is often built over.

Elsewhere, in parts of Suffolk, Hertfordshire, Essex and the Chilterns, villages did not move en masse to the edge of common land, but straggling hamlets emerged around greens and commons as settlements expanded.[17] Some of these hamlets still retain this form, such as Croxley Green in Rickmansworth or Roe Green in Sandon (both in Hertfordshire), but in many cases this pattern of settlement has been obscured by subsequent enclosure. At Littlebury Green in Essex, for example, the straight road through the hamlet is bordered by nineteenth- and twentieth-century houses and barns, but behind the buildings on each side lies a row of older structures, set well back from the road, and reached by straight side tracks. The more recent buildings date from the enclosure of the green on to which the older houses used to front in 1805.

The building of houses on the edge of the commons was probably stimulated by the shortage of grazing which occurred in the medieval period. As common grazing fell to the plough, areas of pasture became islands of grass amidst seas of arable. Woodlanders were attracted to the margins of these islands, partly because of the convenience of proximity, but perhaps also because their presence on the edge of the common reinforced their claim to the grazing within it. The absence of effective communal controls in the woodland areas, which would otherwise have ensured a fair distribution of common rights, may have made a physical presence necessary. The complexity of manorial arrangements and the high proportion of free tenants in medieval East Anglia probably goes a long way towards explaining why settlement was so mobile in this area, and why so many entire villages upped sticks and moved to the edge of the commons. Moreover the location of settlements around the areas of common pasture probably indicates the importance of this resource in the woodland regions, a reflection of the large number of smallholders, who were economically dependent on the maintenance of their grazing rights.

The loss of pasture also had other consequences. It led to a reduction in the number of animals which a medieval community could keep, and this meant that less manure was produced. The ever increasing arable lands

Carleton Forehoe, Norfolk
Isolated churches, left stranded when their villages migrated to neighbouring areas of common land, are a characteristic feature of the East Anglian landscape.

could no longer be fertilized with the intensity they once were, and so the productivity of the fields began to decline. This process was accelerated by the shortage of woodland: as in some Third World countries of the present day, the absence of an adequate source of fuel led many people to burn their manure, instead of returning it to the soil. As a result yields dwindled, encouraging the further decimation of pasture in order to increase arable production.

It seems that it was the champion regions in particular which laboured in this vicious circle. The population levels of these regions were often lower than those of the woodland areas, but their communal organization ensured that not only their resources of wood and timber but also much of their grazing was destroyed at an early date. Moreover, the strips produced by clearance were sited further and further from the settlement and were poorly fertilized and increasingly difficult to work because of the inconvenience of their location. The problems in clayland areas were particularly acute, because heavy rain severely limited people's mobility and the soil was only suitable for ploughing and sowing for limited periods of time. Furthermore, the paucity of organic material in the soil resulting from the lack of manure made it progressively less absorbent and less easily worked, compounding the effects of a climate that was getting wetter.

Although arable acreage was increased in champion areas, there was a decline in arable production per acre, and some remarkably inefficient farming methods were practised. The expansion of arable agriculture was both a cause and a consequence of this inefficiency, as the farmers had to clear more land to counteract their declining yields.

The landscape of today still shows signs of the extent to which open-field farmers extended their cultivation. In former champion areas of the Midlands there are many parishes (such as Naseby or Welton in northwest Northamptonshire) which, until recently, were completely covered in ridge and furrow, apart from where there used to be water meadows. These landscapes indicate that when the tide of medieval expansion was at its height the whole of the waste was eliminated, and almost every inch of land fell under the plough.

In woodland regions the weak communal ties ensured that the arable was not expanded at the expense of the waste as much as it was in champion areas. Common wastes tended to survive better, especially where there were large numbers of free smallholders. Furthermore, in certain woodland areas pressure on arable land combined with the individualistic organization of farming produced some highly innovative farming methods, in contrast to the inefficient practices seen in the champion.[18]

The most important innovation was what was later called 'convertible' or 'up-and-down husbandry'. Under this regime, instead of being put down to fallow every second or third year, a plot of land was ploughed up and cultivated as arable for a few years, and then for the next few years laid down to grass. This regime increased the quality of both pasture and crops, and was widely practised in such woodland areas as Kent, Suffolk, Devon, Norfolk and Sussex, and in areas like the fens where communal controls were weak. Up-and-down husbandry was by no means first introduced in the post-medieval period, as has frequently been supposed.

Recent research in Norfolk and Sussex has shown that even in the early medieval period entrepreneurial farmers in these areas used all sorts of advanced agricultural methods. They were planting peas and beans for fodder, instead of letting their fields lie fallow. Rotations were flexible and individually determined and crops were densely seeded. Farmers were stall-feeding their animals and spreading the manure, and assiduously using all the fertilizing agents available. This was all very labour intensive, but labour was not short in thirteenth-century England.

On the other hand, it would be misleading to suggest that all woodland regions were occupied by thriving entrepreneurs, while the champion lands languished under the inefficient exploitation of hidebound village communities. Freedom from conservative restraints, and from traditional practices and customary controls, could produce very bad as well as very good forms of agriculture. Sometimes, as in south Norfolk, methods of farming were practised which can only be described as environmentally disastrous, with land being cropped for years on end without ever being allowed to 'rest' as fallow.

Thus the economic upheavals of the twelfth and thirteenth centuries produced considerable changes in the landscapes of England. Wastes and woods were cleared, settlements were expanded, and, as trades and industries proliferated, many people became divorced from the soil. But the changes were not uniform across the face of the country; they were mediated by variations in soil and topography, by the nature of individual communities and by the pattern of power in the land.

Any generalized picture is inevitably a simplification which ignores significant differences between communities on a local scale, but none the less it is useful to draw a general distinction between woodland, upland and champion regions. As the population and the extent of arable land grew in the twelfth and thirteenth centuries, the settlement of woodland and upland areas remained dispersed and often became even more scattered. Although areas of waste were enclosed, large tracts of common still survived. The woodland landscape was thus essentially varied, with farmsteads dotted about amidst a mixture of open fields, commons, woods, deer parks and hedged closes of various sizes.

In champion areas the situation was very different. Comparatively little remained of the wastes, particularly in the highly manorialized champion heartlands of the southern and central Midlands, and there were few of the features of private property which enlivened woodland landscapes. Instead nucleated villages stood isolated in a landscape of bare, unenclosed arable, which formed an ever more striking contrast with the varied woodland landscapes.

Then, in the mid fourteenth century, the years of expansion came to an end as the Black Death decimated woodland, champion and upland areas alike. It swept the country, and ushered in a new phase of social and economic development.

The Black Death first struck in 1349. It returned in the 1360s, and recurred over the following three hundred years. In its first onslaught in particular it decimated the population of England on an almost unimaginable scale. Some people suggest that the population fell by over a third, and the effects of this decimation would have been particularly acute because it occurred within a relatively short space of time. Some impression of its effects can be gained from its impact on three Hertfordshire manors belonging to the Abbey of St Albans. In 1349, sixty-five people in the village of Codicote died, that is, about half the abbey's tenants; at Barnet eighty-five tenants died, and at Abbots Langley eighty-two.[19]

Such a sudden reduction in population was, of course, bad news for those who suffered a horrible death, but it was good news for most of those who were lucky enough to survive. Although the population decline caused some economic contraction, the cake did not shrink anything like as fast as the population. With fewer people land and food were abundant and labour was scarce. The situation experienced in the early medieval period was therefore in many ways suddenly reversed and as a result there were fundamental changes in the structure of English society. The Black Death profoundly affected the relationship between landlord and peasant, and also led to a great change in attitudes to the community, to custom, to change and to social class. Its effects were perhaps similar to the changes which took place in Europe after World War I. The conceptual framework of the old society was disrupted by the dramatic changes and the alterations in ways of thinking were in many ways as significant as practical developments in the social and economic spheres.

The demise of large sections of the labour force strengthened the hand of those who survived in the years following the onslaught of the disease.[20] As peasants capitalized on rising wage rates and falling rents, there was a great increase in the geographical mobility of the labouring population. Villeins were still in theory tied to the manors of their birth, but in practice they could move if they wished. The lords of manors into which they moved would not have readily turned them away. They needed the income from their rent rolls, and were quite prepared to turn a blind eye to breaches of manorial discipline in order to attract tenants to their holdings.

At the same time the lords found it increasingly difficult to compel their villeins to perform their customary dues and services. The balance of power had shifted away from the lords and the villeins were not slow to take advantage of the new situation. Furthermore, as the profits from agriculture slumped many lords got out of demesne farming as rapidly as they could by leasing out their demesne lands and thus had less need of labour.

But the lords did not take the new power of the labourers lying down. They sought to legislate against it, and in 1351 the Statute of Labourers was passed. This was a rearguard action which attempted to control wages, and to restrict geographical mobility. It totally failed to achieve anything of the kind. The economic cards had, for the time being, played into the hands of the workers, and in the short term it was the peasants and labourers who gained from the social upheavals of the fourteenth century.

Yet even in this halcyon era peasant farmers and labourers did not have it all their own way, as was revealed in the defeat of the abortive Peasants' Revolt of 1381. This was sparked off by the institution of a poll tax, or capitation tax, an idea that has recently been revived after 600 years. An armed rising in the southeast was accompanied by demands for the abolition of the ecclesiastical hierarchy and the disendowment of the monasteries; an end to villeinage, manorial regulation and the payment of manorial dues; and the introduction of fixed rents of four pence an acre. After initial successes the peasants were tricked into defeat, but despite this reverse there was a gradual slackening of the chains of villeinage. The old form of personal servitude came to an end, although it was eventually replaced by inequalities that were unrestrained by the power of custom.

There is no doubt that the Black Death dramatically altered the pattern of agricultural exploitation, but it did not have the kind of immediate effects on the landscape which used to be suggested by historians. In many parts of England the humps and bumps of deserted medieval villages can still be seen, the grassy mounds serving as monuments to the decimation of the population that took place in the fourteenth century. But very few of these settlements were deserted as a direct result of the plague. Some very small settlements were entirely destroyed by its onslaught, such as the hamlet of Hales in Northamptonshire, where, as a document of 1356 records, 'nobody is dwelling there or has dwelt there since the Pestilence', but on the whole the desertions and settlement shrinkages were the product of a far more gradual process. They were a consequence of the complex social changes that were brought about by the Black Death.

Villeins now had much greater choice over where they would farm. They could easily take up tenements on land where the rent was low or the soil good, and desert the poor soils or high rents of their home. Thus on areas of marginal land, such as the sandy Brecklands of Norfolk, and the Wolds of Yorkshire and Lincolnshire, there were extensive desertions in the fourteenth and early fifteenth centuries, and these areas are dotted today with the earthworks and

sometimes the crumbling churches of these deserted medieval villages.[21]

In woodland areas many scattered hamlets and subsidiary settlements were also abandoned. Harold Fox's study of the parish of Hartland in Devon, for example, has shown that many of the minor hamlets contracted to become single farmsteads, while those on the poorest soils were often completely deserted.[22] Similarly on the boulder clays of Essex it was the hamlets on the best soils which were the least affected by the population decline.

Hound Tor, Dartmoor, Devon
The drastic population decline of the fourteenth century encouraged considerable mobility, and led to the shrinkage or desertion of many villages, hamlets and farmsteads. This hamlet was established on the lower slopes of Dartmoor in the eighth century, and was abandoned in the early fourteenth.

In some places it was the human rather than the physical environment which spurred the tenants to decamp. If a reactionary landlord attempted to impose unreasonable restrictions on his villeins, the tenants simply voted with their feet. At Hatton in Warwickshire the Bishop of Worcester attempted to extort ridiculously high cash rents from his villeins, as well as some limited labour services. As a result the villagers drifted away one by one until the village was deserted. They simply took up tenements in other more desirable locations.[23]

Many settlement desertions took place in the fifteenth century rather than the fourteenth. These were not simply a consequence of increased mobility, but were rather the culmination of changes in the landholding structure which had been taking place since the outbreak of the plague. These changes involved not only great alterations in the terms and patterns of ownership, but also the growth of new attitudes to property and the emergence of new forms of power in the land.

Before the eruption of the Black Death in 1349, the English peasantry were becoming increasingly polarized, and this trend was accelerated in the years after the plague. The sudden abundance of land made it possible for the more prosperous peasants to increase the size of their holdings and the fifteenth century saw the emergence of a flourishing yeoman élite. This was in part a consequence of the relaxation of manorial authority following the plague and in particular of the weakening of manorial control over the sale of land.

The economic changes of the fourteenth century also disrupted the terms under which much land had been traditionally held. As many families died out, large acreages of customary land reverted to the lords.[24] When this land was let once again it was not on the original customary terms, but on something more akin to a private contractual arrangement between landlord and tenant. This contract took the form of a copy of the manorial court roll which recorded the admission of the farmer to his holding and the terms on which the land was held. At the same time, much demesne land which had never been customary land was now being made available to farmers as the lords got out of demesne farming. Such land was held by leasehold, a private cash transaction entirely independent of the manorial court. All this served to weaken the customary controls over land.

In time many farmers came to hold their land as copyhold, but there were various forms of this copyhold tenure and considerable variations in the rights and security enjoyed by the tenants. 'Copyhold for years', for example, meant that the farmer only had security for the number of years that were stated—often as few as twenty-one or forty years. 'Copyhold for life' or 'for lives', on the other hand, meant that the family's tenure was secure for the duration of a farmer's life, or for his life and his son's life, and perhaps even his grandson's life too. At the end of this period, the next generation could take over the holding only on payment of a fine. The level of this levy was no longer decided by custom, but was fixed by the manorial lord to whom it was paid.

These agreements reflected the new ideas about land that were emerging in the fourteenth century. Since the thirteenth century the lord had begun to be seen as the owner of the manorial waste. From the mid fourteenth century he was regarded in practice, and increasingly in law, as the owner of copyhold land held for lives or for years. The tenements were his private property, over which he had ultimate control, and the tenant was increasingly seen as a tenant in the modern sense of the word. His rights over the land which he held were strictly limited.

Some copyholders, however, who held their land by 'copyhold of inheritance', had greater security than those who held 'for lives' and 'for years'. These farmers had to pay a fine when their holding passed from father to son, but in the case of a dispute such fines were still set by the manorial court. In areas where the community remained strong and assertive, the copyholders by inheritance could enjoy considerable security of tenure, and most copyhold of inheritance eventually came to mean much the same as free tenure.

As ideas of private property developed, free tenants gained complete security of tenure and the land they held began to be seen as belonging to them. The inflation of the years before the Black Death had usually reduced their rents to almost nothing. They paid a mere token, a peppercorn rent, to their manorial lords, and in most cases these renders were eventually forgotten altogether. As free tenures and the most secure of the copyhold tenures became freehold, these men became the owners of the land.

There were thus considerable variations in the kinds of tenure enjoyed by the farmers of England, and these were to have a substantial influence on the evolution of the countryside. The regional distribution of the various forms of tenure and tenant communities was the product of the way in which these communities developed both before and after the plague.

In woodland areas, and especially in the south and east, there were large numbers of landless labourers and small copyholders, but also a flourishing class of prosperous freeholders. Such men not only enjoyed secure tenure in their own holdings, but often leased substantial quantities of additional land. They were thus in a much better position than their insecure copyhold neighbours, and the juxtaposition served to indicate the extent to which the population of these areas had been polarized before the arrival of the plague. Communities of this kind also developed in some champion vills, and in particular in eastern champion areas such as Cambridgeshire, where manorial control was weak or divided.

Elsewhere in the champion regions communities had generally maintained a much greater degree of coherence. In some villages, particularly those which had formerly been heavily manorialized, strong communal controls had prevented the disintegration of holdings and thus the polarization of the community. The villeins of these villages often formed strong and assertive communities, able to stand up to the manorial lords as the terms of tenure changed. Thus, when agricultural prices picked up again in the late fifteenth century, these villages were characteristically inhabited by moderately wealthy farmers, who held by freehold or copyhold of inheritance.

In other, and usually smaller champion communities, however, the lords managed to maintain much of their manorial authority. In many of these villages the most enterprising tenants, having failed to extort a reasonable deal from those who owned the land, upped sticks and moved elsewhere. Those who remained succumbed to the landlord's power, and became vulnerable communities of weak tenants, holding by insecure forms of copyhold.

In the fifteenth century changing economic conditions encouraged many landlords, and many prosperous tenants, to rethink their agricultural strategy. Arable farming was labour intensive and costly, and as food prices dropped it brought increasingly low returns. Sheep farming, in contrast, was becoming an ever more attractive proposition. It required little labour, and the international price of wool was invitingly high. There was a great inducement, therefore, for landlords to convert what they increasingly regarded as their own land to sheep farming, and to try and get rid of the farming communities and tenants who had traditionally exploited the lands as arable. They could then either farm the lands themselves, or lease them to one of the rising class of tenant farmers.

This removal of arable communities was not universally approved and various attempts were made to legislate against enforced depopulation, particularly under the early Tudors. As the preamble to an Act in 1489 pointed out:

> Great inconveniences daily doth increase by desolation and pulling down and wilfull wast of houses and Towns within this . . . realm, and laying to pasture lands which customarily have

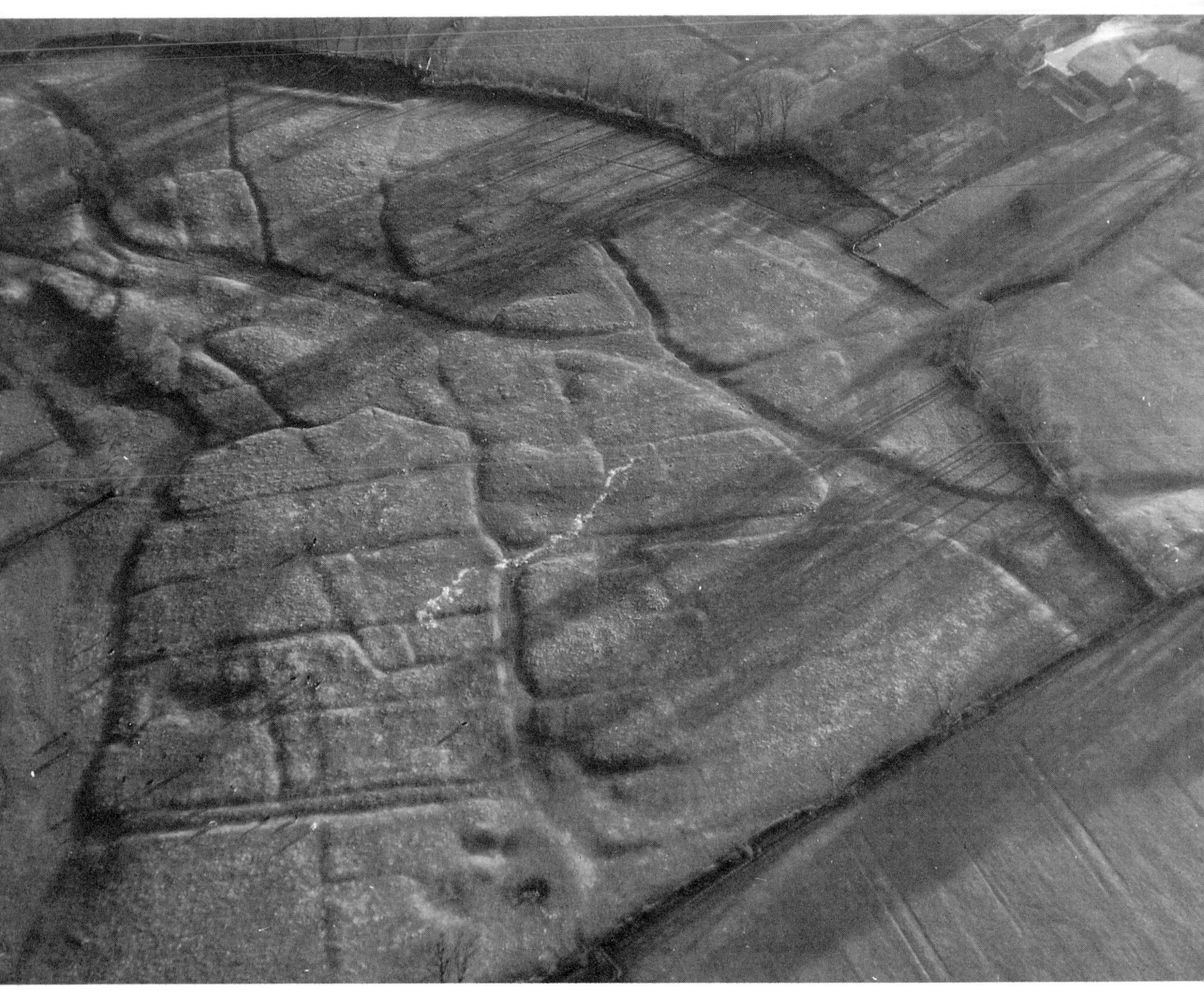

been used in tillage, whereby idleness — ground or beginning of all mischiefs — daily doth increase, for where in some Towns two hundred persons were occupied and lived by their lawful labours, now be there occupied two or three herdsmen and the residue fallen in idleness; the husbandry, which is one of the greatest commodities of the realm, is greatly decayed; churches destroyed; the service of God withdrawn; the bodies there buried not prayed for; the patron and curate wronged; the defence of this land against our enemies outwards feebled and impaired; to the great displeasure of God, to the subversion of the policy and good rule of this land.[25]

Despite such controlling legislation, forced evictions continued, although they were only successful under particular circumstances, and in certain parts of the country. A village could be destroyed only if it was under the control of a single manor and it was generally only small weak communities of insecure tenants who were successfully removed. Most evictions took place

Burston, Buckinghamshire
When John Swafield enclosed Burston and converted it to grazing in 1488, he destroyed the village and evicted its sixty inhabitants. The earthworks of the village are preserved in these large fields which are typical of the enclosed pastures of the late medieval period.

among the champion communities of the Midlands, and in particular among those of Warwickshire, Leicestershire, north Buckinghamshire and Northamptonshire. As the author of the sixteenth-century *Treatise Concerning the Staple* remarked, deserted villages occurred 'in the middle parts of the body of the realm'. In 1488, for example, John Swafield evicted sixty people from the village of Burston in Buckinghamshire. As a result, the value of the land rose from £13 1s 8d per annum to £40. Twenty years later when the antiquary John Leland passed through the parish he commented on the excellence of the pasture.[26]

Where the tenants held by copyhold for years, the lord merely had to wait until the copyhold was completed. Where copyholds were held for life or lives, the lord could charge exorbitant fines on the death of a tenant, making it impossible for sons to take over their fathers' holdings. In villages where there were only small numbers of freeholders, they could be bought out. This latter policy was often followed by the monastic institutions, which could afford to invest in agricultural specialization and long-term planning. Thus the villagers of Stormsworth in Leicestershire were gradually bought out in the fifteenth century by their manorial lords, the monks of Selby Abbey.[27] Clearing the land in this way could take a considerable time, and on occasions unscrupulous landlords looked for more rapid results, resorting to effective but illegal methods. The freeholders of Over Shuckborough in Warwickshire, for example, complained that:

> Thomas Shuckborough of late of hys grete power and myght hath enclosed, severed and taken from ye sayd orators . . . certyn ground . . . and all thys he hath doon to wery your seyd besechors to dryfe theym from the seyd towne to the entente he myght laye it all to severall pasture as he hath doon the forsayde grounde.[28]

But whatever the means of removal, the net results were the same. Small, weak, champion communities were destroyed, and the open fields replaced by the pastures of sheep or, in some cases, cows. It was this that produced many of the deserted medieval villages of England, rather than the fatal impact of the plague. The earthworks, house platforms, traces of roads and fragments of churches that we see today are monuments to a change in the balance of power in the land.

As the medieval period drew to a close, the complex property system of the customary landscape was in decline. Some peasant farmers had begun to gain outright ownership of their lands, while others found themselves the tenants of a manorial lord. Yet the clarification of customary tenures was a gradual process, and continued in some peripheral areas of England into the seventeenth century. The physical and administrative features of the customary landscape, the common fields, common wastes, manorial courts and by-laws did not disappear overnight. They gradually became less important in the post-medieval period as the proportion of land in the hands of small farmers declined.

The creation of sheep farms in the champion lands of the Midlands was but a prelude, a mere taste of the changes to come. The privatization of the landscape and the growth of agricultural specialization gathered momentum from the sixteenth century. The consequence of these developments was a revolution in the landscape of England with the enclosure of both common arable and common waste. Yet the progress of this revolution was in part determined by the tenurial variations established in the medieval past.

FIVE

After the Middle Ages: The Progress of Enclosure

THE LANDSCAPE OF LOWLAND ENGLAND is essentially a landscape of hedges. Thick, winding and species-rich, or flimsy, rectilinear and hawthorn, the varied hedges criss-cross the countryside. In the highlands of England grey stone walls are at one with the desolate terrain, but they are also a reminder of the human endeavour that has shaped even these hostile surroundings. In lowland England it is the banks and hedges which give the landscape its peculiar intimacy; they create an air of privacy, with limited rather than boundless prospects. Nostalgic ex-patriots dream of the hedges of England, and recently the hedge has come to symbolize what is most to be valued and most threatened in our landscape.

In many parts of the country, the landscape has been well hedged for centuries. In woodland areas individual holdings began to be enclosed from the Middle Ages or even earlier. These areas are characterized today by their ancient sinuous hedges, made up of a multiplicity of species: hazel, dogwood, bramble, hawthorn, maple, sloe, oak, elm or even spindle. Each of these hedges is unique in its blend of colours, shapes and species, reflecting its long history.

Some old and interesting hedges are found even in the champion areas, particularly on parish boundaries or around the edges of the former open fields. Enclosure for sheep farming from the fifteenth century in a number of champion regions also led to many hedges being planted around the large grazing pastures which replaced the open-field strips. So although most boundaries in the former champion areas date from the large-scale enclosures of the post-medieval period, these regions also have many older hedges.

Moreover, the varying ages of the more recent boundaries themselves mark successive phases of enclosure in the post medieval period. They are thus central to the narrative of this book. Enclosure did not merely involve the consolidation of scattered property and the fencing and hedging of fields, but also represented the triumph of individual ownership over the rights of the rest of the community. Walls and hedges serve a practical agricultural purpose, but they also have a wider, symbolic significance as the boundaries of a private landscape.

Enclosure involved two distinct processes: the enclosure of common waste and the enclosure of common arable. These have a great deal in common, for they both represent the conversion of land used by many into land that is owned by a few, but it is useful to distinguish between them. In some parts of the country it was largely waste, and in other parts of the country largely arable which was enclosed in the post medieval period.

An ancient hedge
Despite the widespread belief that hedges can be reliably dated by counting the number of shrub species which they contain, there is no strict relationship between the age and species content. Nevertheless, old hedges such as this tend to be composed of a greater number and range of shrubs than those created by post medieval enclosure.

The enclosure of common waste and arable from the fifteenth century was one aspect of a long and complex process of agricultural change which began at this time. Farming gradually became a capitalist industry based on a sophisticated market economy, but this development was only possible because of the evolution of concepts of absolute ownership, and the emergence of a few wealthy landowners and large farmers in place of the former multiplicity of peasant proprietors.

The origins of these developments can be traced back to the medieval period, and were rooted in a whole nexus of social, economic, tenurial and technical factors. Of all the processes involved, the increase in regional specialization, the increase in agricultural innovation and the decline of the small owner-occupier were particularly important in the evolution of the English landscape.

As the economy of England became more complex and sophisticated, farmers began to concentrate on particular agricultural products rather than on producing a wide range of commodities to satisfy the needs of the local community.[1] They chose the crop or animal to which their land appeared most suited, taking account of the climate, the soil and the location, and they produced that crop or animal for sale on the national market. Thus regions developed which were primarily devoted to a single type of agriculture. These regions were not always static; some changed their speciality as the centuries went by. None the less, much of the basic pattern of regional variations was maintained from the sixteenth to the eighteenth century.

There is still a basic distinction between the primarily pastoral west of England and the primarily arable east, but in the early modern period the pattern of regional variations was far more complex than this simple dichotomy. As we saw in the last chapter, areas of Leicestershire and Northamptonshire were given over to the production of sheep and cattle in the fifteenth century. This was one of the earliest specialized landscapes, and in the subsequent centuries they became much more widespread. Much of Norfolk and Suffolk, for example, was devoted to dairy farming in the sixteenth and seventeenth century, a far cry from the intensive arable agriculture seen in these areas today.

Of course, post medieval systems of agricultural specialization are not comparable to the kind of monocultural production on which modern farming is based. Up to the twentieth century the great majority of farmers practised some form of mixed agriculture, with a particular bias towards a certain type of production, and the pattern of specialization varied considerably from village to village and from farm to farm.

The development of this specialization was partly a response to an increasing demand from the rapidly rising population of the sixteenth and seventeenth centuries. After more than a century of demographic stagnation agricultural prices were high, which encouraged many people to invest in farming, while some large landowners began to resume the direct management of their demesne lands. Many farmers realized that by concentrating on the production of a single lucrative crop they could maximize the returns on their capital. Moreover, increased investment made possible various forms of innovation and experimentation.

Birstwith, North Yorkshire
A fine parliamentary enclosure hedge—straight as a ruler, and almost entirely composed of hawthorn.

Although the price of agricultural goods, particularly cereals, declined in the second half of the seventeenth and the early eighteenth century, the trend towards intensified agricultural production and improved agricultural methods did not stop.[2] Farmers, many of whom were tenants encouraged by their landlords, tried to maintain their levels of profit by increasing the quantity of food which they produced. Thus the process of agricultural innovation was maintained, and it was further stimulated in the late eighteenth century when agricultural prices picked up once more.

Any kind of pastoral farming or stock rearing was easier within a hedged landscape. And in arable farming it was far easier to invest and experiment where land was individually rather than communally worked. In many woodland areas where much land had been held in severalty for centuries, and where farming was frequently very individualistic, sophisticated agricultural techniques had long been practised. From the sixteenth century, however, advanced methods such as up-and-down husbandry began to be more widely applied, and numerous new techniques were developed. Since these techniques could be most successfully employed on enclosed land, they served to encourage the spread of enclosure.

Many of these new techniques were aimed at

solving a problem which had bedevilled medieval agriculture, namely a lack of grazing. This deficiency had limited the number of animals kept, and so had restricted the amount of manure produced and available to use as fertilizer. In the highlands of England there were considerable areas of marginal land which provided large quantities of poor grazing, but in many parts of the lowlands the shortage of fodder was acute, especially in the winter and spring when the grass did not grow. Partly in response to this problem, the ingenious agriculturalists of the early seventeenth century developed the technique of floating water meadows.

These involved the construction of a complex system of channels and sluices which could be used to flood the meadows in spring, ensuring that they were dressed with rich river sediment and also that they were protected from the damaging touch of the frost. Grass grew richer, greener and earlier in these meadows than in those which had not been treated. In some river valleys, such as that of the Nadder near Salisbury cathedral, or of the Avon at Lower Woodford, these channels and sluices can still be found.

From the seventeenth century a number of farmers began to try out new crops, particularly various types of root. The turnip, the carrot and the parsnip gradually revolutionized agricultural practices in England, as farmers began to sow them in land which had previously been left fallow. These crops could now be used to feed livestock while they stood in stables and stalls, so animals no longer had to scour the fallow fields for whatever weeds they could find. As a result

Floated water meadows near Salisbury, Wiltshire
The photograph shows maintenance work being carried out on the elaborate system of sluices constructed for the flooding of water meadows. Many such systems were still in use in the Avon and Wylye valleys of Wiltshire in the inter-war years.

of this supply of fodder, the numbers of animals which could be kept vastly increased, and the manure they provided indoors could now be well rotted and efficiently used. Its nitrogen was less likely to leach away or disperse into the atmosphere than when it was spread by animals roaming at large.

Dwarf rape and cabbages were planted as fodder, and a variety of fertilizers were employed. Soot, sawdust, coal dust and industrial refuse were ploughed into the ground, and relatively cheap lime began to be available as a by-product of coal production. What is more, the availability of coal further increased the fertility of the soil, for cow pats were no longer burned as fuel and could be returned to the land as manure. The quality of the land was also improved by the use of nitrogen-fixing crops such as sainfoin and clover.

In the eighteenth century these innovations encouraged a great intensification of arable agriculture on the lighter soils, particularly in eastern England. A system was developed under which 25 per cent of arable land was put down to the new improved grasses and clovers, which provided grazing in the summer as well as hay for the winter; 25 per cent was used to grow turnips for fodder; a quarter was used for spring crops (barley, oats, beans or peas); and a further quarter was used for winter crops (wheat, rye, and field beans). This was a highly efficient system of arable farming, and it also facilitated tremendous improvements in animal husbandry. Not only were more animals kept, but individual beasts were healthier and much larger.

Moreover, from the seventeenth century great improvements in the quality of stock had been made by selective breeding. First sheep, then cows and horses were carefully crossed and recrossed to produce humanly devised ideals. Agricultural shows and awards acted as a further stimulus in the eighteenth century, and an indication of the enthusiasm for this form of improvement can be found in numerous paintings which commemorate particularly vast and nowadays seemingly monstrous beasts. A popular folk song, *The Derbyshire Ram*, eulogizes one such creature.

To some extent these innovations directly encouraged the enclosure of the landscape, but they also served as an indirect stimulus, since they accelerated the decline of the small owner-occupier. The small farmers lacked the capital to introduce new improvements, and they were progressively less able to make a living from agriculture in the competitive markets of the sixteenth and seventeenth centuries. Their problems were increased in 1692 when a land tax was introduced, and the slump in agricultural prices of the late seventeenth and early eighteenth centuries served further to speed their decline. In November 1690 one of Sir John Newton's agents reported that two farms in the Midlands had been given up by their tenants, and could not be relet without some decrease in the rent. This situation was attributed to:

> ye extreme badness of the times . . . For what can a farmer do with barley at 10/- per quarter, beans 12/-, wheat 20/-, oats 7/-, rye 12/-. Best wool is at 16/- per tod and small wool 12/- and these are the best prices that are given. Horses cannot be sold at any rate, and beasts and sheep are fallen to just over half of what they were a dozen years since. All men complain sadly and that man counts himself most happy that deals least.[3]

In such circumstances many freehold farmers fell into debt and eventually had to sell up. By 1800 perhaps as little as 15 per cent of the land of England was in the hands of small proprietors, that is, owners of less than 50 acres. At the same time, the average size of the tenant farm was growing, with the result that the number of people involved in farming gradually declined. At a local level, of course, the rate of change was influenced by the policy of individual estates. Some landowners encouraged the movement towards larger farms, whereas elsewhere this process was retarded by

Old-fashioned Chinese Black
As eighteenth-century farmers and landowners became increasingly interested in selective breeding, even the stock of the humble pig was improved. But as this oil by J. Clark indicates, the portraits which were sometimes painted to celebrate the prize beasts often exaggerated the size and proportions of their subjects.

a paternalism which favoured the survival of small leaseholders and insecure copyholders.

As farming became more specialized and sophisticated, control over the land increasingly fell into the hands of those who had most to gain from enclosure. For the substantial landowner an enclosed landscape had numerous practical advantages, on top of the freedom it gave for agricultural innovation. An agreement made in 1630 to enclose land at Marston in Lincolnshire outlines some of these advantages. It states that through planting hedges enclosure will alleviate the chronic shortage of wood and timber which afflicted Marston, while the ditches beside the hedges would aid drainage. Moreover, the existence of hedges and a clear division of property would reduce the incidence of trespass, and the resultant quarrels and litigation.

Larger landowners were not prepared to forego such advantages merely because the enclosure of the landscape affected the livelihoods of the poorer members of the community. Indeed, the fact that many smaller freeholders and tenant farmers depended on the maintenance of common rights for their survival often provided powerful landlords with an additional incentive for removing the commons. As the concept of absolute ownership emerged in the post medieval period landmarks increasingly came to think of the commons as 'their' property. They regarded ancient customs and common rights as part of a rather old-fashioned tenurial system, which was also essentially subversive, and a dangerous threat to the discipline of the labour force. Common lands provided poor cottagers with a certain amount of independence. They could gain a portion of their subsistence through exploiting the wastes, and were therefore discouraged from entering full-time employment as labourers. To many landlords this limited independence seemed far from desirable. It encouraged insubordination, and made it difficult to cultivate the kind of malleable and submissive workforce which they saw as essential for good labour relations.

The larger commons were a particular problem, for they were frequently settled by squatters: landless families who erected insubstantial cottages and hovels, kept a few animals and eked out a living as craftsmen. They provided a pool of labour which encouraged the development of industry, especially in the north and west, but they were seen by many as a threat to the stability of society. Many large commons were outside the control of the manorial courts and the Church, and were notorious for their lawlessness. As one pamphleteer commented in the seventeenth century, 'The poor increase like fleas and lice, and these vermin will eat us up if we do not enclose.'[4] Various attempts were made to outlaw squatting, but none of them succeeded. A law was introduced in 1589, for instance, which prohibited the erection of any cottage without four acres of land, but this, like many similar laws, was almost impossible to enforce.

These law and order problems were a particular feature of woodland and forest areas, for it was in these regions that extensive areas of commons survived. In the champion much of the waste had fallen to the plough in the Middle Ages, and manorial control also tended to be much stronger. Many champion villages, and in particular those in the central and southern Midlands, had a single manorial lord who was the dominant landowner. He was therefore in a much better position to control his tenants and maintain order and harmony, particularly since these communities contained increasingly few owner-occupiers.

In the woodland and forest areas, in contrast, extensive tracts of commons often lasted into the nineteenth century. This made it possible for many small freehold farmers to survive, as well as numerous independent cottagers and part-time craftsmen. These people generally resented restrictions and interference and tended to be individualistic and independent. As John Norden wrote in 1607, 'the people bred amongst the woods are naturally more stubborn and uncivil than in the champion countries'.[5] The enclosure of the wastes was therefore not merely a means of maximizing the profit of the landowners, but was seen as a way of curtailing the independent spirit of the poor. It replaced a landscape of rights and customs with a landscape of private property, and in doing so it reflected not only a change in the attitude to social control but a change in its function. The old system of customs and common rights was seen to be highly undesirable in the increasingly hierarchical and authoritarian society of post medieval England, associated as it was with a community of truculent and independent farmers and smallholders. The new system of landholding was based on a new concept of the role and social status of the poor. In the seventeenth century, for example, Adam Moore argued in favour of enclosure on the basis that it would 'give the poor an interest in toiling, whom terror never could enure to travail'.[6]

As enclosure progressed, a multiplicity of independent producers was replaced by a three-tiered system of large landlords, tenant farmers, and landless labourers. The timing and process of enclosure varied greatly from parish to parish and region to region, but as far as the appearance of the present landscape is concerned, the most important distinction is between *piecemeal* and *general enclosure*.[7]

Piecemeal enclosure has a very long history and involved the gradual enclosure of areas of common arable through a series of transactions between individuals, with a landowner buying, selling or exchanging strips of land until he had an area large enough to surround by a hedge or wall. General enclosure was a rather different business. It was based on the decision of a community (or at least of the most powerful elements within it) to enclose its common land, instead of on the unilateral action of individual landowners. Under general enclosure, therefore, the whole of the open fields and commons in a village were usually enclosed at once, as the landscape and landholding system were totally reorganized. The enclosed fields were distributed amongst the villagers, in proportion to the amount of land and rights that they were deemed to have had under the previous system.

Following this reallocation of land, many tenant and freehold farmers moved out of the nucleated village into new farmsteads set amongst consolidated holdings. This change enabled them to work their new fields with ease, but it also reflected their increasing exclusivity, as they distanced themselves from their landless social inferiors within the village.

The overall planning involved in general enclosure ensured that the landscapes that it produced have an appearance of coherence, with regular and often rectilinear fields. These are a striking contrast to the landscapes of piecemeal enclosure, where irregular fields are common.

There was a certain amount of piecemeal enclosure in the champion regions from the medieval period, and in many areas the extent of the open fields was very substantially reduced. But this form of enclosure predominated in the woodland and upland areas, where open fields had never been exploited with the co-operative enthusiasm that had characterized the champion, and where the number of farmers involved in each open field was often not very large. Where open fields contained only the strips of the farmers who lived nearby, these strips could be consolidated relatively easily in a kind of tenurial game of Happy Families, in which strips were exchanged to produce enclosable blocks. But in the champion, where the cards had been dealt out to large numbers of people, it was more difficult to eradicate the common arable through private deals between interested parties.

Piecemeal enclosure was practised so extensively in the woodland that the vast majority of open fields had disappeared by the seventeenth century, even in areas such as south Norfolk which had had quite large areas of open fields in the early Middle Ages. None the less, there were some exceptions to this trend, such as northeast Hertfordshire, where patches of woodland open fields survived into the eighteenth and nineteenth centuries. In many woodland and upland areas the signs of piecemeal enclosure are evident in the landscape today. The hedges that were planted usually followed the boundaries of the strips and many still have the sinuous profile which reflects this origin. Indeed there are areas of England, such as the southern or White Peak regions of the Derbyshire Pennines, where the majority of field boundaries are shaped in this way. In Brassington in Dovedale, or in the area around Eyam and Wardlow, the characteristic curves of medieval strips are clearly visible, picked out in the landscape by stone walls and hedges. In places such as west Hertfordshire these boundaries have been adopted in the pattern of urban development. In part of the new town of Hemel Hempstead the roads follow the reversed S's that divided property in the earlier landscape.[8]

Piecemeal enclosure had less impact on the common wastes of the upland and woodland areas than it had on the open fields. Small greens and commons were often enclosed by

Landscape of walls, near Wardlow, Derbyshire
This beautifully preserved pattern of dry-stone walls was almost entirely created by the piecemeal enclosure of irregular open-field arable in the late and post medieval periods.

informal agreements between commoners, but where the wastes were extensive and rights were widely shared they could normally only be enclosed by the process of general enclosure, and often survived largely intact into the eighteenth and nineteenth centuries when Enclosure Acts were passed. In upland areas in particular, there is often a marked contrast between former arable lands and former wastes. The arable fields show all the signs of having been enclosed piecemeal. They are irregular, with sinuous boundaries, and tend to be located on the best land in each parish, close to scattered farmsteads and hamlets. In contrast, the poorer soils that used to be open grazing have been divided into large geometric fields, bounded by walls or neat hawthorn hedges, and criss-crossed with straight roads. Such contrasts can be seen across the upland regions of England, from the Pennines to Cornwall.

It was, however, across central England, in champion country, that general enclosure had the most profound impact on the landscape. The earliest form of general enclosure was 'enclosure by unity of possession', which occurred when all the land in a village fell into the hands of a single owner. It was this kind of enclosure which took place in the late medieval period, when areas of arable were turned over to the production of sheep. This process continued in the sixteenth and seventeenth centuries, when it affected not only the Midlands, but also the northeast of England, and in particular the coastal lowlands of Northumberland and Durham. Even at this late stage this form of enclosure could occasionally lead to the depopulation of villages. The village of Seaton Delaval in Northumberland, for example, was cleared at the end of the sixteenth century.

This method was, however, gradually superseded by 'enclosure by agreement', which took place when a number of proprietors in a village agreed to extinguish the rights of common and enclose. Such agreements were sometimes reached amicably but could involve a greater or lesser degree of coercion. They usually required the appointment of an external body who worked out the details of the enclosure. This commission of arbiters acted at the behest of the landowners, and usually gave a twelfth of the land of the village to the lord of the manor. The rest of the land was divided between the freeholders, according to the size of their holdings in the open fields and the extent of their rights to the waste. In many cases, the agreements drawn up by the commissioners were subsequently ratified by some kind of legal authority, most notably by the courts of chancery.

Enclosure by agreement was much more widespread than the work of many historians would suggest.[9] Indeed, in the seventeenth and eighteenth centuries as much land may have been enclosed by this method as by the best-known method, that of 'parliamentary enclosure'.[10] From the mid eighteenth century, however, parliamentary enclosure became the usual form of general enclosure, initially involving the landowners of a village petitioning Parliament for an act which allowed them to enclose their fields and wastes. As with enclosure by commission, this necessitated the allocation of land by independent commissioners, although after the general enclosure act of 1836 a separate act of Parliament was not required for each enclosure.

Different forms of general enclosure produced distinctive landscapes. Enclosures by agreement do not have the rigid formality which was to characterize landscapes enclosed by act of Parliament. Their fields and hedges are roughly rather than precisely straight, and some of their features fossilize elements of the earlier landscape. Some of the hedges were planted on top of the old furlong boundaries, although this did not happen as often as in areas where enclosure occurred piecemeal.

In September 1658 in the parish of Great Linford in Buckinghamshire, the lord of the manor, Sir Richard Napier, and the other freeholders drew up an agreement to enclose. This brought about a striking alteration of the landscape, as is revealed in the contrast between the map of the parish dated 1641 and that dated 1678. Common grazing and open arable depicted on the earlier map are replaced by new fields and some new sections of road. But perhaps the most striking consequence of enclosure was the drastic reduction in the number of tracks and wide driftways which crossed the parish. Many of the old routes were lost completely, and those that remained were considerably straightened and narrowed.[11]

These early general enclosures were often associated with the conversion of land to pasture, which often led to a certain amount of depopulation. Unlike the clearances which took place in the fifteenth century, this rarely caused the total desertion of villages, but tended to produce a dramatic contraction in the size of the settlements, as occurred in the village of Haselbech in Northamptonshire. This was enclosed at the end of the sixteenth century by an agreement between the majority landholder, Sir Thomas Tresham, and eleven other freeholders. Tresham's land was held by tenants and farmed as arable before enclosure, but afterwards it was laid down to pasture. Desperate for money in order to meet the fines he had incurred by refusing to renounce his Roman Catholic faith, Tresham demanded rents which his tenants were unable to pay. As a result, sixty farmers were evicted from his land, on top of those removed by the other freeholders. Haselbech was not completely deserted, but shrank considerably: the en-

closure map of 1599 showed twenty-nine houses in the village, but today only six houses remain.[12]

Parliamentary enclosure seldom led to the shrinkage of settlements, partly because it tended to occur in villages with numerous landowners, but largely because it took place at a time when the rural population was rising rapidly. The landscapes produced by this form of enclosure are highly distinctive, being characterized by their geometric rigidity and by field divisions which pay scant attention to the boundaries of the earlier landscape. Although elements of the extant road pattern were sometimes maintained, in many areas, and in particular where patches of open grazing were enclosed, the roads were completely redrawn.

Despite the mass-produced and rather monotonous quality of the landscapes of parliamentary enclosure, there are various subtle differences between the earliest and those which were drawn up later. Up to the late eighteenth century, roads within these landscapes were laid out with wide verges, giving a total road width of between forty and sixty feet. This ensured that road users could pick the best course along the track, when inclement weather made it muddy and difficult. Towards the end of the eighteenth century, improvements in road construction ensured that such wide verges were no longer necessary, and their use

Panorama of 'planned countryside' from Combe Hill, near Wendover, Buckinghamshire

Agricultural intensification has simplified but not erased the characteristic rectilinearity of this predominantly eighteenth- and nineteenth-century pattern of fields. Even in areas such as this, in which the field pattern was largely created by parliamentary enclosure, there are often a number of earlier boundaries. In this picture, for example, some of the fields in the middle distance appear to result from the earlier piecemeal enclosure of open-field strips.

by gypsies provided an additional incentive for their removal. As a result, roads laid out from the late eighteenth century are usually under forty-five feet in width.

The geographer Michael Turner has indicated what impact this change in policy had on the countryside in his descriptions of travelling through the parishes of Kilby, Arnesby and Shearsby in Leicestershire, which were enclosed in 1771, 1794, and 1773 respectively. On crossing the parish boundary between Kilby and Arnesby, the road narrows from around sixty to around forty feet, but widens to sixty feet again on the boundary between Arnesby and Shearsby.[13]

Even within the planned landscapes of general enclosure, there was considerable diversity, which has contributed to the varied fabric of the countryside. Yet although the effects are so well recorded, the conditions which produced general enclosure, and the nature and timing of what happened on a local level, are still not wholly understood. General enclosure was encouraged by the development of agricultural specialization, and in particular by the need to convert land to pastoral production, but it was also stimulated by agricultural prosperity. The process of enclosure was difficult and expensive, whichever method was used, and so it tended to occur when landowners were in an optimistic frame of mind. There was a great wave of parliamentary enclosure, for example, particularly on the lighter lands of the east, when grain prices rose in the course of the Napoleonic Wars. But one of the most important factors in the progress of general enclosure seems to have been the pattern of power in the land — that is, the relative numbers of large landowners and small freeholders. Enclosure was clearly far easier when it required the agreement of only a few people.

Wherever there were large numbers of small freeholders, the general enclosure of the landscape tended to come late. This was not only because there were large numbers of individuals whose consent was required, but also because there was good reason why many of the small men would not be in favour of enclosure. Those who had the smallest farms were most dependent on their common rights and, in particular, on the exploitation of commons and the grazing of the harvest shack. As time passed, however, the various methods by which land could be enclosed were adapted, and they made it progressively easy for those who wanted enclosure to impose it on the landscape.

One of the important features of parliamentary enclosure was that it articulated the principle that general enclosure could take place without the consent of the majority of the proprietors involved. As the legal writer H.S.Homer stated in 1766, 'where a general consent cannot be obtained, a concurrence of so many of the parties as are possessed of four-fifths of the property is now considered sufficient grounds for an application to the legislative to inclose by Act of Parliament'.[14] This ruling made possible the enclosure of almost all the country's extant common land. Even in areas where strong communities of small freeholders had survived and which held out against enclosure much longer than anywhere else, the most prosperous members of the community were eventually able to impose their will on the landscape.

The progress of general enclosure was thus tied to a nexus of changes in agriculture and the basis of landholding. Land was enclosed in different ways, at different times, in different parts of the country. Despite the complexity of the process, however, it is possible to pick out various factors which gave a regional dimension to the distribution of different types of enclosed landscape. For the spread of enclosure was intimately connected with the evolution of specialized farming regions and regional communities. Certain types of farming particularly encouraged enclosure, but in addition some forms of farming encouraged the more rapid decline of those whose holdings were small.

Parliamentary surveyors at work, Henlow, Bedfordshire
This sketch, painted on an Enclosure Award in Bedfordshire Record Office, gives a rare view of the surveying work which preceded each general enclosure.

In general, the decline of the small landowner was more marked in regions which specialized in arable agriculture than in those which were devoted to dairying or livestock production. This trend was encouraged by the fact that the most expensive innovations of the post medieval period were devoted to the improvement of arable rather than pastoral production. Arable agriculture tended to favour the large producer, who was able to benefit from economies of scale and could afford to introduce the new methods. Moreover, arable farming was far more labour intensive than pastoral, so that even the small arable farmers had to rely on some outside labour. This was a serious financial burden in the late seventeenth and early eighteenth centuries, when prices were low, and when larger farms with their new methods were becoming increasingly productive and competitive.

In the areas with a bias towards pastoral farming, small farmers tended to be rather better off than the small men of the arable regions, for then, as now, pastoral production was viable on a fairly small scale. There was less scope for capital-intensive improvements in this form of agriculture than there was in arable husbandry, and in the seventeenth and eighteenth centuries the prices of dairy products and meat did not slump as much as the price of corn. Yet not all forms of pastoral farming were equally suited to production in very small units. While livestock rearing, which was largely concentrated in the upland regions, required little labour and little investment, dairy farming needed rather more, although even in dairying regions the small farmers could survive far better than in arable lands. Fattening animals for slaughter, on the other hand, was capital intensive and was often practised by wealthy gentleman farmers.

To some extent, the distribution of arable and pastoral agriculture in the post medieval period was determined by the nature of the environment. In the upland areas of England, where the climate was cold and wet and the pasture was poor and unsuitable for dairying, farmers tended to specialize in the breeding and rearing of livestock. In lowland England, however, the pattern of specialization was not wholly determined by such natural factors as soils, climate or topography. Although pastoral farms tended to be concentrated in wet regions and on heavy clays, by no means all such areas were exploited by dairy or stock farmers because the ability to change from one form of agriculture to another depended on the patterns of land ownership which had been inherited from the medieval past.

By the end of the medieval period most woodland areas contained holdings of various sizes, farmed by men with varying degrees of security of tenure. Many were smallholders, but some were substantial freeholders, working farms of a hundred acres or more. Where the soils and climate permitted, many of these yeomen were able to move into pastoral farming because their land lay either in hedged closes or in small open fields which could be easily enclosed piecemeal.

Many woodland areas also contained substantial tracts of common, making it possible for even fairly small farmers to introduce some form of livestock farming. The holder of only a handful of acres could survive by running a few animals on the common, although many also subsidized their incomes by part-time wage-labouring or by practising some kind of craft.

So the tenurial structure of the woodland regions encouraged the development of pastoral farming where soils and climate were suitable, and made it possible for fairly small landowners to survive. This form of agricultural specialization was particularly prominent in the warm wet west, where the climate was peculiarly appropriate, but dairying also flourished in much of the southeast, stimulated by the great markets provided by London and the growing towns. Small landowners also survived well in many of the forest areas of the champion Midlands and in the Fens of Cambridgeshire and Lincolnshire, where there were substantial tracts of common grazing in the post medieval period.

Thus, in the pastoral economies of forest and woodland, upland and fen, the decline of the small landowner tended to be slow. Indeed, some areas may have seen an increase in the number of smallholders, especially in the sixteenth and seventeenth centuries, partly as a result of the division of holdings through partible inheritance. Even when large areas of land were eventually absorbed into the estates of the aristocracy or gentry, many small farms were still managed by tenants, unless, as in parts of nineteenth-century East Anglia, they were converted to arable production.

Although in many areas pastoral farming tended to be associated with the survival of small farmers this was not invariably the case. In those champion areas with heavy clay soils, a slow shift into grass throughout the post medieval period was accompanied by the decline of the small farmer. These soils were not so suitable for intensive arable as the lighter soils of chalk or limestone, and although some improvement resulted from the introduction of up-and-down husbandry, they were too heavy for the new systems of rotation based on root crops. Turnips were difficult to lift from the claggy clays, and they tended to rot. So when grain prices declined from the mid seventeenth century, much of this land was put down to grass and used for grazing. By the late eighteenth century, large areas of Warwickshire, Northamptonshire, Leicestershire, Bedfordshire and north Buckinghamshire had evolved a system of specialized livestock farming on improved, fertilized, permanent pasture. Many parishes were like Fawsley in Northamptonshire, described in 1800 as 'without a single blade of corn, being wholly on grass and applied to feeding'.[15]

The trend towards grass slowed slightly in the late eighteenth and early nineteenth centuries, when grain prices were high, but it resumed soon afterwards. By the middle of the nineteenth century the landscape of the Midlands was dominated by the 'continuous sheet of greensward' which William Marshall had observed in Leicestershire in 1790.

To a certain extent, convertible or up-and-down husbandry could be introduced within the landscape of open fields, for strips or groups of strips could be put down to grass and animals tethered upon them. In the early eighteenth century, for instance, 20 per cent of the open fields of Wigston Magna in Leicestershire were under permanent grass.[16] This development was particularly necessary in the Midland parishes, where there was often little or no common grazing. Nevertheless, a thoroughgoing system of pastoral agriculture could only be introduced within an enclosed landscape and this put open-field farmers under considerable pressure. Their arable agriculture was increasingly less competitive when compared with the output from the lighter lands of eastern England, yet their strip fields were difficult and prohibitively expensive to enclose. As a result, these open-field communities went into decline, and their lands were gradually absorbed into the estates of large landowners.

Wealthy magnates had the resources to enclose land and to convert it to pastoral farming. For example, when the Verney family enclosed Middle Claydon in Buckinghamshire in 1655 the whole parish was turned over to grassland, and the same happened when the family enclosed East Claydon in the 1740s. Most of the large farms produced by enclosure in this way were leased out to wealthy graziers.[17]

The parishes affected by general enclosure in the sixteenth and seventeenth centuries were usually those dominated by one or two great landowners, and enclosure was often accompanied by the termination of insecure copyhold tenancies. Elsewhere, general enclosure tended to occur later, as economic forces produced a general reduction in the number of freeholders, and thus made enclosure by agreement easier to achieve.

The regional variations in the communities of the Midlands therefore had a considerable influence over the progress of enclosure. Those villages which had emerged as strong freehold communities in the late medieval period were often able to resist enclosure for a very long time, maintaining themselves by adopting elements of the new agriculture, especially the up-and-down husbandry, and often growing industrial crops such as woad or hemp. Many of the farmers subsidized their income from their holdings by some other part-time activity, often using their idle teams to hire themselves as carters. In Leicestershire and Northamptonshire many became involved in framework knitting or other home-based industries. For example, Daniel Vann, of Wigston Magna in Leicestershire, left three cows, a pig and four knitting frames on his death in 1680.

Even in those Midland parishes dominated by one or two great landowners, the presence of substantial numbers of freeholders could delay enclosure. In 1737 the parish of Eakring in Nottinghamshire was largely owned by two men — the Duke of Kingston, who held 1011 acres, and Sir George Saville, who had 753 acres. But there were also thirty-seven freeholders, who held 633 acres between them. The largest of these farmers had seventy-seven acres, but fifteen of them had less than two acres. To add to this confusion, thirteen of the freeholders also rented land from either the Duke of Kingston or Sir George, with three of them renting lands from both. In such parishes any attempt at enclosure by agreement was fraught with difficulty.[18]

In some cases enclosure was delayed for the simple reason that the landowner was not interested in agricultural improvements. This was true, for example, of the second Duke of Kingston, who held extensive estates in the east Midlands. Even in villages where he had a majority of the land, enclosure did not take place until his death in 1773. Sometimes failure to enclose was motivated by paternalism rather than apathy, some great landowners, like Edward Laurence, being unwilling to turn 'poor families into the wide world by uniting farms all at once'. Elsewhere enclosure was retarded by disputes between the major landlords.[19]

As time passed, however, enclosure became easier, partly because of the decline in the number of smallholders but also because legislative changes required the agreement of those who held the majority of land in a parish, rather than of the majority of landholders. Most of the parishes on the Midlands clays which, for one reason or another, had long held out against enclosure eventually succumbed to the massive spate of parliamentary enclosure which occurred from 1760 to 1780.

Because the conditions in any particular parish were so important in determining the chronology of enclosure, it is possible to find a Midlands parish enclosed in the fifteenth century next to one enclosed in the late eighteenth century. Burston in Buckinghamshire was enclosed in the late fifteenth century, yet in the neighbouring village of Whitchurch the majority of the open-field arable survived until the parliamentary enclosure of 1772. The village of Salford in Oxfordshire was not enclosed until 1770, but it lies next to the pastures laid out when Little Rollright was enclosed and depopulated in the fifteenth century. Even within parishes there is often a contrast between areas of early piecemeal enclosure and those which were only enclosed later by some form of general enclosure. The gradual development of pastoral agriculture across the Midland plain therefore both accompanied and symbolized the decline of small owner-occupiers in the post medieval period. Nowadays, only the ridge and furrow created by their ploughs remains to testify to their existence.

The impact of the development of pastoral farming on the structure of landholding thus varied markedly in different regions. While in some areas it ensured the survival of the small freeholders and tenants, in others it was associated with their decline. The consequences of the development of specialized arable areas were far more straightforward. In both woodland and champion regions, arable agriculture brought about a reduction in the number of small farmers.

These specialized arable areas had been devoted to what is known as 'sheep-corn husbandry' prior to the improvements of the seventeenth century. Under this traditional agricultural system, the common pastures and fallows were used to support flocks of sheep, which provided dung to fertilize areas of open-field arable. In their unimproved form these light soils tended to be poor and unprofitable, but they were particularly amenable to the new methods of farming introduced in the seventeenth and eighteenth centuries. Those who lacked the capital to invest in the new methods, principally the smaller farmers, gradually went out of business, and as they did so the dry sheep pastures of wold, breck and downland were bought up by the large landowners, improved and ploughed. From the chalk downlands of Wiltshire, Berkshire and Dorset to the limestone uplands of the Cotswolds, from the heaths and wolds of Lincolnshire and Yorkshire to the sands of Norfolk and Suffolk, the small freehold farmers went into decline and their lands were absorbed into large estates.

In those parts of the woodland areas of eastern England where specialized arable farming developed, such as the Chiltern Hills or south Hertfordshire, the enclosure of the open fields was brought about piecemeal, and at an early date. In areas with more regular field systems, although large areas of common arable were often enclosed piecemeal, open fields only disappeared through general enclosure as the number of small farmers declined. As in the clayland areas of the Midlands, however, there were considerable local variations in the rate at which this decline took place. Many of the strong freehold communities survived for a considerable time, particularly in areas of very fertile soil, such as the foot of the Chiltern escarpment in Bedfordshire, Buckinghamshire and Hertfordshire. These communities were able to incorporate elements of the new systems of rotation into the pattern of open-field agriculture. Elsewhere, the freeholders adapted to the new economic conditions by producing specialized industrial crops such as saffron, which was widely grown in south Cambridgeshire.

But in general, the numbers of small farmers on light arable lands declined through the sixteenth, seventeenth and eighteenth centuries, although there was not quite such a direct impact on the progress of general enclosure as in those areas which developed a pastoral system of farming. There was less incentive for people to undertake the expensive business of general enclosure where the land was mostly devoted to crops. Even in parishes where there were few freeholders, land was often not enclosed until there were good economic inducements to do so, although strips

Fields near Blubberhouses Moor, North Yorkshire
These straight dry-stone walls were the product of the enclosure of open moorland in the late eighteenth century, producing a landscape that is typical of many of the upland areas of England. The more sinuous wall at the bottom of the picture is probably an earlier feature, the result of the piecemeal enclosure of arable lying in the more sheltered valley. The large field in the centre of the picture is marked with the earthworks of 'narrow rig', a diminutive form of ridge and furrow which is usually associated with the expansion of arable cultivation on marginal land at the time of the Napoleonic Wars.

A Mill on a Common
This mezzotint by David Lucas (1830) based on an oil sketch by John Constable shows East Bergholt Common in Suffolk under the plough, a year after the common was enclosed. The post-mill in the background was owned by Constable's father, but it no longer survives.

were increasingly consolidated through purchase and exchange. As a result, many of the common fields and wastes on the lighter arable lands survived until the wave of parliamentary enclosure that came at the time of the Napoleonic Wars, when abnormally high grain prices encouraged investment in agriculture and made enclosure seem both desirable and economically viable. An additional incentive was that all existing leases were terminated on the passing of an enclosure act, so that all tenants who held long leases at fixed rents could be evicted and their farms let again at higher rates.

The gradual spread of enclosure was therefore associated with changes in the social structure of farming communities. Although there were still villages which were dominated by small freeholders in the nineteenth century, especially in areas of woodland, forest and fen, open fields and common wastes gradually disappeared throughout the country, to be replaced by a landscape of walls, hedges and private property.

In many places, however, and in many sections of society, there were those who deeply and bitterly resented the enclosure of the landscape. It not only deprived small farmers and cottagers of their rights to the commons and put them to the expense of fencing their newly enclosed lands and paying any legal costs involved, but it also meant the end of a means of subsistence that was a valuable safeguard against unemployment and economic hardship. In the seventeenth and eighteenth centuries there were various sporadic incidents in which people voiced their objections to the changes in the landscape. For example, in 1639 the men of Corby in Northamptonshire marched to Thackley Green and spent three days pulling down the hedges of the enclosing landlord Sir Christopher Hatton. At Ashill in Norfolk an anonymous letter sent to a local paper in 1816 threatened the enclosing farmers and landowners with death, claiming that 'you do as you like, you rob the poor of their common rights, [and] plough the grass up that God sent to grow'. As late as 1870 the stakes and railings dividing the common at Fakenham in Norfolk were pulled up and burnt.[20]

William Cobbett, while more renowned for his expression of social truths than his historical accuracy, vividly portrayed how important the commons were to the labouring community in his *Political Register*. He frequently inveighed against a system of government which 'draws property into great masses . . . gives to cunning the superiority over industry . . . makes agriculture a subject of adventure . . . puts down all small cultivators; [and] encloses every inch of that land which God himself seems to have intended for the poor'. And he repeatedly dwelt on the extent to which the commons provided a hedge against starvation for the poor. Thus he looked back nostalgically to the days before enclosure:

> I used to go around a little common, called Horton Heath, on a Sunday. I found the husbands at home. The common contained about 150 acres; and I found round the skirts of it, and near to the skirts, about thirty cottages and gardens, the latter chiefly encroachments on the common, which was waste (as it was called) in a manor of which the Bishop was the lord. . . . I remember one hundred and twenty-five or thirty-five stalls of bees, worth at that time ten shillings a stall, at least. Cows there were about fifteen, besides heifers and calves; about sixty pigs great and small; and not less than five hundred heads of poultry! The cattle and sheep of the neighbouring farmers grazed the common all the while besides. The bees alone were worth more annually than the common, if it had been enclosed, would have let for deducting the expense of fences.[21]

The details of Cobbett's calculations may be debatable, but recent work by a number of historians has left little doubt that enclosure caused considerable hardship to the poor. There was almost invariably a dramatic increase in the number of people claiming poor relief in the period following enclosure.[22] Small landholders and labourers often saw enclosure as robbery, and felt themselves to have been treacherously wronged. Although the hedge is now eulogized in England, and symbolizes the countryside we all have a right to enjoy, not so long ago it was hated by large sections of the people as a symbol of tyranny and despotism. To many the hedge meant enclosure, and a system of property which disregarded not only the rights of the people, but also the traditional way of life which had formerly protected those rights.

Many looked back to the time before enclosure as a golden age of rural harmony and happiness, as exemplified in William Cobbett's attack on the society that had brought about the enclosure of Horton Heath.

> I learnt to hate a system that could lead English gentlemen to disregard matters like these! That could induce them to tear up 'wastes' and sweep away occupiers like those I have described! Wastes indeed! Give a dog an ill name. Was Horton Heath a waste? Was it a 'waste' when a hundred, perhaps, of healthy boys and girls were playing there of a Sunday, instead of creeping about covered with filth in the alleys of a town?[23]

Cobbett's views on the England of the old days are often tinged with a romantic nostalgia, but none the less there is a great deal of truth in what he says. Enclosure had revolutionized the landscape of property and represented the concentration of ownership in the hands of the few.

SIX

The Rise of the Great Estates

THE ENCLOSURE OF THE ENGLISH LANDSCAPE and the concentration of land in the hands of a small élite were accompanied by a fundamental revolution in attitudes to landed property. These new concepts of land and land ownership stimulated changes in the way that the countryside was used. In the Middle Ages there was no large-scale manipulation of the landscape in the display of personal status. The pattern of landholding would have made it difficult for any individual to make a large-scale alteration to the fabric of the countryside; furthermore, the nature of society was such that this was neither sought nor desired. It was only with the evolution of private property that the landscape began to be deliberately and extensively shaped for social and aesthetic purposes. For the first time the social élite displayed their power directly in the land.

The spread of enclosure was therefore accompanied by a growing interest in the appearance of the environment amongst the landed élite. This is seen most clearly in the evolution of the landscape park, but it also applied to the wider rural landscape. The design of schools, churches, cottages and barns all began to reflect the personal tastes of individual landowners. The local customs and traditional practices in both architecture and agriculture which had shaped the landscape for centuries gradually decayed. Standardized farming methods and building styles were introduced all over the country, as the eighteenth- and nineteenth-century landscape began to display the aesthetic preferences of the class by whom it was owned.

Imagine what a manorial hall in the medieval period was like, and the chances are that your mind will be full of images of noise and life. Servants are everywhere, fetching and carrying great plates of food. There are blazing fires and a number of tenants and yeomen entertaining their lord with samples of earthy rural wit. But think of an eighteenth-century house and the picture is markedly different. Discreetly silent servants in powder and elaborate wigs attend a supercilious gathering of ladies and gentlemen in an elegantly appointed room, or indeed, an apparently deserted Georgian country house lies surrounded by beautiful but empty parklands.

These twentieth-century images of the past are stereotypes, but the contrast between them is significant. They reveal that the medieval house is associated with activity and the community, and the estates of the eighteenth century with the exclusion of the everyday world of the mass of the population.

From the sixteenth century the landed élite gradually isolated themselves, and became divorced from the world of agriculture and rural labour. The landscape parks which they created around their country seats revealed their desire to shape their immediate environment and the increasing limitation of the lower classes' rights in the land. In their carefully

Averham Park, Gloucestershire, from the east
This picture, painted by an unknown artist around 1720, is of immense historical interest. In the foreground it shows open-field strips, which are rarely represented in visual art. Each strip has been individually ploughed, and is separated from its neighbour by a deep furrow. In the newly enclosed parkland beyond the arable fields, earthworks of ridge and furrow show that this area was also cultivated in strips until relatively recently. The hill is topped by a country house which dominates the surrounding countryside. The painting thus encapsulates the fundamental processes of landscape change in the post medieval period, as the customary landscape was replaced by a landscape dominated by a local landowning élite.

placed clumps of trees, their sweeping lawns and lakes, the landscape parks provided a sanitized, stylized form of what was seen as the 'natural' landscape, and represented the landed wealth on which the aristocratic ethos was based. Yet this landscape also served as a barrier between the house and the rural community, and in its exclusion of the realities of rural life denied the importance of labour within agriculture and as an essential part of the production of wealth.

The landed élite's impact on the countryside varied considerably in different parts of the country. Some areas came to be dominated by the massive landscaped layouts of the great estates, but in others there were only the more discreet parks and other features created by the minor gentry. Like the progress of enclosure, the creation of the great estates was fundamentally influenced by the complex history of agriculture and landholding. Although the decline of the small freeholder and owner-occupier was a continuous theme of the post medieval period, the main beneficiaries of this process changed over time. During the sixteenth and for much of the seventeenth century, it was the local gentry who tended to increase their share of the land of England. From the late seventeenth century, however, land increasingly fell into the hands of the owners of very large estates.

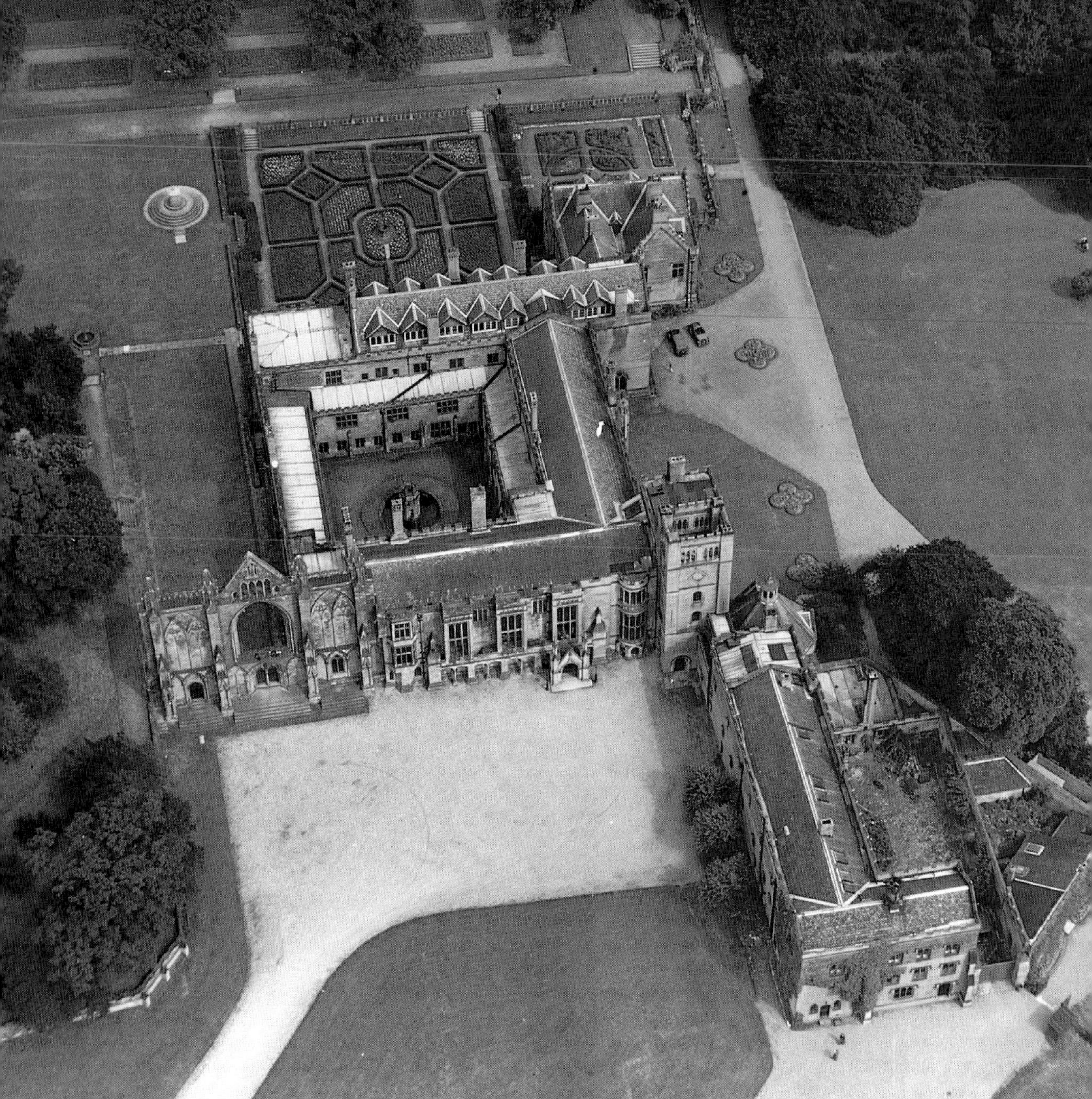

Newstead Priory, Nottinghamshire
The Augustinian priory was acquired by the Byron family in 1540, and converted into a great country house. Much of the original structure is incorporated into the building, which is set around the priory cloister. On the left is the ruined west front of the priory church.

The Dissolution of the monasteries in the 1530s ushered in a period of massive upheaval in the system of landholding. Vast acreages (up to 25 per cent of the total area of England) were suddenly more or less up for grabs. Although the Crown initially took over the estates of the monastic institutions, by 1550 most of these lands had passed into private hands in order to raise revenue to fund abortive continental military adventures. In the hyperactive land market that resulted, property was sold and rapidly resold in a complex series of transactions.[1]

The landscape still bears signs of the impact of this upheaval and it is recorded in the names of many stately homes. The estates around Woburn Abbey or Newburgh Priory, for example, are largely made up of former monastic land, and some country houses incorporate elements of earlier ecclesiastical buildings. An example is Thame Park in Oxfordshire. The house has an elegant Palladian front, which looks out over its now decaying parkland, but if you go round the back of the house it has a different aspect altogether. The building is rambling and irregular, an antique amalgam of extensions and piecemeal additions. These were the lodgings of the old abbots of Thame, and they tell a rather interesting story. In common with many other monastic houses, the building was clearly extensively altered in the years leading up to the Dissolution. Many monastic establishments seem to have anticipated some confiscation of their liquid assets, although not total dissolution, and therefore tried to spend their ready money as quickly as possible. As a result, many great schemes of building and redecoration were carried out. Thame Park, for example, contains, amongst other sixteenth-century additions, a set of sumptuously decorated rooms in the Italian Renaissance style. These were built between 1530 and 1539, for Abbot Robert King.[2]

Much of the land that came on the market at the Dissolution was taken over by great magnates, landowners of national rather than local importance, but on the whole it seems to have been the local gentry who benefited most. In the fifteenth century there had been a considerable increase in the importance of this group of landowners, and the lands they obtained at the Dissolution further augmented their power. As many gained land, and as agriculture became more capital-intensive and specialized, the gentry became more closely involved in the details of agricultural production. As Thomas Wilson wrote in 1600:

> The gentlemen, which were wont to addict themselves to the wars, are now for the most part grown to become good husbands, and know as well how to improve their lands to the uttermost as the farmer or countryman, so that they take their farms into their hands as the leases expire, and either till themselves or else let them out to those who will give most . . . whereby the yeomanry of England is decayed.[3]

Not only was there an increase in the proportion of land held by the gentry, there was also an increase in the number of people belonging to this social class, so that there were many villages which had a resident member of the landed gentry for the first time in the sixteenth century. This was partly because the expansionary economy of the fifteenth and sixteenth centuries had provided a certain amount of scope for upward mobility. Edward VI observed in 1551 that 'the gentleman, constrained by necessity and poverty, becomes a farmer, a grazier, or a sheepmaster; the grazier, the farmer, the merchant become landed men and call themselves gentlemen, though they be churls.'[4]

In the seventeenth century, however, the pattern of landholding changed again, as the rise of the gentry was succeeded by the rise of the great landowners. The large landholding units had been expanding to some extent in the sixteenth and early seventeenth centuries, but from 1680 there was a rapid increase in their share of the national property cake. The great magnates began to pick up the land of the waning smallholders, and they may even have made some gains at the expense of the gentry.[5]

Taxes on land and the stagnation of the agricultural economy towards the end of the seventeenth century affected many of the gentry as well as small freeholders, and those who were involved in primarily arable pro-

duction were particularly badly hit. While the small-to-middling men foundered, however, the greater resources of the large landowners enabled them to weather the storm. The owners of many of the great estates were able to draw on various forms of non-agricultural income, such as lucrative government offices. Pensions, sinecures, ambassadorships, governorships, army commissions and so on all provided the means for members of the élite to subsidize the income from their estates. The Paymaster, for example, who was responsible for the payment of the forces, was entitled to a salary and allowances worth some £4000 a year in the early eighteenth century, as well as such perquisites as the interest on the money that was reserved to pay the army. The Duke of Chandos was reputed to have built his great house, Cannons (Greater London), on the profits he made as Paymaster from 1705 to 1712.[6]

Many landowners were also able to subsidize their estates with the profits from their commercial ventures. The Earl of Derby owned coal and lead mines in Lancashire, invested in canals and turnpike roads, and also had a cotton factory in Preston. Daniel Defoe, in his *Tour Through the Whole Island of Great Britain*, noted the alum mines in Yorkshire, 'from whence Lord Musgrave, now Duke of Buckinghamshire, has his title as he has also a great part of his estate'. The social upheaval in the aftermath of the Civil War also saw the

Leicester Square Farm, South Creake, Norfolk
As the great estates became more directly involved in agriculture in the late eighteenth century, some landowners began to build architect-designed model farms. This great brick barn is one of several on the Holkham estate in Norfolk designed by Samuel Wyatt.

demise of those taboos which had formerly prevented large landowners from becoming involved in the practicalities of agricultural production. Instead of merely living off rents, many landlords started to take an interest in their estates, and in the details of investment, innovation and improvement. In the course of the eighteenth century, therefore, it was they rather than the gentry who were in the forefront of the agricultural revolution.

The involvement of large landowners in agricultural innovation was initially indirect. They sought, through the provision of capital, plant, and moral support, to encourage their tenants to make various improvements in methods, and thus to increase both yields and rents. But gradually, as food prices rose and farming became more profitable in the eighteenth century, the big landowners began to be more directly involved in agriculture, and the exploitation of their estates became centralized and increasingly efficient. Many developed their home farms as models for the edification and stimulation of their tenants. The late eighteenth century was a period when great landowners became involved as never before in the active administration of the land.[7]

This development had a considerable impact on the landscape, for the big landowners were able to finance far larger improvement schemes than could be carried out by their tenants or the gentry and had the resources to concern themselves with areas like the wolds of Yorkshire or the sandy East Anglian heaths, where the soils were light and infertile. Before the eighteenth century these areas had been considered marginal, and large stretches were given over to the farming of rabbits and sheep. Immense quantities of sheep dung were needed to coax a crop from the small areas of arable, but new agricultural methods introduced in the late eighteenth century, in particular the new rotations, made the revitalization of even these light soils possible. Great landowners such as Sir Christopher Sykes on the Yorkshire Wolds or Thomas Coke on the 'good sands' of western Norfolk invested heavily in improvement schemes. A memorial tablet in West Heslerton church in North Yorkshire proclaims: 'Whoever now traverses the Wolds of Yorkshire and contrasts their present appearance with what they were cannot but extol the name of Sykes.'[8] Signs of this phase of agricultural intensification can be seen today in the landscape of west Norfolk, where thousands of marl pits still pock the ground. The sandy soil of this area is underlain by chalk which was dug out in the process known as marling and spread on the land to improve the texture and fertility of the soil. This was an important element in many land improvement schemes.

It was the landscapes of these eastern areas which came to be most strikingly dominated by the great estates in the eighteenth and nineteenth centuries. Their sandy or chalky soils were ripe for improvement, but the small freeholders could not afford the investment required. Many were defeated by the lean years of the early eighteenth century, selling their arable land at a cut-price rate, and abandoning their rights to the areas of common grazing.

Even in these areas, however, some tenant farmers were reluctant to abandon their holdings and held up the process of enclosure. William Windham's plans to enclose and improve the common fields and heaths of Felbrigg in north Norfolk were dependent on the acquisition of 'one small farm, of seventy pounds a year, belonging to a young man, a yeoman, just come of age'. In William Marshall's words:

> Steps were taken towards obtaining the desired possession; not, however, by threats and subterfuges, too commonly but very impoliticly made use of upon such occasions; but by open and liberal proposals to the young man, who was made fully acquainted with the intention: and frankly told, that nothing could be done without his estate.[9]

In this instance the tenant, a Mr Priest, was relatively well treated, and sold his estate in return for a considerable sum.[10] But as Marshall made clear, many yeomen did not fare so well at the hands of the acquisitive landlords of the late eighteenth century.

The great estates also increased their hold on the marginal upland areas of the north and west, where tenures were often insecure. Much of this land was unsuitable for arable agriculture even when improved, so that the schemes of enclosure and land improvement introduced by the great estates were usually aimed at improving the quality of the grazing. Such capital intensive improvements were possible because of the rise in the price of agricultural products which took place in the eighteenth century. With the war against Napoleon, the profits of agriculture soared. The great estates had a particular impact on cheap and marginal land, but they increased their hold all over the country and on all sorts of soils, from the arable lands of Lincolnshire to the dairy lands of Devon. The buoyant market for agricultural produce certainly encouraged this development, but it was primarily the fruit of important legal and social changes.

In the years following the Commonwealth, for example, there was a considerable alteration in the terms under which land was inherited. Primogeniture had been standard practice amongst the upper classes since the early sixteenth century, but from the late seventeenth century the freedom of action of heirs to estates was significantly circumscribed because of the legalization of the process known as 'strict settlement'. This prevented heirs from dividing or selling any part of the family estate, so those who came into property could no longer dispose of a few fields or farmsteads in order to pay off the debts of their youth. Each incumbent was not so much the owner as the trustee of the property, responsible for maintaining it for the heirs that were to come. He was, indeed, merely a tenant for life, and it was not until 1882 that a law was passed enabling such tenants to alienate their lands, although before this it had been possible to break settlements through a private act of parliament. As Edmund Burke put it, in his *Reflections on the Revolution in France*, the landed interest represented 'a partnership . . . between those who are living, those who are dead, and those who are to be born'.[11]

The introduction of strict settlements had various consequences, including an increase in the size of the settled estates. This was more or less inevitable, for the purpose of settlement was to ensure that estates could grow, while preventing fragmentation. But it also caused considerable stagnation in the land market since it prevented vast quantities of land from changing hands. This was a handicap to those upwardly-mobile barons of industry and commerce who sought to validate their position by acquiring an estate. They had to create estates piecemeal, by buying up the farms of failing yeomen and minor gentry, or they could take a short cut into the landed élite by marrying a daughter of the nobility. Such marriages were very common and convenient for both parties, bringing élite status to the wealthy and wealth to the élite. In particular, contracts of this kind helped to counteract the chronic shortage of cash amongst the landed classes, which turned out to be one of the side-effects of the settlement of their estates. As Sir J.B.Burke noted in 1873:

> One cannot help perceiving that the chief houses still existing have been built on the foundations laid by feudalism, largely increased at the Dissolution of the monasteries, and constantly enriched by the heritage of lady ancestors.[12]

Wealthy people of all kinds enriched the landed families by marrying into them. Those who had made their money in law, the professions or in government service tried to connect themselves to a family that still had ties with the land. The daughters of great magnates were naturally sought after, but so were the offspring of the greater gentry. William Blathwayt, for example, Secretary of State and Secretary at War under William III, joined the ranks of the landed when he married Mary Wynter, heiress to the Dyrham estate in Gloucestershire.

The stable system of property ownership which resulted from the English revolution of the 1640s was probably even more important than settlement in encouraging the rise of the great estates. Before the Revolution the possession of land had been a prerequisite of power and status, but it had also been fraught with uncertainty and insecurity. From the early Middle Ages to the seventeenth century there are innumerable examples of families falling from favour and losing their estates, casualties of the dynastic struggles which were common in the Middle Ages. In the words of the medieval lawyer, Bracton, a man who supported the losing side ran the risk of 'the loss of all his goods and the perpetual disinheritance of his heirs, so that they may be admitted neither to the paternal nor to the maternal inheritance'.[13] In the troubled years of 1450 to 1500 some 400 people were required to forfeit their estates as a result of the Acts of Attainder passed by Parliament, although as many as half of these may have managed to have their acts reversed.

Even when the establishment of a strong monarchy under the Tudors brought an end to the internal warfare which had wracked late medieval England, the maintenance of estates could still be precarious. Factions plotted and vied with each other to influence and control the Crown, since the monarch was the source of both lucrative pensions and patronage. Estates could be won and lost as men fell in and out of favour, but with treason punishable by execution and confiscation of land, the court was a dangerous place to fall.

Estates could also be ruined by the cost of maintaining the display that was necessary at court. In the early seventeenth century Sir John Oglander had expenses which were £1000 in excess of his income. As a contemporary, Arthur Wilson, commented, the court is 'a kind of lottery, where men that venture much may draw a blank, and such as have little may get a prize'. E.P.Shirley observed in 1859 that many of the oldest families in England had survived and prospered due to their *lack* of prominence in the Tudor and Stuart courts.[14]

There were also various institutional impediments to the maintenance of great estates. Foremost amongst these was the institution of wardship, a hangover from the feudal system perpetuated by the Crown. Under this system, if a tenant-in-chief died leaving a minor as his heir, the Crown could take control of the estate until the heir became of age. The Court of Wards usually farmed out the right to administer these estates and those they appointed were not always the dedicated public servants that in theory they should have been. Heirs were often lucky if they reached their majority before their estates had been plundered beyond repair.

The survival of wardship until the overthrow of King Charles I, despite its deleterious effects on the landed classes, indicates the relationship between property and power that existed at this time. It suggests that continuity of land ownership was comparatively unimportant in a society that revolved around the power of the king. The fluidity of the landed élite would not radically disrupt society while the king was a dominant political force. This all changed, however, with the political upheavals of the seventeenth century.

The Revolutionary government confiscated the estates of those it branded traitors, and many royalist families were ruined by their support for the losing cause. But landed wealth was safer after the Revolution than it had ever been before. The arbitrary power of the Crown had been abolished; the Court of Wards had ceased to exist; and the country was under the control of men who had most interest in the protection of landed property. Following the Glorious Revolution of 1688, Parliament was finally established as the supreme governing body and it was dominated by large landowners. The stability of political administration was rooted in the stability of landholding.

In this environment the very large landholding units flourished, for every care was taken to make the political and social system congenial to their interests and needs. Despite the development of an increasingly diverse economy, and the emergence of new forms of commercial and industrial wealth, land was still seen in many quarters as the basis of national prosperity. Large quantities of literature were produced which discussed the political role of the landholder and land, and justified the preferential position of the landed interest in the political system. This literature indicates something of the ideology which underlay the adaptations of the landscape which were carried out in the eighteenth century. Although many writers emphasized the economic importance of non-agricultural production, the arguments used were conducted in a rhetoric which represented land as a very special form of wealth.

Only the owner of a great estate could assess the needs of the country. Only he could recognize what would be for the benefit of all. The great landowner was mythologized as a wise and powerful figure, who embodied the aspirations of the community which he served. His benevolent omniscience was a result of his landed status, for as an owner of part of the nation he was seen to be able to understand its needs. Moreover, the fact that his wealth was rooted in land was thought to convey an impartiality denied to those more closely tied to the means of production. Merchants, financiers and industrialists were seen as biased by self-interest, but the landowner's wealth was in the nation, and his interest was thus the national good. He was therefore seen as the natural statesman, and things could not go too far wrong while he was at the helm of the ship of state.[15]

In Joseph Addison's *Spectator*, the periodical which became so important in the early eighteenth century as the definitive model of literary style and taste, the ability of the 'spectator' to provide an impartial analysis of society is in part connected with his ownership of land. The fictitious narrator of Addison's papers gives the following account of himself:

> I was born to a small Hereditary Estate, which, according to the Tradition of the Village where it lies, was bounded by the same Hedges and Ditches in *William* the Conqueror's Time that it is at present, and has been delivered down from Father to Son whole and entire, without the loss

or Acquisition of a single Field or Meadow, during the space of six hundred Years.[16]

Addison satirizes the pride of contemporary landowners in the antiquity of their holdings, while he exploits the traditional concept that it is independent landowners who are best able to observe, comment on and control society.

Of course this image of the independent landowner conveniently suppressed the dependence of many great estates on non-agricultural forms of income, but it indicates the tremendous cultural importance of landed property in the eighteenth century. As society became increasingly dependent on commercial and industrial wealth, the possession of land became an ever more powerful symbol of social status. Political rhetoric associated the estate with both power and political judgement, and the ownership of land became the aspiration of all those who had profited in other walks of life. Landowners sought to own increasingly large estates, but they were also anxious to use the landscape to display the extent of their power.

The consolidation of estates which had begun during the later Middle Ages was accelerated in the eighteenth century, for the estates that could most clearly demonstrate the extent of their owner's domain were those in which the lands were most compact. Through judicious sales and purchases and the shrewd use of the marriage contract, landed families began to concentrate their holdings in large blocks of land, in contrast to the far-flung estates they had once possessed. This process was in part stimulated by social attitudes to landed wealth, but it was also encouraged by sound practical considerations. Once estates began to be managed as single units and run from an administrative centre, there were considerable advantages in holding a compact estate. Management was much easier and boundary disputes were minimized. Such disputes frequently ended up in the courts and could be both expensive and time-consuming. They were also very common, since landowners were extremely jealous of their property rights, and inclined to be obstinate if they thought they had been deprived of land.[17]

By the seventeenth century the strength of a landowner was no longer gauged by the manpower he could raise. His power was based on his wealth, and on the extent of his political influence, and both of these were enhanced by the consolidation of estates. For consolidation not only made agriculture more efficient and productive, and thus improved the income that could be gained from the land, but also meant that a landlord's tenants lived nearer to one another. This increased the chances that they would form the majority of voters in at least one parliamentary constituency, and thus that the landlord would get the representative he favoured returned to parliament.

The great estates flourished in the areas where land was relatively cheap, and where large estates and landscaped parks could be created at relatively little expense. Even today there are areas on the edge of the sandy Breckland in Norfolk and Suffolk where it is possible to go for many miles without losing sight of a landscape park, and where other signs of the large estates are prevalent. In the environs of Thetford, for example, it is possible to pass from the estate of Elveden, with its estate village and park dominated by exotic conifers, to Euston, with its park designed by Repton, to Kilverstone, Shadwell, Wretham and Croxton. All these parks, or former parks, lie within a few miles of each other, and the countryside around them bears all the marks of estate land, with the characteristic estate farms, cottages and plantations.

Another important factor in the formation of great estates was the ease with which unified blocks of land could be acquired. In areas where there were numerous villages owned by a single manorial lord, it was fairly easy to combine a number of these villages into a single large estate. In much of north Buckinghamshire, for example, a single landowner owned at least 90 per cent of over a third of the parishes

Brocklesby, Lincolnshire
The size and continuity of great landed estates was emphasized in the nineteenth century by the standardization of estate architecture. The farms and cottages on the Earl of Yarborough's estates, for example, have a visual unity that shows that they are all part of a single landholding unit. They are adorned with a characteristic repertoire of drip-mouldings, barge-boards, and gable posts.

by the late eighteenth century, so that families like the Verneys could amass a large and continuous estate with relatively little trouble. It was partly for this reason that the great estates flourished in many former champion areas, particularly in parts of the east Midlands, such as the middle Trent Valley, between Stone and Newark, and in the triangle between Grantham, Leicester and Stamford.

There were considerable regional variations in the distribution of large landed estates. By the nineteenth century many areas were dominated by large landowners — that is, by estates of 7000 acres or more. These tended to be located on the edges of what had been the champion heartlands, and in particular on the lighter lands which lay around the clayland core of the Midlands. They were a particular feature of the great sandy areas of northwest Suffolk and west Norfolk, of the light chalk soils of the wolds of Yorkshire and Lincolnshire, of the sands around Sherwood Forest and of many chalkland areas, especially in Wiltshire, Berkshire and Dorset. In addition, by the mid nineteenth century the great landowners had taken control of vast areas of the uplands, much of which was poor quality grazing and moorland. Some of this was improved and converted to productive farmland, but much, especially during the nineteenth century, was left as it was and used for shooting.[18]

The medium-sized estates, of 1000 to 7000 acres, were more widely distributed by the late eighteenth and nineteenth centuries than those at either extreme. They were found throughout the length and breadth of England, but were particularly prominent in some areas, such as parts of Shropshire and Herefordshire, and in the old woodland counties of Middlesex, Essex, Hertfordshire and Surrey in the environs of London. The estates near London were relatively small because of the high price of land. Some landowners here had much larger estates in more inexpensive but less fashionable parts of the country, but many of these 'home counties' estates were owned by businessmen, merchants and financiers, who liked to play the role of the country squire but could not move far from the capital. Others were farmed by small landowners, who exploited the profitable markets of London. As a result, a complex property landscape emerged in these areas, made up of a patchwork of small and medium-sized estates, and this pattern was to influence the subsequent evolution of the woodland landscape in the home counties.

The impact of large landed estates on the appearance of the landscape was not simply a consequence of their size and continuity. One complicating factor was the strength of their tenant communities. In the pastoral areas of the north and west, such as Nidderdale, where the tenants were numerous, fairly prosperous and of an independent turn of mind, the landowner's control over the appearance of the landscape was circumscribed. He could not easily enforce any degree of standardization in the architecture of either domestic or agricultural buildings. Generally, large-scale adaptation of the environment could be brought about most easily in those areas where communities were economically most closely tied to the landlord. Such areas tended to be devoted to primarily arable agriculture, with a few, large tenant farms and a great many landless labourers.

But above all, extensive landscaping was easiest where the countryside was relatively featureless. Thus in various parts of the uplands and the east, where land was poor and farms were cheap, great tracts of land were acquired by estates and formed into elaborate landscapes. Bare open wastes of heath and moor were replaced by fields, farms and roads, which could be drawn on the landscape as on a blank slate. These new landscapes could be constructed to a uniform plan, using standardized techniques of building and planting, to create an environment that was clearly the product of a single family and a single period.

In the Wallington region of Northumberland, for example, large quantities of barren moorland were enclosed and improved between 1730 and 1780 at the behest of Sir W.H.Blackett. The arable fields, woods, trees, roads and numerous buildings that resulted make up a landscape that is clearly planned and has a striking visual unity, in marked contrast to landscapes that have developed gradually.[19]

Such 'great estate landscapes', in which the wealth of the landlord and the extent of the estate are revealed in practical agricultural features, can be found in a number of areas. A notable example is on the poor soils of Exmoor, on land that was open moorland until it was enclosed in the early nineteenth century. John Knight of Wolverley Hall in Worcestershire bought 10,000 acres of this newly-enclosed land, and over the next sixty years he and his son brought about a transformation of its appearance. Although the venture was a failure in financial terms, the results of this transformation can still be seen today. The landscape is divided into large rectangular fields, hedged with earthen banks topped with beech trees. Dispersed amongst these fields are long, narrow belts of conifers, and seventeen slate-roofed farmhouses, both revealing the nineteenth-century origins of the landscape. The whole estate is bounded by a 29-mile wall.[20]

Perhaps the most spectacular great estate landscape was that created by the Yarborough family on the Lincolnshire Wolds in the late eighteenth and nineteenth centuries. Made up of 30,000 acres of enclosed and improved wold land, the estate is a monument to the interest of its owner in almost every aspect of rural life. The roads, fields, houses, schools and even the station were laid out in an elaborate status landscape, with the individual architecture of the buildings clearly showing their dependence on the great Yarborough estate. They are all constructed in distinctive yellow brick produced by the estate yard in Kirmington, and they all share the same decorative details. The houses, schools and station are heavily ornamented with barge-boards, gable-posts, and panelled and studded doors, and they all have elaborate drip mouldings above the windows.[21]

Extensive planned landscapes such as these form a striking contrast to the landscapes that have been shaped and moulded by innumerable hands over the centuries. Yet although they are exceptional, these planned estates are not outlandish for they are merely the most striking products of a far more general change. The general enclosure of open fields and wastes provided both the opportunity and the stimulus to shape the landscape and to use it to display taste and status. In the old enclosed landscapes of the woodland, on the other hand, there was far less potential for such aesthetic display, and thus the impact of the landed estates tended to be more limited.

The landowners who were most interested in adapting their estates were those who took up residence there, as there was clearly little point in an absentee landlord concerning himself with the aesthetics of an estate that he hardly ever saw. A similar principle was at work within the estates themselves, most of which exhibited what may be called 'distance decay'. This was the tendency for estate buildings and other features to be progressively less ornamented the further they were from the house. Cottages

Nineteenth-century landscape improvement on Exmoor
Two views of the landscape created by the reclamation of Exmoor by the Knight family in the mid nineteenth century. The earth banks crowned with beech trees around the newly-enclosed fields and the straight road bordered by a beech hedge are characteristic features.

clustering on the margins of the park would be decorated in accordance with the latest taste, while the more distant fields and farms were far less carefully adorned. On the Yarborough estate, for example, buildings near the estate centre at Brocklesby are far more lavishly ornamented than those further away. This feature is also evident on the Gunton estate in Norfolk. Barns and buildings on farms around the park at Gunton, such as Tops Hill Farm, Dairy Farm and Park Farm, are far more sophisticated and ornate than those on more distant farms. But this principle did not always operate. On the nearby Holkham estate there is much less evidence of distance decay, for substantial and well-built late eighteenth-century neo-classical farms are scattered right across the area of the estate.

The growth of the large unitary estates had a profound effect on the whole fabric of the landscape. The clearest symbol of this development was to be found at the very heart of the landed estate, in the country house, with its park and gardens. The evolution of these features reveals much about the changes that were taking place in the social and tenurial organization of the great estates, and also in the agricultural landscape as a whole.

SEVEN

A Place in the Country

Have we not seen, at Pleasure's lordly call,
The smiling, long-frequented village fall?
Beheld the duteous son, the sire decay'd,
The modest matron, and the blushing maid,
Forced from their homes, a melancholy train,
To traverse climes beyond the western main.[1]

TO SEVERAL EIGHTEENTH-CENTURY WRITERS, the image of the village cleared to make way for the parkland of a country house powerfully symbolized the decadence of a luxurious age. The removal of a community which had long inhabited and worked the land seemed a betrayal of the landlord's traditional paternalistic responsibility, and the magnificence of the new country houses was seen as a departure from the frugality of the past. Nowhere was this extravagance more evident than in the creation of elaborate parks, out of land which had formerly been used for productive agriculture. Alexander Pope, while no enemy of landscape gardening, condemned some of the excesses of eighteenth-century taste. Nowadays, with the countryside dotted with the ploughed remains of eighteenth-century parkland, there is a prophetic quality to his words, as he looks forward to a time when a particularly vast and tasteless park will once again be used for arable agriculture:

Another age shall see the golden Ear,
Imbrown the Slope, and nod on the parterre,
Deep Harvests bury all his pride has planned,
And laughing Ceres reassume the land.[2]

This chapter looks at the process which led farmland to be converted into a landscape of display, and traces the history of that acme of eighteenth-century taste, the English country-house landscape. As Alexander Pope was well aware, the parks and gardens of the aristocracy tell us much about élite ideas of land, wealth and status.

But before we consider the changing styles of the landscape park itself, we must take a look at its centre, the heart of any landed estate, the English country house. The evolution of country-house architecture reflected the changes in society which were to be so important in determining the form of the landscape park. In particular, alterations in the organization of the country house revealed the gradual demise of medieval face-to-face communities and a move towards the spatial separation of social classes.[3]

The decline in the importance of the hall, which had begun in the Middle Ages, continued through the post medieval period. By the sixteenth and seventeenth centuries, this room had begun to serve primarily as a common room and dining-room for the servants, and was only occasionally used as the venue for great communal feasts. From the end of the Middle Ages there was a gradual reduction in the number of formal rituals and ceremonies which were carried out in the households of the landowners. There was less incentive to maintain activities which had formerly bound communities together as power, and the wealth it brought, began to be based on access to the court, rather than on the support of large numbers of tenants and dependants.

As landlords became less interested in the maintenance of social intercourse with their inferiors, the private chamber replaced the communal hall as the most important room within the house. In the greatest households this development took place in the Middle Ages, but it spread through the lower ranks of landed society in the sixteenth century. As it did so, landowners began to lavish money and attention on the furnishing and decoration of their chamber, and to use it as the room in which they would entertain and impress guests. These visitors tended to be their social equals, near equals or superiors—rarely their inferiors.

Thus, as the size of their households declined, both the great barons and the lesser gentry increasingly divorced themselves from the local community. They no longer needed to be surrounded by hosts of dependants, since political power and personal prestige had ceased to be based on the strength of the fighting force which an individual could raise in an emergency. Landowners began to see themselves as part of a national élite, set apart and unified by their adoption of an exclusive and cultured lifestyle identified by common standards in taste and fashion.

As power gradually assumed a political and financial base rather than a martial foundation, towers and crenellations stopped being used to adorn manorial halls. Castles were abandoned or extensively altered, and some, like Nottingham Castle, were quarried for stone. As landlords began to identify themselves as a national ruling class, they increasingly sought to display their familiarity with the classical culture which this group supposedly shared. A style of architecture loosely based on Greek and Roman models became fashionable, and houses were built on classical principles of symmetry.

At first, a symmetrical facade concealed an irregular arrangement of rooms. But as the hall lost its primacy and gradually declined in size, traditional lopsided house-plans were superseded during the seventeenth century by designs in which the internal layout had a rigid symmetry. The hall, while still used sporadically for great occasions, principally served as an imposing entrance, from which stairs led to the upper floor. The country house ceased to provide a place in which tenants, casual visitors and dependants of all kinds could congregate, and servants' rooms were moved to the basement. Flights of back stairs were incorporated into new houses, allowing servants to move about the house without being seen. This indicated not merely the increasing segregation of classes, but a decline in the status of servants. By the later seventeenth century the households of great men no longer included the younger sons of gentry families, but were exclusively made up of menials who were increasingly kept out of sight.

In the symmetrical houses of the late seventeenth and early eighteenth centuries, the arrangement of rooms was carefully structured to accord with the growing formality of social relations. The most important rooms were organized in a sequence with one leading off from another. The more public rooms led to rooms that were more private and exclusive. Under French influence, the chamber was renamed the 'saloon', and was usually located on the ground floor behind the hall. From this led various suites of carefully ordered rooms, in which an antechamber preceded a bedchamber, which was followed by a closet or cabinet. While the saloon served as a relatively impersonal space, in which casual visitors and social inferiors could be entertained, the final rooms in the sequence were used only for private discussions with social equals or superiors. In the late seventeenth and early eighteenth centuries, this arrangement of rooms was suited to the conduct of financial and political business based on close personal contact. Inferiors solicited superiors for patronage and favours, and while the hierarchical fabric of society was maintained, social dominance ceased to be demonstrated by the public display which had traditionally taken place within the hall.

It was not only great landowners who exerted powers of patronage. The local gentry had the right to nominate the parish clergy, and, of course, they also made appointments to offices on their own estates. They used their gift of these positions to gain the support of social inferiors, the more prosperous tenants or affluent freeholders. Thus, like the great landowners, they too established their social position through a series of personal relationships of obligation. As a result, the formal plans which facilitated and articulated these relationships were not only used in great mansions, like Blenheim Palace or Chatsworth, but also in some relatively small country houses, such as Nether Lypiatt Manor in Gloucestershire, which was built between 1700 and 1705. The use of these formal plans in the houses of the gentry was, however, motivated as much by their desire to emulate their superiors as by the way that they ordered their lives.

Although the status of the hall declined, it did not entirely lose its earlier functions, even in the formal houses of the late seventeenth and early eighteenth century. It was still sporadically used for entertaining, and as late as 1756 Isaac Ware wrote that the hall was 'a good apartment for the reception of large companies at public feasts'. Tenants were often still entertained at Christmas, and on the days when they paid their rent. Dinners were also sometimes given to local freeholders if a landlord was standing in a contested election, for although open voting ensured that he could count on the support of his tenants, he still had to win the allegiance of the freehold farmers.

Towards the end of the seventeenth century, when the highly formal house-plan was in fashion, considerable alterations were made in the external appearance of the country house. As the growing popularity of the Grand Tour amongst the upper classes led to the dissemination of knowledge about classical civilization, the details of classical architectural design became increasingly sophisticated and ever more accurate.

Under the influence of the Italian architect Palladio, the standard eighteenth-century house took the form of a classical temple, with a portico and rusticated base. Houses built in this style, such as Stowe in Buckinghamshire, Gorhambury in Hertfordshire and Holkham in Norfolk, have been frequently seen as embodiments of Augustan refinement and elegance. Elements of this style percolated down to the homes of lesser landed classes, and were also used in the 'villas' which sprang up around the metropolis.

The earliest Palladian houses, such as Wentworth Woodhouse in Yorkshire, maintained the formal plan of the previous tradition. But as the lifestyles of the landed rich changed in the course of the eighteenth century, there was a gradual alteration in the organization of their homes. During the eighteenth century the gentry and aristocracy became increasingly divorced from smaller farmers, prosperous tenants and small freeholders. As many parliamentary seats came to be apportioned by local agreements between magnates, contested elections became increasingly rare. Great landowners no longer needed the support of the small freeholders, who were declining both in number and economic strength. At the same time, links between the aristocracy and gentry were becoming ever stronger and more intimate. These two groups made up the 'polite society' that dominated eighteenth-century culture. Similarly educated and often closely related, the gentry and aristocracy shared an abiding interest in the maintenance of the property system. They cemented their alliance through a multiplicity of social engagements — dinners, routs, concerts and balls — which served to reinforce their intimacy and social exclusivity. This could not be more clearly displayed than in that most eighteenth-century of entertainments, the masquerade or masked ball. In theory, this entertainment gave a novel freedom to social relations, since all those attending the ball were required to turn up in disguise. But as a character in Fielding's novel *Tom Jones* points out, in practice it was very different. As Lady Bellaston informs Tom Jones:

You cannot conceive any Thing more insipid and childish than a Masquerade to People of Fashion, who in general know one another as well here, as when they meet in an Assembly or a Drawing-room; nor will any Woman of Condition converse with a person with whom she is not acquainted.[4]

To cater for this extensive entertaining, eighteenth-century houses developed ornate suites of public rooms, arranged not in a hierarchical linear sequence but in a circuit to allow for informal circulation. At the same time, the hall still continued to decline, and in smaller country houses, such as Harleyford in Buckinghamshire, it became a mere vestibule, too small to be used for any social gathering at all. As transport improved, it became fashionable to visit neighbouring country seats, and this development culminated in the great house parties of the nineteenth century. The entertainment of house guests led to the

Stowe, Buckinghamshire
The spectacular south front at Stowe was rebuilt in 1774 to the design of Robert Adam, and epitomizes the elegance of eighteenth-century Palladian architecture. The park in which the house stands has gone through a series of changes in style and layout, and the octagon lake in the foreground is now a misnomer, since its formal geometric outline was greatly modified in the 1750s to present a more natural appearance.

development of specialized rooms for billiards, breakfast and, ultimately, smoking. Meanwhile, servants were moved even farther from the centre of the household, with kitchens, stables and offices often located in a separate wing of the house. This development had been encouraged in the late eighteenth century by the invention of the bell-pull, and by the evolution of gothic architecture.

The adherents of the gothic style scorned the formal symmetry of classical houses, and favoured the creation of rambling and irregular piles. Extra wings and rooms could be added at random to gothic houses, without detracting from the overall effect. The earliest houses constructed in this style were fantastic mock-medieval creations, like Ashridge in Hertfordshire. This was built between 1808 and 1817 by James Wyatt and Jeffry Wyatville, and is romantically situated on the beech-covered crest of the Chiltern Hills. Later in the nineteenth century, a more 'Tudoresque' manor-house style became fashionable, like that used at Whitewick Manor near Wolverhampton, which was constructed in the 1880s, or at Shadwell in Norfolk. Like many country houses, Shadwell was an amalgam of additions and alterations built over numerous years, and in its final phase of rebuilding, in the 1850s, it was converted into an assymetrical Elizabethan pile. Many of the houses built in this style, such as Knebworth in Hertfordshire, incorporate genuine late medieval or sixteenth-century buildings.

This architectural change was part of the Victorian attempt to create a romantic myth of medieval England. As the country industrialized, and the disaffected poor became identified as a threat to the status quo, many

Knebworth House, Hertfordshire
Built largely between 1815 and 1820, but incorporating parts of a genuine late medieval building, this rambling gothic creation is a good indication of the fantastic nature of Victorian ideas of medieval architecture.

landowners looked back with nostalgia to the close-knit communities of the past. Mock-gothic castles and manor houses were created, and in some Victorian country houses, such as Ketteringham in Norfolk, the open hall was reintroduced.

This architectural revival in no way represented a genuine return to the community households of the medieval past. Within nineteenth-century houses servants continued to be carefully hidden, spatially segregated from their social superiors. Moreover, the desire of the landed classes to be socially isolated influenced the surroundings as well as the architecture of their houses. From the late seventeenth century landlords began to shape their grounds in order to display their divorcedness from the local community, and this led to the evolution of the great landscape parks of the eighteenth century.

The landscape park revealed the status of its owner by an apparent lack of any practical purpose; it was an aesthetic adornment to the country house and its form was dictated by fashion. It was a place in which the taste and wealth of the owner was displayed, and it served to insulate the country house from the neighbouring labouring community. As such, it was very different from the parks in which medieval lords had kept their deer. How did this change in the nature of the park come about? How did the house become surrounded by a park, instead of being sited in the village? And what motivated the stylistic alterations that were made in the appearance of the landscape park?[5]

In the sixteenth and early seventeenth century, many deer parks were destroyed and converted to farmland, as landlords sought to profit from the high prices of the agricultural boom. In his *Survey of Cornwall* (1602) Richard Carew noted that a number of parks had disappeared within living memory, and described how some owners were 'making there Deere leape over the pale to give bullocks place'. After the Dissolution many of the monastic parks were converted to agricultural use, and during the period of the Commonwealth numerous families got rid of their parks in order to raise money to pay fines.

Nevertheless, there were many deer parks which were not destroyed, but merely underwent a transformation of their function and form. In some cases, when it was first becoming fashionable to isolate the hall, it was relocated in the deer park. The park as hunting reserve evolved directly into the park as pleasure ground. Indeed, there was sometimes a subsequent adaptation, when the pleasure ground was formed into a municipal open space. Cassiobury Park in Hertfordshire, for example, began as a hunting park belonging to the abbots of St Albans. Following the Dissolution it became the setting for the country house of the Earls of Essex. Now it is a park maintained by Watford Council, who bought it in the 1920s when the Cassiobury estate was sold.

In most cases, however, the manorial hall was not resited in the deer park, but the park was extended to encompass the manorial hall. This was often relatively straightforward, because many of the parks backed on to the houses to which they belonged. It was therefore in part because the majority of deer parks were located in woodland or upland regions of the country that the earliest landscape parks tended to occur in these areas too. Yet this was not the only reason.

Woodland or upland areas were usually enclosed at an early date, and parks could only be formed or extended in land where enclosure had taken place. It would not have been possible for a landowner to develop an elaborate 'status landscape' without having first eradicated the rights of other people to the land. There would have been no point in planting an avenue or an ornamental clump of trees if the cattle of the peasantry were free to browse the carefully sited saplings. Moreover, a landlord's pleasure in the prospect of his park might have been considerably diminished if he were constantly faced with the sight of local villagers wandering across it.

In woodland areas a landowner could either relocate his house in a deer park, extend a deer park to encompass the house, or create a new park to surround it. In many champion areas, however, the slow progress of enclosure meant that emparcation was delayed. Parks only appeared as landlords gathered strips together piecemeal, or, more usually, as general enclosures revolutionized the appearance of the landscape. With the spread of parliamentary enclosure, landscaped parks proliferated until they were found in almost every part of the country.

The isolation of a landowner's house often required more than the mere accumulation of a compact block of enclosed land. It necessitated the reorganization of the fabric of the landscape. Roads and footpaths had to be redirected, and on many occasions the pattern of settlement had to be altered. Sections of villages or even whole communities were flattened in order to make way for pleasure grounds. Landscape parks produced in this way dramatically symbolize changes that have taken place in the distribution of control over land. They indicate the social divide which had developed between the landed élite and the local community, as power became concentrated in a landlord's hands. By the eighteenth century, if a landowner did not like the sight of one of the villages which he owned, he could simply move it, or even have it destroyed outright.

Ickworth Park, Suffolk
The church of St Mary was left isolated in the magnificent park when the village was destroyed by emparking in the early eighteenth century. The manor house remained next to the church until the end of the century, when it too was demolished and replaced by the unusual circular building which can be seen in the far left of the picture. It was begun by Frederick, Bishop of Derry and Earl of Bristol and a member of the Hervey family, lords of the manor since the fifteenth century. It has the same circular shape as a house which the bishop had previously begun, but not completed, at Ballyscullion in Derry.

Some villages were moved more than once. In 1737 Thomas Anson moved the village of Shugborough in Staffordshire in order to lay out a large park around his house. In the nineteenth century his descendant, Thomas Lord Anson, moved the village again when the park was enlarged. Recent research has suggested that the clearance of villages or parts of villages occurred far more often than was previously thought. In a survey of parks and gardens in Hampshire, for instance, over half were found to contain village earthworks or an isolated parish church, and the majority of these features were probably the direct result of emparking.

On many occasions, however, the creation of a landscape park required the alteration of village plans, rather than the total destruction of settlements. In Northamptonshire eight villages were entirely cleared for emparking during the eighteenth and nineteenth centuries, but in addition to these there were twenty-five which had to be radically changed. In Thorpe Malsor, for instance, the houses on one side of the main street were removed in the eighteenth century.

Villages that have been annihilated or extensively reshaped by emparking can be found all over England, but they tend to be most common in champion country. In these areas manorial halls were most frequently sited amidst sizeable villages and these would have to be removed if the hall was to be emparked. In contrast, the great houses found in woodland regions were often fairly isolated, so that the creation of a park could require the removal of only a handful of homes. Furthermore, a landlord could only remove those settlements which he owned outright, and it was in the champion regions that the landowners were most frequently in possession of entire villages.

For many years most landlords were content with removing the parts of a village in the immediate precincts of their house. Between 1550 and 1700 many cottages were cleared, but they were usually replaced by small formal gardens rather than extensive landscaped parks. These gardens gave some degree of privacy to the landowner's house and separated it a little from the rest of the village. But, unlike later parks, they did not create a massive private landscape in which a country house could be wholly protected from the sight of local people.

In 1580 Christopher Hatton, one of the most important men in England, began to lay out a formal garden around Holdenby Hall in Northamptonshire. This garden was unusually large for the period, and its creation involved the removal of cottages in the southern half of Holdenby village. Despite its proximity to one of the greatest houses in England, the rest of the village was not cleared. Instead it was rebuilt on a rather neater plan than before, with the houses clustered around a square green. The village became a feature of the landscape when viewed from the house, observable through decorative arches in the garden wall.[6]

From the late seventeenth century tastes changed, and landowners increasingly wanted their houses to be totally secluded. Villages began to be moved not merely because landowners wanted their sites, but also because it was unfashionable for such features to be seen from the heart of a landscape park. None the less some landowners reconstructed the villages in a suitably tasteful style, which enabled them to be incorporated in the great estate landscapes on the margins of the park itself. We will be looking at such 'model villages' in more detail in the following chapter.

In many cases, however, villages that were destroyed were never replaced, and their inhabitants were merely absorbed into neighbouring settlements. Although there are some exceptions, such as Milton Abbas in Dorset (which was almost a minor market town), the majority of the communities evicted for emparking were relatively small. They were often settlements that had been in decline for years, and it was this which made it easy for landlords to destroy them. The village of

Bryanston in Dorset was cleared in the eighteenth century to make way for parkland around Bryanston Hall. In the Middle Ages this had been a prosperous settlement, but in 1662 it was made up of only six households.[7] Likewise, part of the village of Croxton in Cambridgeshire was destroyed to make way for a landscape park in 1812, but earthworks reveal that the village had already declined considerably before emparking.[8]

Many deserted villages are discernible in the parks of our great country houses as irregular humps and bumps in landscaped lawns. It is often still possible to trace the course of their routeways and to make out house platforms which mark the spots where buildings once stood. Elsewhere, landowners removed even these meagre traces of former inhabitants, by having village earthworks flattened. In most places, however, when a village was removed to make way for a park the parish church was not destroyed. Left isolated within the park, it usually continued to serve as a centre of worship, either for rehoused villagers, or for workers on the estate. Today the presence of such churches may indicate that emparcation occurred at some stage.

In some woodland areas, however, the church and house may have stood together, apart from other buildings, for centuries, as a result of the dispersed settlement pattern. Moreover, the deserted settlements within areas of parkland were not all produced by emparking. The park at Easton Neston in Northamptonshire, for example, contains the earthworks of a village that was depopulated in the Middle Ages, when the area was turned over to sheep.[9] Such enclosures facilitated the conversion to parkland at a later date.

At the end of the eighteenth century, the rate at which villages were being destroyed sharply declined. Labourers' cottages began once again to be incorporated into the élite landscape, provided they were placed at a convenient distance from the house. Thus, many villages began to be 'landscaped' themselves and adapted in accordance with aristocratic taste. This ensured that they could redound to the status of their landlord, and become, in Repton's words, 'among the ornaments of (a) place'.[10]

In many ways, however, it is not very satisfactory to explain these developments purely in terms of changes in élite taste. Why were there so many changes in the form of the landscape garden, and what was the significance of the various styles? Furthermore, what was the function of these parks, and why did they develop?

It is not easy to appreciate the appearance of the earliest parks and gardens, for very few have survived intact. Gardens are very transient. As tastes change, a previous style is liable to be swept away. From the early seventeenth century, however, not only maps but also paintings, in particular portraits, occasionally represented areas of park or garden. These give us some idea of what the originals might have looked like. Like the later parks, seventeenth-century gardens underwent numerous changes of fashion, adopting and adapting ideas derived from Italy, the Low Countries and France.

Terraces, flights of shallow steps, gravel walks arranged in rectangular patterns and symmetrical beds of flowers were recurrent features in the seventeenth-century garden. Many included topiary work and orderly rows of statues. They were groups of gardens rather than one unified whole, consisting of various independent elements rather than following a uniform plan. They were full of individual beauties and elaborate detail, arranged in a precise and geometric order. Such gardens were not very extensive, but tended to be restricted to a few courts around the house, enclosed within walls, earthworks or hedges.

These gardens formed a striking contrast to the working agricultural landscape, with its open expanses of fields, woods and commons. The outside world was made up of broad prospects and irregular lines; but gardens were composed of straight lines and strictly confined views. This contrast was particularly obvious in champion regions, where the countryside tended to contain few hedges and trees. Enclosed and private land did not yet dominate the countryside, and the status landscapes of the élite were clearly divorced from the environment produced by the community and by work.

Nowadays, there is little to be seen of the vast majority of these gardens. Most have been totally destroyed, and only earthworks remain of many others.[11] Although the sixteenth- and early seventeenth-century gardens were usually not very large, their creation often involved the movement of considerable quantities of earth, to form extensive terraces and mounts. In some places pavilions and garden buildings have survived, like the fine early seventeenth-century garden building at Bawburgh in Norfolk, now somewhat incongruously situated amidst a modern housing estate.

At first, relatively few formal gardens around country houses lay in parkland. Most were bordered by ordinary agricultural land. As late as 1700 the map in Chauncy's *History of Hertfordshire* depicted 147 houses of status sufficient to be deemed 'gentlemen's houses', but of these only thirty-five are shown to have a park. Once again, it is mainly through illustrations that we can gain some idea of the appearance of these sixteenth- and seventeenth-

RIGHT **Bawburgh, Norfolk**
These seventeenth-century garden buildings have survived to the present day, even though the house with which they were associated, Bawburgh Hall, was demolished long ago. They are now sited somewhat incongruously amidst a modern housing development.

Strixton, Northamptonshire
These low earthworks are all that remain of the terraces of the sixteenth-century formal gardens of Strixton manor house (now demolished).

S L

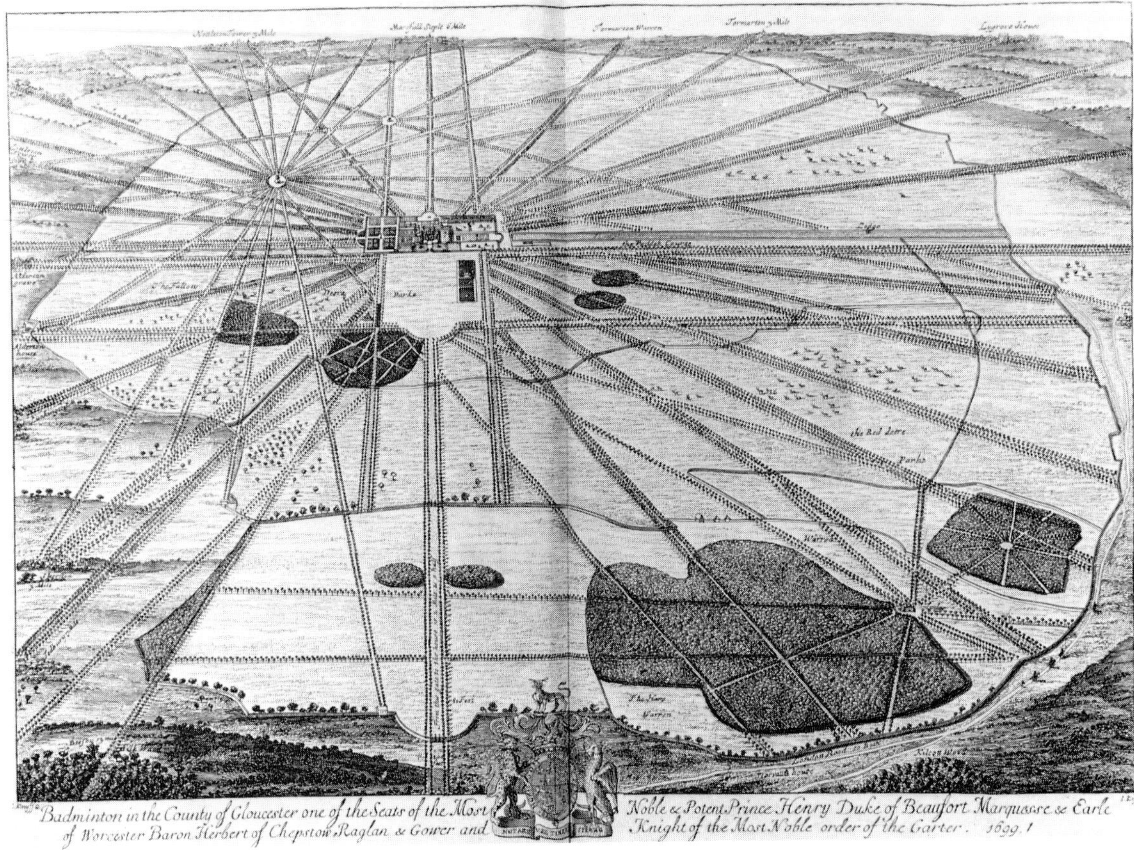

century parks, although, of course, these need to be interpreted with some caution. We cannot always be sure that an artist has portrayed the landscape as it actually appeared, rather than as he or his patron wanted it to look. None the less, in the absence of other sources, paintings and prints give us some useful clues. Among the most revealing seventeenth-century illustrations is a series of engravings carried out by Wenceslaus Hollar in the 1630s, depicting Albury Park in Surrey.[12] The house is surrounded by a small walled garden, and beyond this lies the park, an area of grassland dotted with single trees and tree clumps. This park contained more formal elements than was usual for the period. Most notably there was a large terrace and a canal, each some 400 metres long, but apart from these somewhat incongruous features the park looks like a deer park, which is what it was.

During the seventeenth century walled gardens around the country house began to become more elaborate and extensive. Terraces became increasingly substantial, and the artificial mounds known as 'mounts' became more common. These provided those within the garden with a view over the garden wall, and a prospect of either the park or the agricultural landscape. Such features reveal an increasing interest in the less ordered and formal environment beyond the bounds of the garden. Nowadays mounts often survive as neglected but quite striking earthworks. They are sometimes buried within the woodland of a later landscape, and because of their size they are occasionally mistaken for mottes.

Badminton, Avon
In the late seventeenth and early eighteenth century a number of landowners had vast geometric landscapes laid out around their homes. This late seventeenth-century engraving by Johannes Kip shows the Duke of Beaufort's seat at Badminton surrounded by a host of radiating paths.

In the seventeenth century it became increasingly common for country houses to be approached by an avenue of trees, but it was not until the final decades of the century that the élite began to adapt their gardens extensively, and also to shape the parks and agricultural land around the house. Walled gardens were increased in size and various formal features began to be established outside the confines of the garden wall. Long avenues and lines of trees or canals continued the main axes of the formal house and garden far into the surrounding countryside, which was further enhanced by geometric plantations, through which straight rides were cut.

This grandly formal, geometric landscaping was based on the principles of Le Nôtre and imported from the court of Louis XIV. It became fashionable in England in the late seventeenth century, and influenced the landscape of a number of country seats. We can get some idea of the appearance of these landscapes from the engravings of Leonard Knyff and Johannes Kip, although there is some doubt as to whether these pictures exaggerate the extent of formal layouts. Their illustrations of places such as Brympton in Somerset, Lowther in Cumbria, or New Park in Surrey depict the house at the centre of the landscape, surrounded by a host of radiating paths. To convey the scale and complexity of the landscaping, the scene is represented as if viewed obliquely from the air, a perspective that graphically portrays the landlord's circle of influence.

In England, as in France, these landscapes were seen as symbolic and as an embodiment of the power of the landed élite. The avenues and alignments running out into the landscape showed the areas under the owner's control and emphasized the country house as a pivotal point in the landscape. They were usually extended as far as possible into the countryside; indeed the Duke of Montague is supposed to have contemplated an avenue which would run between London and Northampton, a distance of seventy miles! Such developments were made possible by the increasing consolidation of estates. As landowners ceased to be perpetually on the move, they had the incentive as well as the opportunity to establish their dominance over the appearance of a particular locality.

People sometimes express surprise that so little remains of these massive layouts today. There are various relict features, such as the octagonal pond at Wimpole in Cambridgeshire, and avenues in particular have survived better than is often supposed. At Buxted in East Sussex, for example, there is an avenue of limes planted around 1630, and the lime avenue which Moses Cook planted at Cassiobury in Hertfordshire in 1672 can still be seen, although it now runs through a golf course. Despite changes in fashion, the owners were inclined to cherish these signs of their influence, and incorporated them into later landscape designs. Thus when George Lucy had his park remodelled in the latest style by Lancelot 'Capability' Brown in the 1760s, he expressly forbade Brown to remove an avenue of trees. In a few places there are rather more extensive remnants. At Hampton Court Palace in Greater London, for example, a series of magnificent formal canals and avenues radiates from the house. But on the whole, there is not much to be seen of the great status landscapes of the seventeenth century.

Later landscape styles have tended to survive better than earlier, and this is not simply because they were formed more recently. Little remains of early formal layouts not only because they were destroyed to make way for more informal fashions, but also because they were not very common in the first place.

Extensive formal landscapes like that at Wimpole Hall, Cambridgeshire, which had an avenue three miles long, could be created only if the landowner was in control of a large and unified block of land. At the time when the formal style was popular, relatively few landowners were in this position. The decline of the small landowner, and the enclosure of the open fields and commons, took place only gradually from the seventeenth to the nineteenth century. By the time the landscape gardener Humphry Repton was designing his parks at the end of the eighteenth century, there were far more people who were able to make an extensive park than there had been a century earlier and the possession of a park was almost a prerequisite of respectability in high society. Each successive style had a progressively wider distribution, until by the end of the nineteenth century parks were found across the length and breadth of the country.

In contrast, extensive formal layouts were concentrated in areas where medieval deer parks were already common, especially in the areas around London and other parts of the southeast. According to contemporary illustrations, most gentry houses were set amidst pale and diminutive imitations of the kind of thing depicted by Knyff at Wimpole or at Badminton in Avon. If they had a park, and in 1700 many did not, the formal landscaping often only extended to a few avenues through the deer park. Elsewhere the avenues just ran through fields.

Another reason why so little remains of these landscapes is that the style was so short-lived. Almost as soon as it began to be accepted, it started to be simplified and its rigid formality toned down. Indeed, the change in fashion was so rapid that it elicited comment from contemporary writers. As Sir Thomas Robinson wrote to Lord Carlisle in 1734, 'The celebrated gardens of Claremont, Chiswick and Stowe are now full of labourers to modernise the expensive works finished in them since everyone's memory.'[13]

The story of the rise of the informal landscape style has been told many times. According to the orthodox view, it was largely inspired by Continental landscape art and scenery. In the first half of the eighteenth century fashionable young men were despatched on the 'Grand Tour', travelling through France and Italy in quest of society and culture. Here they saw the highly influential landscape paintings of Salvator Rosa, Claude Lorrain and Nicholas Poussin, depicting classical subjects amidst wide expanses of idealized romantic scenery. They could also see for themselves the Italian *campagna* which was the landscape model for many of these paintings. So impressed were the sons of privilege by what they had seen on their European tour, that they attempted to embody the Italian masters' attitude to nature in their own estates.

The formal elements in the park were gradually removed, and this was followed by the destruction of the enclosed gardens around the house. Instead of ordering the landscape to impress man's authority on it, landscapers began to aspire to a harmonious blending of nature and art. The landscape of geometric formality was replaced by a landscape of natural curves, featuring sweeping lawns and loosely grouped clusters of trees. As William Kent observed, 'nature abhors a straight line', and nature was the model for the parks of the eighteenth century.

The first phase of this development was characterized by the work of Vanbrugh, Stephen Switzer, Charles Bridgeman and such amateur enthusiasts as Henry Hoare. Winding walks were laid out through woods, and pools were given less rigidly geometric shapes. Although the landscape was still organized around the axis of the house, this was not emphasized by the use of features such as lines of trees. But it is William Kent who is generally held to be the first gardener to introduce the informal style. He made extensive use of the winding walk, the serpentine lake and the irregular tree clump, and he also popularized the ha-ha. This was a most ingenious form of sunken fence, which kept stock away from the house and gardens but did not interrupt views across the park. Yet despite his use of numerous informal features, Kent's creations had much in common with the previous formal tradition, elements of which he often used. At Holkham in Norfolk, for instance, in the landscape which Kent created for Thomas Coke, Earl of Leicester, there were eight straight radiating vistas laid out through a wood to the south of the house, as well as a dead straight, three-mile avenue, much of which still survives. Moreover, like his predecessors Kent filled his gardens with classical and gothic buildings, obelisks, urns and inscriptions. These were redolent with allusions to mythology and the ancient world, and emphasized the importance of symbolism in gardening. Kent's landscapes were formed around the houses of only a small, cultured and extremely wealthy élite and were on an appropriately vast scale. They combined informality with an air of austere grandeur.

From the late 1740s the work of 'Capability' Brown brought the informal landscape style to its apogee. It was Brown who finally banished the formal garden, and ensured that even the kitchen garden was concealed. It was Brown who developed Kent's use of informal clumps of trees and stretches of water, creating apparently 'natural' landscapes which were in reality carefully designed. But it was in his use of the tree belt that Brown departed most clearly from the previous tradition of landscape gardening. Kent had designed his parks so as to give views across the surrounding countryside, but Brown used the tree belt to exclude all sight of the landscape beyond the pale. He removed the distinction between garden and parkland, and emphasized that between the park and the outside world. Thus, while mid eighteenth-century landscapers strove to create a seemingly 'natural' landscape, they did so within a space that was thoroughly insulated from the working countryside.

Brown designed more than 180 landscape parks for country houses of all sizes in England and Wales. Harewood, Blenheim, Audley End and Chatsworth are amongst his most famous creations, but there are many more surviving examples of his style and skill. He was received in the highest society and his landscaping talents were in very great demand. He worked on commissions from many of the rich and famous, including twelve dukes, thirty-four earls and nine viscounts. Brown even worked on some of the royal parks, such as Richmond in Surrey and Hampton Court, although he also had a talent for creating new landscapes at relatively little expense.

The number of parks grew so rapidly in eighteenth-century England that even the industrious Brown could not landscape them all. Many other landscapers emerged at this time to cater for those who could not gain, or could not afford, the services of the great man himself. These men have been often unfairly described as Brown's imitators, although Richard Woods and William Eames, for example, were accomplished landscape gardeners in their own right, even if not as widely known as Brown, or his successor Repton. Indeed the emphasis on the work of the major landscapers in the conventional histories of the English landscape park has tended to prevent any analysis of the range of people who were involved in the business of landscape gardening. There are many parks in England which were not created by anybody famous, but are the work of minor landscape artists, jobbing gardeners, or even the landowners themselves. Out of around 150 parks in Norfolk at the end of the nineteenth century, less than thirty can be reliably attributed to one of the great names. We simply do not know who designed the rest. The importance of Kent, Brown and Repton in the history of the landscape garden is therefore partly due to the fact that they epitomized, and to a great extent initiated, more general tastes and styles.

A number of the landscapes produced over this period are explicitly based on the paintings of Poussin and others, lending credence to the theory that English landscape gardening was influenced by styles in Italian art. At Stourhead, for example, the arrangement of the Palladian bridge, the Pantheon and the Temple of Flora closely imitates the arrangement of ruins in Claude's *Coastal View of Delos with Aeneas*.[14] In other places, however, the connection between art and the parkland is rather less direct and obvious. The similarity lies in the scope of the landscape, in the wide prospects and in the relationship between the foreground and more distant objects, rather than in the contouring or even the flora of the

landscape. The pine trees and low shrubs of the Italian *campagna* have little in common with the stout oaks and beeches of eighteenth-century English landscape parks, and in the work of Brown and his contemporaries rocky crags are conspicuous by their absence.

Despite the sprinkling of classical temples which adorned the parks of England, their origins appear to lie only in part in Italian landscape paintings. Indeed, there are signs that the revolt against formal landscaping had already begun before the work of Claude and Poussin had been widely seen in Britain and was part of the development of a more general sympathy for nature and the natural order. As Anthony Ashley Cooper, third Earl of Shaftesbury, wrote in 1711, 'I shall no longer resist the passion growing in me for things of a natural kind, where neither art, nor the conceit or caprice of man, has spoil'd their genuine order.'[15] Likewise Pope appealed for sympathetic landscaping, based on the mediation of nature by art.

As we have seen, however, there was very little in the English landscape which could be

LEFT **Stourhead, Wiltshire**
The arrangement of the bridge and other features around the lake echoes Claude Lorrain's *Coastal View of Delos with Aeneas* (*below*). The landscape paintings of Claude, Poussin and Rosa were one of the influences on the development of the informal, natural style of landscaping which became popular in eighteenth-century England.

described as 'natural' by the eighteenth century. Almost every landscape was the product of some form of human intervention, and it is very significant that the eighteenth-century landscape park, that feature which has been described as the most distinctive contribution of the English to the arts, resembled nothing so much as a traditional English deer park. It was a wide, grassy vista, dotted with single trees and irregular tree clumps against a backdrop of blocks of woodland. The organizational principles derived from landscape art were thus utilized in the context of a traditional English landscape that had considerable social significance.

The deer park was a landscape which had always been private and enclosed. It had conferred status on the landed élite, and was devoid of any association with either agriculture or the agricultural producer. The absence of overt signs of cultivation made these landscapes appear natural, but their private status set them apart from the wastes of the common people and from the associations with raw and untamed nature which were so upsetting to the upper classes for much of the eighteenth century.

As shown in Kip's illustrations, such as that of Melton Constable in Norfolk, many of the early formal landscapes were simply superimposed on deer parks. Once the avenues and other geometric features were removed, this original landscape was exposed, and could be incorporated into the designs of the landscape gardeners. Oliver Rackham has suggested that even Brown (who of all gardeners had the most cavalier attitude to the existing landscape)

Melton Constable, Norfolk
This engraving by Kip shows how the formal elements in late seventeenth- and early eighteenth-century parks were often imposed on earlier deer parks. The landscape which re-emerged when these were removed formed the main inspiration for the 'informal' landscape style of the mid eighteenth century.

Ickworth Park, Suffolk
A view across typical English parkland. As in the design of many other landscaped parks, the layout of Ickworth was planned to utilize many trees that were already standing in the hedges and fields of a working agricultural landscape.

based his designs on the incorporation of existing trees, as well as on a programme of planting new ones.[16] To a large extent, even Brown's parks were created by adapting surviving parks rather than by creating them anew. He usually added a lake, removed the formal elements, and surrounded the whole by a belt of trees. His art was a process of subtraction as much as addition. And this was even more true of his successor to the mantle of master gardener, Humphry Repton.

The great landscape gardeners showed their artistry in the blending of the new with the old. Thus the sweeping lawns and clumps of trees derived from the deer park were endowed with additional grace and grandeur by the skilful siting of a serpentine lake. By the late eighteenth century, however, landscape gardeners often had a much more positive role for many parks were being created out of agricultural land. Where possible, existing hedgerow trees or other standing timber were incorporated in the designs, as in the park Brown created at Heveningham in Suffolk, but otherwise the landscape was completely altered. Nevertheless, the traditional English deer park still provided the model for these new designs.

The successive landscape styles which characterize the eighteenth century were in part a result of the development of a consumer society economically dependent on frequent changes in fashion. But why did the informal landscape become fashionable, at a time when more formal styles were still *de rigueur* in the rest of Europe? The answer seems to lie partly in the prevailing political climate and partly in the social structure of England.

Eighteenth-century philosophers and moralists stressed the ideological significance of changes in landscape style. Formal gardens in the spirit of Le Nôtre, with their origins in France, were seen to symbolize a political absolutism that was anathema in England after the triumph of constitutional monarchy in the Glorious Revolution. Shaftesbury condemned the geometric style as, 'the formal mockery of princely gardens,'[17] and the blending of art and nature that was advocated by Pope was an appeal for political moderation as much as an aesthetic judgement. The eighteenth-century landscape was thus seen to symbolize the harmony of the English constitution. It avoided both the rigid absolutism of autocracy and the unrestrained excesses of democracy. Indeed, in the early phases of the informal landscape style there was a great deal of overt political statement. At Stowe, for example, the garden buildings included the 'Temple of British Worthies', which housed busts of such ideologically resonant figures as Milton, Cromwell and Hampden — all of whom had important roles in the English Revolution.

The popularity of the informal landscape park was also associated with an increase in the number of people able to create a park. During the fifteenth and sixteenth centuries parks had become less common than in the Middle Ages, but even so they were described in 1598 as being 'common throughout England', and they were far more numerous here than in any other European country. They feature prominently on the maps of Christopher Saxton, published in the 1570s, where they are depicted cartographically by characteristic wooden palings. While the number of parks declined further during the seventeenth century, by the eighteenth century they were once again on the increase, and between 1760 and 1840 they spread dramatically. This was both a cause and an effect of the change in landscape style, for such proliferation would not have been possible if the formal style had been maintained.

The extensive landscapes of Le Nôtre were labour intensive and expensive to maintain. They were only really suitable for the very largest estates. This landscape style was thus inappropriate to the social structure of England which, in the eighteenth century, was far less polarized than that of France. There were a great many members of the minor gentry who were anxious to display their status, and who were increasingly able to create parks as a result of the spread of enclosure. The English landscape park needed little maintenance and could be adapted to fit fairly small estates and so was ideally suited to the needs of this class.

The development of the informal style seems in part to be a reaction to changes in the landscape beyond the park. The proliferation of parks had been made possible by enclosure, but the spread of enclosure may also have influenced their form. The small formal gardens of the sixteenth and seventeenth century, and the short-lived extensive layouts of circa 1700, revealed their élite status in their striking dissimilarity to the agricultural land in which they lay. With the progress of enclosure, however, the appearance of much agricultural land changed. A landscape of enclosed fields came to replace the open arable lands of the champion and the commons of the woodland areas, and those parts of the country affected by general and especially parliamentary enclosure were characterized by geometric patterns of fields and roads.

The curves and 'natural' lines of the informal landscape park therefore contrasted not only with the industrial landscapes that were becoming increasingly common in England, but also with the enclosed landscapes of agricultural labour which were often rigidly geometric in their layout. The landed élite surrounded themselves with landscapes ostensibly divorced from productive agriculture, but which still emphasized the nature of their power and status. The layout of trees and lawns was usually contrived so that the house appeared to blend into a supposedly 'natural' landscape and to be in complete harmony with the surrounding environment. In this way the landed élite appeared to be a natural part of the rural order, but their dominance of that order was reinforced by the contrast between the park and the landscape of labour.

None the less, despite the sharp, visual distinction between the aesthetic landscape of the park and the working landscape of the countryside beyond, in practice most landowners made money out of their pleasure grounds. Indeed, it has been suggested that the returns from timber and grazing in the parks often exceeded the rent from an equivalent area of arable land in the eighteenth century and many landowners were not averse to exploiting non-agricultural resources.[18] Limestone was quarried in the parkland around Calke Abbey in Derbyshire, and when a substantial remodelling of the park involved the removal of a few hills, the Harpur Crewes made a considerable profit from the limestone.[19] The economic exploitation of landscape parks was, however, never as important as their role in displaying status, taste, and wealth.

Between the eighteenth and nineteenth centuries there were further changes in the style of the landscape park, largely instituted by Humphry Repton. Although he maintained a broadly Brownian style for many years, he gradually departed from this tradition and introduced innovations of his own. Unlike others in his profession, Repton wrote extensively about his work and its aesthetic significance,[20] and he attacked what he saw as the excesses of Brown's imitators, although many of the features he criticized had been developed by Brown himself.

Repton particularly disapproved of the fact that the country house often stood 'solitary and unconnected' in Brown's parks, isolated amidst a vast sea of grass. It was set apart from the local community, but also from its own ancilliary buildings, its stables and kitchen garden, which were kept out of sight. Repton found this practice both aesthetically and socially distasteful, because he believed that the landscape park ought to embody a landowner's paternalistic role in the rural community as well as displaying his status. The isolation of the house within an exclusively private park symbolized an abrogation of that role.[21]

Repton's designs began to break down some of the barriers which Brown had established between the park and the outside world. The continuous belt of trees was often abolished as a 'boundary scarce less offensive than the pale itself', ensuring that the parks became more integrated with the landscape of agricultural toil. Indeed the farmland of the estate began to be considered intrinsically beautiful, and to provide a pleasing backdrop to the domesticated scenes of the park. This change in attitudes was associated with the increasing involvement of the landlords in the practicalities of agriculture. The landed élite began to define their status in terms of their connection with the agricultural environment, rather than seeking to emphasize their divorcedness from it, and their houses began to look out over the landscape which they owned and farmed.

Repton not only de-emphasized the boundaries between the park and the estate beyond, but also began to manipulate the working countryside to create a wider landscape of aesthetic display. The dairy farm, he wrote, 'is as much a part of the place as the deer park, and in many respects more picturesque'. Likewise, he believed that if labourers' cottages 'can be made a subordinate part of the general scenery, they will, far from disgracing it, add to the dignity that wealth can derive from the exercise of benevolence'.[22]

This development was connected with a more general social change. At a time when the events of the French Revolution were providing a striking indication of the potential power of the poor, many landowners sought to limit or defuse such power by cultivating the image of the organic rural community. The landscapes Repton created presented an image of the country house as a central part of the working countryside. The connection between the landlord and the land revealed the basis of his political power, but also the extent of his paternal influence over the locality. The cottage and the great house both had a place in a harmonious landscape, which was none the less under the control of the landed élite. Repton and many other Tory thinkers believed that social revolution could only be forestalled by the benevolent paternalism that this landscape idealized.

This idea of unifying a multiplicity of disparate parts also influenced the kind of landscapes that Repton developed within the park. The visual homogeneity of Brown's sweeping lawns and clumps of trees was now rejected and Repton began to break up the deer park landscape, reintroducing the gardens of flowers and flower beds around the house. He sometimes provided a terrace, to give the house a more dignified setting, and even allowed surviving avenues to remain. However, these components were not seen as individual features, as they had to some extent been in the gardens of the early seventeenth century, but as interrelating parts of a single landscape. Each occupied its rightful place in a totality which was ordered by the taste of the landlord and dominated by his country house.

These landscapes symbolized the landowners' view of his role within rural society. The individual features all fitted together in a harmonious whole, representing the peaceful coexistence which should characterize all human relations. Every part of a landscape, from the clumps of trees in the foreground to the labourers' cottages in the distance, had its own particular place and function, just as all the individuals had their place within the hierarchy of the village. While the status landscape was arranged around, and dominated by, the country house, so the landowner dominated the rural community. The landlord was therefore represented in the landscape as the most important figure within local society, who was able to dictate the position and the needs of everyone else. This image of the role of the landowner had considerable political implications; the landed élite frequently justified their dominance of political power on the basis of their ability to understand the needs of the community.

One sign of the increased interest in the landscape beyond the park was the growing popularity of prospect towers. These features provided wide views across the landscape, and while they were rarely built in the early eighteenth century, they became much more common from around 1780. The tower at Little

Berkhamsted in Hertfordshire was built by Admiral Stratton in 1789. Local tradition claims that the Admiral built it to look at his ships in the Thames, but since the Thames is miles from Berkhamsted, way out of sight of the tower, it seems more likely that it was built for the sake of the fine views it gives across the country.

Repton's ideas were not, however, universally accepted, and were challenged most

Stratton's Folly, Little Berkhamsted, Hertfordshire
Local tradition asserts that this tower was built by Admiral John Stratton in 1789 so that he could inspect his ships in the Thames estuary. But since the Thames is over 40 miles away, it seems more likely that the tower reflects a growing interest in panoramic views, like similar features built in the late eighteenth century.

directly by the movement that became known as the 'picturesque'. This involved a long and acrimonious dispute between Repton and the proponents of the picturesque, notably Uvedale Price and Richard Payne Knight. Price and Knight believed that landscape gardens should not merely imitate nature, but should imitate nature in the raw. They scorned Brown's parks as being too bland and stereotyped — as representations of a nature that was domesticated and uninteresting. Their view was that parks should attempt to capture the true spirit of the Italian artists, and in particular of the paintings of Salvator Rosa. They should have a drama and ruggedness that would serve to inspire awe. Knight's condemnation of Brown as the 'thin meagre genius of the bare and bald' pointed to the fact that the eighteenth-century landscape parks bore little similarity to the paintings on which they were supposedly modelled.

Supporters of the picturesque attempted to create more wild and barren scenes, with the widespread planting of conifers and exotics, and the creation of rocky slopes and waterfalls. This was rather difficult in places like Norfolk, although it could be achieved more successfully in the north and west, as in the grounds of Knight's own house at Downton in Herefordshire. Within these rugged landscapes, a host of picturesque ornaments in the gothic and mock rural style were created. These were more representative of man's struggle for existence against the natural environment than of his harmonious position within it. Moreover, the consciously archaic style of these features romanticized rural communities of the past, and their ability to survive in a hostile and undomesticated landscape.

Such landscapes were recognized as having overt political connotations and there were many at the end of the eighteenth century who did not like what they saw. The cult of simplicity in gardening which Knight and Price advocated was associated with the interest in natural man and natural rights propounded in the writings of the supporters of the French Revolution. As Repton's friend Anna Seward wrote to Dr Johnson, about Knight's didactic poem *The Landscape*:

> Knight's system appears to me the Jacobinism of taste; from its abusing that rational spirit of improvement suggested by Milton in his description of the primeval garden; and realised and diffused by Brown; . . . Mr. Knight would have nature as well as man indulged in that uncurbed and wild luxuriance, which must soon render our landscape-island rank, weedy, damp, and unwholesome as the incultivate savannas of America . . . save me, good Heaven, from living in tangled forests and amongst men who are unchecked by those guardian laws, which bind the various orders of society in one common interest. May the lawns I tread be smoothed by healthful industry, and the glades opened by the hand of picturesque taste, to admit the pure and salutary breath of heaven! — and may the people, amongst whom I live, be withheld by stronger repellants than their own virtue, from invading my property and shedding my blood!! — And so much for politics and pleasure grounds.[23]

Proponents of the picturesque were not, however, advocates of the complete overthrow of society, despite the ideological implications of their creations. Their work had much more in common with Repton's than was recognized at the time. Like Repton they were against the separation of the landscape park from the surrounding working environment, and believed that the latter should ideally be incorporated into the former. The 'marks of industry and habitation' were preferable to 'buildings of parade [which] have a staring, unconnected, ostentacious appearance'.[24] In addition, the landscapes of both Repton and the picturesque school were much easier to adopt for smaller areas than Brown's wide vistas and sweeping lawns. Repton had problems designing the park of Wentworth Woodhouse in Yorkshire because the area he was supposed to work on was simply too big. 'Wentworth

Park', he wrote, 'consists of parts, in themselves truly great and magnificent. The woods, the lawns, the water and the buildings are all separately striking; but, considered as a whole, there is want of connexion and harmony in the composition, because parts in themselves large, if disjointed lose their importance.'[25] The disparate features of the picturesque landscape, the cascade, the rocky outcrop, the pine trees and so on, could be given a visual unity within a relatively confined space.

This was important at a time when parks were no longer confined to the houses of the long-established landed élite. Repton was a social snob, hostile to parvenues and the increasingly wealthy magnates of commerce and industry, but financial necessity ensured that he frequently landscaped the surroundings of these men's villas. The picturesque gardeners, too, were increasingly employed on parks of less than one hundred acres.

This trend towards the intimate and intensive rather than the extensive landscape continued and strengthened into the nineteenth century. In the early Victorian period the gardening scene was dominated by John Claudius Loudon, who introduced what became known as the 'gardenesque' style. This was based on the display of individual features, such as particular trees and flowers, rather than on boundless and harmonious prospects of woods and lawns. Terraces, ferneries and herbaceous borders became popular, and proliferated in the small parks which surrounded the capital. Indeed, the nature of the audience which Loudon addressed was re-

Wentworth Woodhouse, South Yorkshire
Whenever Humphry Repton was employed to landscape the surroundings of a house, he would provide a 'Red Book', showing the landscape as it appeared and the proposed improvements. This illustration shows his plans for Wentworth Woodhouse.

vealed in the title of his book, *The Suburban Gardener or Villa Companion*, published in 1838. The designs he advocated were a far cry from the massive élite landscapes which were created around the great country houses in the eighteenth century. None the less, the basic landscapes of the traditional park, the informal arrangements of trees and lawns, were maintained within the landscape parks as long as they continued to be created — that is, until well into the second half of the nineteenth century.

The history of the landscape park is thus far more than a catalogue of styles and artists. The stylistic developments seem in part to be related to changes in the parks themselves, as they were no longer confined to a wealthy landed élite and became progressively smaller. In part, however, they embody ideas about the social system, symbolizing an image of rural community that was often very different from the realities of rural life. The landscape park mirrored the social system that the rich liked to believe should exist, and the changes in its form revealed the changing nature of this ideal. It was, however, in the landscape outside the park, in the villages and cottages of the labourers, that the clearest signs were to be found of the social attitudes of the landed élite, and of the growth of their power over the countryside.

Cliveden, Buckinghamshire
This formal *parterre*, overlooking the valley of the Thames, was laid out in the late nineteenth century. It shows the extent to which the gardens of the Victorian country house had moved away from the eighteenth-century ideal of the 'natural' landscape park.

EIGHT

Village Architecture and Village Life

TO THE CASUAL VISITOR it is not the pattern of fields, woods and hedges which most clearly characterizes a region, but the style and materials of its buildings. The Cotswolds are associated with cottages of soft yellow stone, the Thames Valley with red brick and flint, whereas the Welsh border counties of Herefordshire and Shropshire abound with black-and-white, timber-framed houses. This architectural variety is to a large extent the consequence of England's very varied geology. Different kinds of building materials were available in different areas, and these determined the styles and methods of building that were developed. Even so, architectural diversity cannot be wholly explained by geology. In some areas there are large numbers of old houses; in others comparatively few. Some villages seem to date very largely from one period; others contain buildings of widely varying styles and dates. Many of these variations reflect the histories of the communities that lived and worked within the landscape.

The distribution of old houses is an indication of the way in which wealth was distributed in the past. For much of the medieval and post-medieval period it was only the most wealthy who were able to have houses which were likely to survive for a long time, and so the earliest buildings are nowadays concentrated in those areas of the country which were formerly most prosperous. There are, for example, far fewer old buildings in the north of England than there are in the south, for until the late seventeenth century most parts of the impoverished north could not support the craftsmen required to construct durable dwellings.

As time passed, however, and standards of living improved, some of those in the poorer areas of the country were also able to afford substantial houses, and so were a number of those from lower social classes within the more affluent communities. In the medieval period, apart from the manor houses of the social élite, houses that would last could be built only by prosperous yeomen or wealthy merchants. But by the seventeenth century the majority of farmers had houses of stone, brick or timber framing, rather than the flimsy, impermanent shacks which previous generations had lived in, and which had had to be frequently rebuilt. Most of the poorer sections of the rural population, on the other hand, had to make do with such makeshift accommodation until well into the eighteenth century.

It was therefore not only the affluence of the community as a whole which determined the extent to which houses survived. The way in which wealth was distributed was also important. In those places where the income of the majority of smallholders was more or less the same, there would not be the substantial high-quality houses that were found in villages with greater extremes of wealth and poverty. Moreover, since the construction of durable houses required a considerable capital investment, it was unlikely that anyone would embark on such a building project unless he had considerable security of tenure. In the late medieval and early post medieval period it was only the freeholders and those who held their land under the most secure forms of copyhold who were prepared to invest in the kind of houses that still stand to the present day. The importance of tenurial conditions in determining housing standards is illustrated by the history of building in the old county of Westmorland. Here there was a considerable dispute over the nature of 'tenant right' in the seventeenth century. In 1656 the government of the Commonwealth declared this local customary tenure to be the equivalent of a full freehold, and this was confirmed at the Restoration of 1660. From this time, when the tenants were finally made secure in their holdings, durable and well-built houses began to appear in abundance. As R.H.Machin, the architectural historian, declared, 'The hundreds of proudly dated houses in Westmorland proclaim a newly won freedom from archaic feudal obligations laid upon a free peasantry, rather than newly acquired farming profits'.[1]

Likewise the very different architecture of two neighbouring places in Dorset has been shown to be a consequence of variations in the security of tenure enjoyed by the inhabitants. At Abbotsbury all the tenants held by copyhold or leasehold for life until the late nineteenth century. As a result, very few buildings in the town contain any pre eighteenth-century elements. In nearby Yetminster, however, the situation is very different. In the sixteenth and seventeenth centuries the tenants held by an unusually secure form of copyhold. Nowadays the village contains a wealth of seventeenth-century buildings, and several sixteenth-century houses.

The importance of tenurial factors in determining the standard of housing has ensured that architecture provides a clear indication of the contrasts that existed between the tenurial structure in various regions of the country. Surviving houses of classes below the level of the gentry dating from before 1500 have a limited distribution. They are largely confined to the woodland areas of England and are concentrated in Kent, Sussex, Surrey, Suffolk and Essex, and to some extent in south Norfolk, Hertfordshire, south Oxfordshire, parts of Hampshire and Berkshire, the south-west Midlands, Herefordshire and the southern edge of the eastern Pennines.[2]

These were areas in which a class of prosperous yeomen emerged in the late medieval period with sufficient wealth and security of tenure to allow the early construction of prestigious and durable houses. Indeed, in Herefordshire, Hertfordshire, Suffolk or Sussex the substantial isolated medieval farmstead is as much a characteristic of woodland landscape as the high hedgebanks, irregular fields or winding lanes. It is thus no coincidence that, in the champion areas of the Midlands, where villages depopulated for sheep farming are most common, surviving early buildings are also most rare. Here there were few wealthy and tenurially secure yeomen farmers in the late Middle Ages. Durable farmhouses only began to appear in these champion areas in the late sixteenth and seventeenth centuries when holdings were consolidated and concentrated in increasingly few hands.

The present distribution of early houses has, of course, also been influenced by the ability of subsequent occupants to maintain and extend the fabric of their dwellings, as well as by later tenurial developments. Where freehold farms were eventually absorbed into large estates, farmhouses and farm buildings were often entirely rebuilt in the eighteenth and nineteenth centuries, in order to attract the right kind of tenant.

The history of the village communities of England is revealed not only in the distribution but also in the changing form of the yeoman farmer's house. The earliest were hall houses with a central room open to the roof, and usually with a two-storeyed section at either end. These two-storeyed sections formed wings of the house or could appear in the main body of the building. In the south and east of England where these early farmhouses are most common, there was no clear-cut distinction between the living standards of the lesser gentry and those of the prosperous farmers in the late medieval period, and there was a great deal of social mobility between these two groups. It is therefore hardly surprising that early yeoman houses often resembled manorial halls in plan.

Within the farmhouse, one of the ends was used as a parlour on the ground floor, while the other was divided from the hall by a passage which ran between two doors across the width of the house, and provided a space in which food was stored and prepared. Once brick was widely available in the sixteenth century, chimneys could be built and this basic structure was replaced by a house which was double-storeyed throughout. There was no longer any need for a large open hall in which smoke could gradually disperse, so new houses were built without open halls and the old ones were floored over. The additional upper chamber created by this innovation was not necessarily used to provide extra accommodation. It was often used as a loft, for storing corn, apples or other produce, since the heat from the chimney made it conveniently dry.

These two-storey houses vary greatly on a local and regional basis, and there are many individual buildings which are highly idiosyncratic. In the sixteenth and seventeenth centuries, however, many displayed some kind of variation on the basic medieval plan. They had three principal rooms arranged in a row on the ground floor, and these were usually a parlour, a hall, and a third room which might serve as a kitchen, store, or occasionally as additional sleeping space. Between this third room and the hall there was a passage, as in the medieval house, which ran the width of the house between opposing doors. The principal chimneystack was either placed between the hall and the parlour, providing a fireplace in both these rooms, or it was built between the hall and the passage, so that the hall would be heated but the parlour would not. In some areas the former arrangement was more common, in others the latter, and these variations may in part have been related to regional differences in the social structure of post medieval England.[3]

In the first house plan, the presence of a heated parlour suggests that the owners of the house were beginning to put a particular value on privacy. It provided a place to which the farmer and his immediate family could withdraw, away from the servants and farm workers who gathered in the hall. The farmhouse hall thus increasingly became a room which served as a kitchen and a place where the servants and farmhands congregated, while the parlour became progressively more important as a wholly private and exclusive social space. In the second type of house there was no heated parlour and here the hall appears to have been still important as a communal space. Instead of shutting himself away in a private room, the employer continued to mix with his employees, and cooking was often carried out in the service room beyond the through-passage.

Houses of this latter kind are a feature of the upland areas of the north and west of England, where farms were relatively small and devoted to primarily pastoral agriculture. This ensured that the relationship between master and men was fairly relaxed, for communities were not marked by radical differences in status. Many of the workers employed on the farms were the sons of neighbouring farmers, who were merely serving their time while waiting to take over their father's holdings.

In the sixteenth century the houses with

The relationship between the chimneystack and the principal entrance of a post medieval farmhouse can often indicate the internal layout of the rooms. These variations in internal organization tell us something about the way people lived in these farms. In the house at **Patterdale, Cumbria** (*above*), the chimneystack is located near the front door. This indicates it stands between the passage across the width of the house and the central hall. The room beyond the hall, on the far left of the building, is therefore unheated, indicating that the communal, public space of the hall was of more importance to the owner than the private space of the parlour. The main chimneystack in the house at **Great Eversden, Cambridgeshire** (*above right*), is located away from the principal entrance. This indicates that the stack lies between the hall and the parlour, providing a major fireplace in both rooms. In such houses, the owner and his immediate family were accustomed to retreat into a purely private room, away from the farmhands and servants in the hall. At **Blyford, Suffolk** (*right*), the chimneystack is positioned directly behind the principal entrance. The door does not open into a cross-passage, but into a small lobby backing onto the stack, from which further doors lead into a heated parlour or the heated hall.

heated parlours were largely found in the lowland areas of the south and east. Here, both arable and pastoral farms tended to be larger than those in the upland areas, and sometimes employed considerable numbers of wage labourers. Some of these workers usually 'lived in', like the labourers on upland farms, but they were generally of lower social status than their upland counterparts. In these areas, therefore, farmers were particularly anxious to emphasize

the social distinction between themselves and their employees.

In the second half of the sixteenth century, some houses were further refined by the development of the 'lobby entrance' plan, which ensured an even greater separation between the farmer and his men. The basic three-room plan was maintained, with the main chimneystack positioned between the hall and the parlour. But the through-passage was done away with and the front door opened into a small lobby opposite the chimneystack, where stairs led to the rooms on the upper level. On either side of the lobby were doors, one leading into the hall (and thence to the kitchen), the other giving access to the heated parlour. The owner of the house could now pass straight into his private room, without having to walk through the communal space of the hall. These houses are extremely common in East Anglia, and are also found in other parts of the southeast of England. But they are rarer in the central Midlands, where even the most prosperous farmer could seldom aspire to a house of this size in the sixteenth and seventeenth centuries. Many lived in homes with only two rooms downstairs, separated by a central chimneystack.

Variations in house plans in the sixteenth and early seventeenth centuries were not wholly the result of social and economic factors, but also reflected constraints imposed by the availability of building material, and the continuing importance of customs and traditions in determining local styles. From the second half of the seventeenth century, however, regional architectural variants were gradually superseded by what is known as the 'double pile' house. This was symmetrical in plan, two rooms rather than one room deep, and made possible a much greater degree of privacy and social segregation. A centrally placed front door led into a passage, from which doors gave access to the ground floor rooms and a staircase led upstairs. A proliferation of chimneystacks made possible a profusion of fireplaces. Servants could be confined to the back rooms, while the owner or tenant and his family enjoyed a considerable amount of privacy in the front. In the course of the eighteenth century these double-pile symmetrical farmhouses became common in all parts of England. Some were built by farmers on their freehold land, but many were constructed by the landlords of great estates. They became a particular feature of the landscape of the Midlands, where stout red-brick farmhouses were constructed outside the villages on newly enclosed land.

The houses of prosperous farmers became more substantial and comfortable with the passing of time, but the housing of the less affluent sectors of the population remained desperately poor. Smaller farmers or 'husbandmen' and growing numbers of landless labourers continued to live in insubstantial dwellings and, indeed, the quality of their houses appears to have declined in the eighteenth century. Enclosure deprived the poor of the materials with which they had traditionally built and maintained their homes and this problem was aggravated by a rapidly rising population and by the increasing reluctance of farmers to allow young labourers to live in. By the end of the eighteenth century, therefore, the majority of agricultural workers in England lived in conditions of squalor. One important factor that affected the standard and provision of housing in rural villages was the distinction between 'open' and 'closed' parishes. The 'closed' parish was one in which the land was entirely owned by one or a small number of very powerful landowners, in contrast to the 'open' village, where there was a much larger number of freeholders and landlords.[4] Landowners in the eighteenth and nineteenth centuries had to pay poor rates, and many believed it to be in their interests to limit the population in a parish by discouraging people from settling there. The number of houses built in closed villages could be controlled, but this was more difficult in the open village where it was in any case of less importance to those who owned the land.

In the open villages the cost of the poor rate was spread across a number of freeholders and landlords, and there were many who could profit from the expansion of the settlement. In the absence of any restrictions on building, considerable sums of money could be made from the provision of cheap, poor-quality homes. Thus while the closed villages tended to be small, and under the strict control of their landlords, open villages were sizeable sprawling settlements of unplanned and often jerry-built cottages. For example, a poor law inspector noted that 1352 new cottages had been built in eighty-six open parishes in Oxfordshire between 1839 and 1849, whereas in thirty-four closed parishes only seven cottages had been built. Gilbert a Beckett, writing of East Anglia in the mid nineteenth century, also observed the contrast between the open and closed parishes:

> In almost every Union where the course of my enquiry has taken me, I have found some one or more densely populated parishes in the neighbourhood of others very thinly inhabited by labourers, and in some instances having scarcely any cottages at all. In the former, the dwellings are for the most part wretched, damp, unwholesome, inconvenient, excessively high rented, and crowded with inmates, to such an extent as to render it impossible that health and comfort should be enjoyed.[5]

The communities who inhabited these large open villages were characterized by a sense of independence, in striking contrast to the subservience of their closed brethren. They often contained not only agricultural labourers, but a range of rural industries, and catered to the needs of neighbouring closed parishes where labour was generally scarce.

By the nineteenth century the standard of housing in closed villages tended to be higher than in the open, reflecting the awareness of the landed élite of a responsibility to provide houses for the poor. In earlier centuries, however, the general standard of building in closed villages was often very bad indeed. Insecure copyholders and tenants were unlikely to spend any of their surplus capital on the construction of substantial homes, or the improvement of existing structures. The extensive house-building programmes of the eighteenth and nineteenth centuries were thus in part made necessary by the low standard as well as by the lack of earlier housing.

As a result few old houses survive in closed villages and they tend to have an architectural uniformity that is not characteristic of the open parishes. The houses of open villages range widely in age and are often irregular in form, indicating alterations and extensions over the centuries. In particular, many open villages contain large houses which were subdivided in the eighteenth and nineteenth centuries to form a number of cottages. This subdivision was often carried out following the enclosure of a parish, when the former occupants of these houses moved out of the village into new double-pile brick farmhouses set amidst their fields. On occasions the problems of rural overcrowding produced bizarre solutions. Sixteenth- and seventeenth-century pigeon houses, for example, were sometimes converted into homes for humans by the insertion of floors, windows and chimneys. One such house can be seen beside the green in the open village of Barrington in Cambridgeshire.

Closed villages were, and often still are, smaller than neighbouring open ones, and they tend to have a more regular form. The closed village of Sandford St Martin in Oxfordshire, for example, is made up of two neat rows of marlstone cottages along a single street. Just over a mile away is the sprawling open settlement of Middle Barton. The history of these two villages in many ways illustrates the contrast between open and closed parishes in the late eighteenth and nineteenth centuries.[6]

By the mid nineteenth century the village of Sandford St Martin was under the control of two large estates, the Park estate and the Manor estate. The houses and cottages along the eastern side of the road belonged to the Park estate and in 1849 this was bought by Dr Edwin

Guest, the Master of Gonville and Caius College, Cambridge; the western side of the street was owned by the Manor estate and in 1862 this was taken over by the Reverend Edward Marshall. These two men worked together to make the standard of housing in the parish approach 'more to what the habitations of a village population ought to be'.[7] Yet while their efforts ensured that their own labourers were reasonably housed, their control over the housing stock of the village meant that its population could not expand.

In contrast, the population of the village of Middle Barton rose rapidly in the nineteenth century, absorbing some of the surplus from Sandford St Martin. This open village had grown up on the border between the villages of Westcott Barton and Steeple Barton, and contained the land of a multiplicity of small proprietors. It was said that on enclosure 'there was not a single proprietor of six acres resident in either Barton', and in 1869 the 150 cottages in Middle Barton were owned by around forty different people. As a result the village was architecturally diverse, and there was also a notable absence of the kind of deference to the landed élite which was fostered in the confines of the closed settlements. One of the consequences of this independent spirit was the growth of religious nonconformity in the village. A Wesleyan chapel was built in 1835, and the primitive Methodists built a chapel in 1860. By this time there was said to be in the village 'an almost universality of Dissent'.

Closed villages can be found all over the country, but they tend to be more common in some areas than others. They are a feature of the champion regions, especially the areas that were enclosed early and converted to pastoral farming, and are also characteristic of the areas which specialized in arable agriculture, such as eastern Yorkshire, Lincolnshire, Nottinghamshire, northwest Norfolk and the Cotswolds. They are least common in woodland areas, particularly those which practised pastoral agriculture; counties such as Hertfordshire, Essex, Surrey, Sussex and Suffolk have very few villages which approximate in any way to the closed form. Their distribution in Norfolk reveals this pattern very clearly, as David Dymond has shown. Closed villages are most common among the nucleated settlements in the north and west of the county, on the light soils of the arable areas. They are much rarer in the south and east, where there were numerous small freeholders, where there was early piecemeal enclosure and where the pattern of settlement is dispersed.

Within any area, however, there was always a mixture of open and closed villages. Some open villages inevitably existed in areas where closed villages predominated in order to provide a supply of labour for the use of the closed parishes. In nineteenth-century Norfolk, for example, labourers from the open settlement of Gooderstone walked to work in the closed parishes of Cockley Cley and Beechamwell, five miles away. The interdependence of the villages is often still discernible on nineteenth-century maps. The large, sprawling and formerly open village of Lakenham in Norfolk had an arc of neat and compact closed villages to its south: Intwood, Keswick, Caistor St Edmund, Arminghall and Trowse.[8]

During the eighteenth century a small number of landowners began to construct villages which were extreme examples of closed settlements. These were 'model' villages — built as units, often to the design of an architect, in order to create a striking visual effect.

On the road from Oxford to Henley, for example, stand the two rows of red-brick, timbered cottages which make up the village of Nuneham Courtenay. This was built by Lord Harcourt in the 1760s, and replaced the old village which was destroyed by the creation of a landscape park around his mansion.[9] The identical semi-detached cottages have an architectural uniformity and a regular plan which is strikingly different from the loose conglomeration of houses of all shapes and styles that is the characteristic open village

New Houghton, Norfolk
Built in 1729 for Prime Minister Robert Walpole, New Houghton is probably the earliest complete model village. Twenty-four identical brick houses and eight almshouses stand at the gates of Houghton Hall. The parish church, isolated within the parklands around the hall, marks the original site of the village. As was common in eighteenth- and nineteenth-century estate villages, the front doors are at the sides of the houses, so that passers-by did not have to look inside.

form. When built, they were seen as an element in the landscape of the Harcourt estate, and were designed to be admired by visitors as much as the classical temple with which Harcourt replaced the old village church. The dependence of the village is also indicated by the pub, *The Harcourt Arms*.

Numerous model villages of this kind were built in the eighteenth and early nineteenth centuries, often, although not invariably, to replace villages destroyed in the creation of a landscape park. In 1729 Sir Robert Walpole commissioned the construction of New Houghton, the first complete model village, to replace the settlement destroyed to make way for the grounds around Houghton Hall. The sturdy slate-roofed houses reveal Walpole's paternal care for the local community, and only the isolated church within his parkland now marks the spot where the original village of Houghton once stood. The sizeable settlement of Milton Abbas was destroyed in the eighteenth century, when Joseph Damer decided to extend the park of Milton House. This was replaced around 1773 by a smaller village, consisting of two rows of identical semi-detached thatched cottages tucked neatly in a fold of the downs.

These early model villages had a rigid

symmetry and uniform design which clearly distinguished them from the settlements which had developed organically. The houses were all clearly built at one time, and had no individual features and no individual history. They were a direct reflection of the occupants' dependence on both the benevolence and the taste of an individual landowner. Each house was but an element of the village, and the village was one feature of a landscape of aristocratic status. In the early eighteenth century these villages tended to be regarded more as spectacles, as part of the property of the estate, than as the home of a working community.

With the development of the picturesque movement, landowners became particularly interested in the aesthetic possibilities of the estate village. Earlier villages had primarily served to replace settlements destroyed by emparking, but by the nineteenth century the model village had come to be regarded as an essential component of the truly picturesque landscape. It was therefore no longer invariably hidden away behind a belt of trees on the outskirts of the parkland, but was sometimes sited in full view of the park, and incorporated into a planned prospect across the countryside. These later villages were, however, stylistically very different from the formal rows of symmetrical houses constructed in the eighteenth century.

Blaise Hamlet in Avon consists of a small group of cottages clustered around a village green. Each is individual, with twisting chimneys and leaning outbuildings, and each peeps anthropomorphically from behind thick hedges and fringing trees. Outwardly, Blaise Hamlet bears some resemblance to the random form of the traditional village but Blaise is, in fact, a parody of these. It was built in 1810, to the design of John Repton (son of Humphry) and John Nash, at the instigation of the Quaker banker John Harford. Standing outside the park of Blaise Castle, it is a classic example of the extravagance of romantic and picturesque taste. For although loosely based on the house plans, building materials and pattern of the traditional village, Blaise exaggerates these features out of all proportion. Each of the cottages (three thatched and six tiled) is made up of a mass of intersecting, sagging, irregular roofs, tall ornate chimneys, and a bewildering variety of porches, sheds and lean-tos. Repton explained in a letter to Harford that although some of the houses would have an internal cellar and pantry, 'if we make them *all* so it will very much injure (if not entirely destroy) the picturesque effect of the different cottages where so much depends on the lean-tos and sheds'.

Blaise was the first example of a new trend in model village building, and was followed by several other 'picturesque' villages, some equally bizarre. The men who built them attempted, by the use of 'traditional' styles and materials, to create an idealized version of the English village. Examples of their work are Somerleyton in Suffolk, Holly Village in Highgate, London, Old Warden in Bedfordshire, and Ilam in Staffordshire. More common are individual cottages, or small groups of cottages, which betray the nineteenth-century taste for the picturesque, and these are found all over England. Sometimes the landowner did not bother to build new houses, but simply adapted existing cottages, adding picturesque features such as porches and gables.

Despite a conscious adoption of traditional styles, the appearance of such cottages and villages is often highly incongruous. They reflect, not the revival or continuation of local vernacular traditions, but the imposition of national, élite concepts of traditional architecture. The formal villages of the eighteenth

Somerleyton, Suffolk
This fine example of a picturesque model village was designed in the 1840s by John Thomas for Sir Morton Peto, owner of Somerleyton Hall. The houses are built in a variety of pseudo-vernacular styles, and each one is individual. They are grouped in 'traditional' fashion around a newly-created village green.

century tended, for practical reasons, to utilize local building materials; Milton Abbas, for example, was built of cob and thatch. In the picturesque village, by contrast, the cottages were often of materials alien to the areas in which they were built, but which could now be obtained from outside the region with the improvements in transport. The designers could thus indulge their romantic, fixed and unrealistic ideas of the nature of 'vernacular' architecture. At Ilam, for example, many of the model cottages have tile-hung gables, a form of cladding which was entirely inappropriate for the local area.

Many houses in picturesque villages are decorated with mock timber-framing. This usually has no structural function, but merely represents the landowners' image of the traditional old English cottage. The net result is that model villages often have a rather curious appearance. They are burlesque versions of the real thing. With their barge-boarding, latticed windows, thatched roofs and half-timbering, their storm porches and ornate twisting chimneys, the cottages are composed of a disjointed amalgam of seemingly heterogeneous features.

The difference between the formal order-

Somerleyton, Suffolk
Curiously ornate chimneys are a particular characteristic of picturesque village architecture. Together with thatched roofs and mock timber-framing, they present a burlesque version of genuine vernacular architecture which could never be confused with the real thing.

liness of Milton Abbas and the rambling romanticism of Blaise is, however, a manifestation of more than simply a change in aristocratic taste. The earlier villages reveal their dependence on their landlord by having a rigidly standardized form. They are strikingly different from the sprawling open villages, where the individualistic architecture displayed the independent spirit of the inhabitants. In contrast, later model villages adopted many of the features which characterized the traditional, organic village, and they consciously mimicked its varied and irregular appearance. This change coincided with new trends in landscape gardening, and the increasing incorporation of the working countryside into the status landscapes of the élite.

By the early nineteenth century landlords had begun to see the landscape as a broad social canvas, in which every aspect of rural life could be shown to have a place. It is therefore somewhat ironic that their representation of a united rural community incorporated, not existing villages, but custom-built imitations of these. None the less, the changing tastes of the landed aristocracy revealed a change in their attitude to the rural community. The spread of general enclosure in the seventeenth and eighteenth centuries had considerably curtailed the independence of many villages, particularly the closed parishes, and as a result they represented much less of a threat to the social order. Landlords could now see the rambling English village as romantic, and no longer felt the need to establish their authority in rows of regimented houses.

As well as forming part of a status landscape, the picturesque village served to create a particular image of the labouring poor. The deliberately dilapidated and poky thatched cottage reflected aristocratic ideas about rural felicity. The rural poor were seen as inherently happy and virtuous, and this moral purity was thought to stem directly from their poverty. They were divorced from the corruptions of the complex modern world, and untainted by the wickedness connected with an excess of material goods. In the paintings of Gainsborough, and in the literature which extolled the life of rural simplicity, this model of a contented peasantry was extensively fostered. Moreover, the construction of a romanticized and supposedly traditional rural environment made it easier for the landlords to believe their fictions about rural life as a whole. The quaint cottage could be regarded as the happy home of the innocent and simple peasant, rather than as the fetid slum of the starving rick-burner.[10]

In a few places the inhabitants of model villages were actually made to wear uniforms which enabled them to harmonize with their surroundings and reinforce this image. At Old Warden Lord Ongley made the inhabitants walk about in tall hats and red cloaks, while the almswomen of Milton Abbas had to wear strangely pointed hats. Elsewhere the landowners were loath to have their embodiment of rural harmony disrupted by the sight of villagers gossiping on their doorsteps, so that at Milton Abbas, East Stratton and many other model villages houses were built with doors at the sides rather than the front. Indeed, in his *Village Architecture* of 1830 P.F. Robinson recommended that care should be taken to conceal the doors from sight when cottages were constructed, 'in order to avoid the appearance of any uncleanly habits'.

Had any of the genteel travellers of Robinson's day peered through the rustic doorway of a pretty estate cottage, it is likely that they would have seen not only uncleanly habits, but a great deal of damp, filth and perhaps rats. Despite the romantic image of a wholesome peasantry which the villages were designed to reinforce, the insides of many estate cottages were squalidly inadequate for human habitation. Indeed, some were little different from the rural slums which they replaced. The landowner's preoccupation with the external appearance of the houses was not matched by a concern for conditions inside them.

The delightfully quaint deep eaves and small windows of a picturesque cottage made the interiors incredibly dark. Newly-laid thatch makes an excellent roofing material, but the sparse and unmaintained thatch of many estate cottages was the source of all manner of ills. Once it became damp and rotten, the inhabitants were showered with rain-water, decomposing roof matter, and the droppings of vermin which almost invariably inhabited the roof. As many landowners did not bother to give model cottages adequate ceilings or floors, rain dripped straight into them, turning their floors into stinking quagmires.

But despite their failings, picturesque houses were better than no houses at all. Although the model villages were designed as much to display benevolence as to respond to the needs of the labouring community, they were more useful than the wholly non-functional forms of landscape ornament. As Charles Waistell wrote in his *Designs for Agricultural Buildings*:

> It has been fashionable with gentlemen to erect buildings in their grounds often merely as objects to look at; it would be happy for themselves, as well as for their poor half-starved labourers, if in ornamenting their grounds gentlemen were to direct their attention to the promoting of the health and comfort of those by whom they are benefited . . . with labourers' cottages instead of useless buildings.[11]

Model villages were the first attempts by the landowners to provide housing for the poor. As the nineteenth century progressed, they began to build better cottages which were more comfortable, and often designed in styles more akin to the local vernacular. Later villages included community buildings such as churches, almshouses and schools, as well as

RIGHT **Ripley, Yorkshire**
Built by William Ingilby in 1854, the 'Hôtel de Ville' is the centrepiece of the model village.

cottages. For example, when William Ingilby built the model village of Ripley in Yorkshire, he included a village hall, rather pompously known as the Hôtel de Ville.

Quite minor members of the gentry as well as great landowners built model villages in the nineteenth century, often easing the financial burden by spreading the work over a number of years. Even in the early twentieth century a few model villages were built. As late as 1917 the lord of the manor of Ardeley in Hertfordshire

BELOW **Ardeley, Hertfordshire**
These picturesque thatched cottages, grouped around a green and embellished with a communal well, were not constructed until 1917.

built Ardeley Green, an attractive group of thatched cottages around a small green.

But it was the introduction of more general house-building schemes which shows how important the landed élite were in the provision of rural housing, and their gradual acceptance of paternal responsibility for workers on their estates. Very large landowners began to build more dispersed groups of cottages, rather than model villages, from the early nineteenth century onwards. The seventh Duke of Bedford built 288 cottages on his estate in Devon and 374 in Bedfordshire, and in 1851 the Duke of Northumberland began building 1000 homes. It was only from the middle decades of the nineteenth century, however, that the building of such cottages became common, and that the smaller landowner also became involved in these schemes.

As Victorian philanthropists drew attention to the evils of inadequate housing and sanitary arrangements, some landowners felt obliged to make provision for the labourers on their estates. They were motivated by a desire to forestall revolutionary discontent, by genuine humanitarian sentiments and by a feeling that some degree of paternalistic responsibility went hand in hand with a landowner's dominance of the social and political system. The importance of this benevolence was expressed in George Eliot's novel *Middlemarch* (1870). The heroine Dorothea spends much time drawing model cottages based on the pattern books of the designer Loudon. She exclaims:

> I think we deserve to be beaten out of our beautiful homes with a scourge of small cords — all of us who let tenants live in such sties as we see round us. Life in cottages might be happier than ours, if they were real homes fit for human beings.

Middlemarch also reveals the practical limitations of humanitarian concern, and the actual inadequacy of landowners' efforts. Like many landlords, Dorothea failed to put her ideas into practice, and despite the existence of numerous estate cottages the general standard of rural housing was woefully poor up to the end of World War I.

The dwellings constructed on an estate usually followed a single distinctive pattern. Not only were their building materials standardized, but so also were details of their design, such as the use of specially moulded bricks, mullioned windows, barge-boarding and ornately shaped gables. This standardization reduced the cost of building cottages, especially on large estates such as the Yarborough estate in Lincolnshire, where the production of estate housing was strongly centralized.[12] It also underlined the 'tied' status of the cottages, the dependence of the inhabitants, and the aesthetic unity of the estates.

Even on smaller estates where only a few cottages were built, the same basic pattern was followed. All around the country it is still possible to spot symmetrical pairs of semi-detached cottages, often of red brick, with small porches, pointed gables, decorative barge-boarding or mullioned windows, often built to the designs in basic architectural 'pattern books'. Datestones inserted in the walls of cottages also make their ownership plain, particularly when landowners included initials or some kind of heraldic symbol derived from their coat of arms. This practice extended to all kinds of estate buildings, from farmhouses to barns. As early as the 1730s Sir Thomas Parkins of Bunny Hall, Nottinghamshire, built several brick barns in the area around Bunny and Bradmore which prominently bear his initials and the date of their construction. These are picked out in black bricks across the sides and gables of the barns.[13] Likewise, in northwest Norfolk the recurrence of the initials T.W.C. testify to the prolific building of Thomas William Coke on the Holkham estate.

The progressive involvement of landowners in the provision of farmhouses and other farm buildings revealed the changes that were taking place in the organization of agriculture, and in particular the fact that the majority of land in

England was now held by the large estates. By the early eighteenth century most of this land was leased to tenant farmers, and as the century progressed the landowners became increasingly anxious to ensure that the tenants were reliable and responsible. They therefore began to create farms and farm buildings that would attract the most desirable occupants. The decline of small freeholders and the rise of the great landowners is thus visually symbolized by the development of increasingly sophisticated farmsteads designed by architects working in the latest national fashion.

As landlords became increasingly interested in agriculture, some even went so far as to build 'model farms' to show off their taste and agricultural sophistication.[14] These can still be seen today, particularly in grain producing areas once dominated by the great estates — in Yorkshire, Lincolnshire, Northumberland and Norfolk, and in coastal areas of Lancashire and Cumbria where large tracts of land were improved in the eighteenth century. Model

Marlingford, Norfolk
Many eighteenth- and nineteenth-century estate cottages have date plaques displaying the initials of the landowner by whom they were built. This example is on the front of our own house in Norfolk.

farms include architect-designed farmhouses to attract the wealthiest of tenants, and the sort of farm buildings that were necessary for the latest agricultural techniques. In particular, the erection of byres and barns for stall-feeding animals made the production of manure more efficient. These buildings were often arranged in a neat quadrangular layout, enclosing a model farmyard. By the nineteenth century model farms began to provide for the mechanization of agriculture, with engine houses for threshing grain attached to the barns.

Before landlords became closely involved in the practicalities of agriculture, they had tended to devote their energies to disguising farm buildings as something else or concealing them behind other features. It was not until the late eighteenth century that a farm became acceptable as a feature of the landscape. In 1762 Timothy Lightholer published his *The Gentleman and Farmer's Architect*,[15] which included designs for farmsteads, granaries, barns and other farm buildings in classical, Chinese and gothic styles. Among them is a particularly striking castellated sheepcote, with two gothic facades 'to place before disagreeable objects'. The gothic style was very popular in the mid eighteenth century, and some gothic farm

Castle Barn, Badminton, Avon
Designed by Thomas Wright around 1750, this grand castellated barn is one of several built on the Duke of Beaufort's estate. It is an example of the mid eighteenth-century desire to embellish agricultural buildings, but also to disguise them.

buildings can still be seen today, especially in the environs of the landscape parks of the larger country houses. At Rousham in Oxfordshire there is a gothic cowshed; at Sledmere, Humberside the home farm is in the shape of a castle; and around Badminton, Avon, there is still a very fine series of gothic farms. These were designed by Thomas Wright in the 1750s for the fourth Duke of Beaufort, and include barns adorned with castellated towers and cross arrow slits.

As undisguised farm buildings began to be acceptable, their architecture became more plain and functional. Many of them, such as those designed by Robert Adam or Samuel Wyatt, were built in the neo-classical style, like the fine farmyard with its huge red-brick barn at Leicester Square Farm on the Holkham estate in Norfolk. A few, however, were constructed in a picturesque pseudo-vernacular, with thatch and latticed windows, often after the whimsical designs of J. C. Loudon and P. F. Robinson. This style was particularly popular for the dairies on home farms, as at Althorp in Northamptonshire, where the building dates from 1786. In some places, whole farmyards were built in this extravagant style, like that designed by P. F. Robinson for Bertie Greathead at Guy's Cliffe in Warwickshire.

Buildings like these represent more than the excesses of aristocratic taste. From cottages to barns, they reflect the growing interest of landlords in the details of rural life, and the increasing control exerted by the landed élite over the appearance of the land. The development of rural architecture manifested numerous changes in taste, but it usually involved the replacement of local vernacular building traditions by nationally standardized styles, in which aesthetic sophistication was more important than everyday practicality. As landlords consolidated their control over the lives of rural communities, their status began to be displayed in their connection with the countryside and signs of agricultural activity began to be flaunted, not concealed. The barn, farmhouse and cottage were no longer hidden or castellated, but became the model for the consciously rural style of the picturesque. The changing tastes of the landed élite have therefore served to shape the landscape, but they were themselves conditioned by the history of the ownership of land.

NINE

Churches and Tombs

WITH ITS SOLID STONEWORK and air of immense age, the parish church is one of the most typically English features of the rural landscape. For centuries it served as a place where the community could come together, and meet in an act of worship on relatively equal terms. It was therefore inevitable that this shared space came to be exploited as a locus for secular display, where the landowners impressed the extent of their families' importance, power and wealth on a receptive congregation.

The most astonishing changes to the exteriors of parish churches were made by rich landowners in the mid eighteenth century as one facet in their landscaping schemes. Churches which had been left isolated within landscaped parks after the removal or relocation of the villages which they had served were often wholly redesigned. This ensured that a church could become part of the aesthetic scheme of a park, and also revealed the extent of the landowners' dominance over the parish. The parish church within Wimpole Park in Cambridgeshire, for example, had been isolated by emparcation and was given a total facelift in 1748 to make it fit in with the architecture of the hall. Everything but its fourteenth-century north chapel was totally demolished, to be replaced by a smaller structure of brick, faced on the west front in stone, and in the fashionable classical style. Like the Victorian estate village beyond the park, the 'Gothic Tower' on a nearby hill, and the serpentine lake created by 'Capability' Brown, the new church testifies to the taste of the landowners, and to the extent of their control over the landscape. Similarly, the marooned parish church of the village of Nuneham Courtenay was converted into a domed classical temple by Simon, first Earl of Harcourt. It was described by Horace Walpole as, 'the principal feature in one of the most beautiful landscapes in the world'. In other words, it had ceased to be seen as the religious centre of the community, and had become a component of an élite landscape of aesthetic display.

Some churches which were drastically modified in the eighteenth century were not already located within a landscape park. Sometimes the landowner destroyed the parish church that stood within the village, and built another more fashionable one in the park. In 1778 Sir Lionel Lyde, a tobacconist and director of the Bank of England, commissioned a church in the form of a Greek temple at his Hertfordshire seat Ayot House. This was built

Ayot St Lawrence, Hertfordshire
The ruined medieval church of St Lawrence on the outskirts of the park of Ayot House (*below*) contrasts with the new church of St Lawrence, within the park (*above*). Designed for Sir Lionel Lyde by Nicholas Revett, the new church is in the form of a Greek Temple, but only the side facing Ayot House is faced with stone: the rear of the building is plain, unadorned brick.

West Wycombe, Buckinghamshire
This hexagonal mausoleum was built by Sir Francis Dashwood in 1763–4 on the eastern edge of the churchyard at West Wycombe. The great golden ball with seats inside which Dashwood added to the tower of the church can be seen in the distance.

at some distance from the village of Ayot St Lawrence, at the end of an avenue from the house. As a result, the parishioners had to walk a considerable way to attend the services because the original building had been converted into a picturesque ruin. Moreover, they were not even allowed to take the shortest route to the church, but had to approach by a circuitous path and enter by a side door. This ensured that they did not pass within sight of Sir Lionel Lyde's house or interrupt his view of the church.[1]

The fabric of the church provides a telling indication of the priorities of its creator. The front of the building, which faced Ayot House, has a stone facade, but the other three sides are simply composed of bare unadorned brick. It did not matter that it was these sides that the villagers saw as they entered the church, for Sir Lionel was only concerned with how the building would look to members of his own class, who would inevitably have approached it from the confines of Ayot House. The building was unashamedly constructed as an adornment to Lyde's estate, rather than as a contribution to the spiritual welfare of the people of Ayot St Lawrence.

In a few places landowners attempted to alter churches that were outside their parks. At West Wycombe, for example, Sir Francis Dashwood transformed St Lawrence's parish church into one of the most excessive churches to be produced in the eighteenth century. This was situated some distance from his park at West Wycombe Hall, within Iron Age earthworks on top of a nearby hill. Although the hill is now largely covered with trees, pictures within the house dating from 1764 show that in the eighteenth century the church was clearly visible from the house and park. It must have formed a strange and striking spectacle, for as well as putting in classical arched windows Dashwood crowned the tower with a huge golden ball with seats inside which could be seen for miles around. In addition he built a massive hexagonal mausoleum in the churchyard, classical in style but constructed, somewhat incongrously, of flint.[2]

The interior of the church expressed Dashwood's bizarre taste even more forcibly. A visitor in 1775 likened the interior to 'a very superb Egyptian Hall', but to modern eyes it resembles a vast and ornately decorated eighteenth-century dining room. The ceiling is covered with elaborate and brightly-coloured paintings; the floor is of highly polished marble, and the nave, which is modelled on the fifth-century Temple of the Sun at Palmyra, is adorned with a frieze and huge Corinthian capitals. Instead of a pulpit there is a beautifully carved and very comfortable looking rosewood Chippendale armchair.

The effect of all this is peculiar and spectacular. It is reminiscent of Pope's description of an eighteenth-century chapel in his attack on the excesses of aristocratic taste, the *Epistle to Burlington*:

And now the Chapel's silver bell you hear,
That summons you to all the Pride of Pray'r:
Light quirks of Music, broken and uneven,
Make the soul dance upon a Jig to Heav'n.
On painted Cielings you devoutly stare,
Where sprawl the Saints of Verrio or Laguerre,
On gilded clouds in fair expansion lie,
And bring all paradise before your eye.
To rest the cushion and soft Dean invite,
Who never mentions Hell to ears polite.[3]

None the less, Dashwood's church was exceptional even by the standards of the eighteenth century, when church fabrics were more frequently adapted to show the landowner's taste than in the preceding and subsequent centuries. The fashion for converting churches was in fact relatively short-lived, partly because it was very expensive, and the number of churches which received dramatic alterations to their exteriors was limited. Where improvements were made, the church was generally adorned with the trappings of some kind of classical style. Churches were not usually given a gothic look, largely because this was the style in which most were originally constructed, and many landlords wished to distinguish their churches from the traditional architecture of the community. The few exceptions include the octagonal gothic church in the park at Hartwell in Buckinghamshire, which was built between 1753 and 1755, and the church at Ravenfield in South Yorkshire which was constructed in the following year.

Even where churches were not landscaped, most contained more discreet displays of secular status, not only in the eighteenth century but also in earlier periods. Monuments ranging from the great and imposing tombs of the wealthy landlord to the humble wooden memorial of the labourer served to demonstrate the standing and wealth of the individuals they commemorated. Despite the conventional image of death as the great leveller, the inhabitants of any rural community were as unequal in death as they had been in life. Nowadays, this inequality is clearly discernible in any church or churchyard, for only the more substantial memorials have survived. As with houses, the older the monument the more likely that the individual for whom it was erected had substantial status and wealth. Initially, durable monuments were the preserve of the very rich alone, and the ability to commemorate themselves in stone only gradually percolated down to other ranks in the population. In the seventeenth century prosperous farmers began to be buried with permanent headstones, but even in the nineteenth century the graves of the labouring poor were usually only given temporary markers.[4]

Status could be conveyed not only in the

appearance of funerary monuments but also by their location. The spatial segregation of classes in death as in life was recognized in the epitaph of Robert Philip, the parish grave-digger of Kingsbridge in Devon, who died in 1795:

Here lie I at the chapel door,
Here lie I because I'm poor,
The further in the more you'll pay,
Here lie I as warm as they.

Only the richer members of the community were buried inside the church; ordinary people had to rest content outside. Even within the graveyard there were obvious social distinctions and most churchyards follow more or less the same basic plan. The large tombs of the rich are usually sited to the south of the church, often on either side of the main path to the south door. The less well off you were, the further your grave was located from this prestigious situation. Indeed, there are usually very few early gravestones of any kind to the north of the church, for this was the very least favoured part of the churchyard. It was cold and dark, and traditionally associated with the devil. Here there were only the graves of malefactors, or of the very poor, and before the nineteenth century these were unlikely to leave any trace of their existence.

The very richest families not only buried their relatives within the church, but commemorated them with immense and impressive tombs. Although the Reformation put an end to the construction of chantry chapels, in the sixteenth and seventeenth centuries some landowners built mortuary chapels within their local church to house the funerary monuments of their families. Such chapels usually appeared in villages which had a single, powerful landowning dynasty, and nowadays they provide quite striking symbols of the continuity as well as the wealth of these great families. On rows of monuments the dates change, the styles change, but the family name stays the same.

The Bedford chapel, for example, was added to the church at Chenies in Buckinghamshire in 1556. Although it was subsequently rebuilt, the large and lavish collection of monuments it contains span the period from the first Earl of Bedford, who died in 1555, to the ninth Duke, who died in 1891. And it was beside another mortuary chapel in the same county at Stoke Poges, that Thomas Gray is said to have written his *Elegy Written in a Country Churchyard.* This commemorates the innumerable people of the village who have no tombs or funerary monuments, and whose lives and deaths are unrecorded. It implicitly contrasts their lack of history with the busts and tombs which record and thereby give importance to the lives of the rich. The construction of mortuary chapels continued in the eighteenth century. At Knebworth in Hertfordshire, the north chancel aisle of the church was rebuilt in 1705 to form the Lytton chapel, which housed the sumptuous monuments of the Lytton family.

During the Middle Ages there had been a gradual increase in the extent to which local dynasties influenced the internal appearance of churches. Not only chantry chapels, but tombs and heraldic displays on walls and windows became more common and more imposing, particularly in the great monastic churches. Yet the overall impact of these features on most parish churches was limited, and the main body of the building was rarely cluttered with the large, free-standing tombs which were to become common later. Before the fifteenth century, monuments to local landowners were usually fairly discreet, often consisting of a brass set into the floor of the church. Moreover, such features would have been far less prominent amidst the brightly-coloured religious paraphernalia and iconography of the medieval church than they are in the electrically lit and bare tranquillity which nowadays characterizes our churches.

From the reign of Edward VI, however, the Reformation brought about a radical alteration in the interior appearance and spatial organization of the parish church. Images and icons were banned on the grounds of idolatry, while the chantries act of 1547 condemned the superstitious belief in purgatory and banned the maintenance of chantry chapels. Wall-paintings were white-washed, statuary was smashed, and roods ripped down. Although many of the earlier fittings and furnishings were replaced under Mary Tudor, for several centuries after Elizabeth's reign many of the basic features of the reformed church were unaltered. Wall paintings were not uncovered, the rood was not restored, and while the rood screen sometimes remained, it was surmounted by the royal arms, a symbol dramatically confirming the dominance of the secular state over the Church.

In the whitewashed setting of the reformed church the tombs and monuments of the local gentry and aristocracy immediately caught the eye. These had survived relatively untouched while the icons and religious symbols were being swept away by the tide of reformist enthusiasm. Moreover, in the decades after the Reformation the tombs and monuments of local lay landowners became increasingly numerous, varied, costly and imposing, as if to represent the growing importance of these individuals in the community.[5]

Medieval tombs had portrayed the dead lying down, looking dead or at least asleep. Tombs of this kind continued to be erected for many years, but in the late sixteenth and early seventeenth century some monuments began to be constructed in various innovative styles, with the use of more animated and dominating figures.

An early phase in this development is represented by tombs like the Fettiplace monument in Swinbrook church, in Oxfordshire. Dating from around 1613 it portrays the dead rather jauntily reclining on one elbow, and looking very much alive if a little uncomfortable. The craze for monuments in this style in the half century after 1570 was immortalized by John Webster in *The Duchess of Malfi*, written a year after the erection of the Fettiplace monument. A character comments:

Princes' images on their tombs
Do not lie as they were wont, seeming to pray
Up to Heaven: but with their hands under their cheeks
As if they died of the tooth-ache.[6]

These reclining effigies were, however, never very widespread and were far less popular than the contemporary fashion for monuments portraying the deceased in a kneeling position, accompanied by a spouse, and by diminutive figures representing their children. There are many hundreds of monuments of this kind in the parish churches of England, such as the tomb of Richard Chernocke, who died in 1615, in Hulcote church in Bedfordshire, or the tomb of Sir Cope D'Oyley, who died in 1633, in Hambledon church in Buckinghamshire. Sir Cope is surrounded by his numerous children, and those who had predeceased him are rather macabrely portrayed holding skulls. Like the accumulation of monuments in mortuary chapels, the imposing upright figures on these monuments serve to reinforce the importance of the local dynasty. It is particularly significant that they not only commemorate the dead, but also honour the children who live on. Such monuments reinforce the importance of hereditary lineage and family continuity at a time when, as we have seen, tenure and the maintenance of family estates were still somewhat uncertain. Some tombs portrayed not only the spouse and children, but also more distant relatives of the deceased. At Holkham in

OVERLEAF RIGHT **The Fettiplace Monument, Swinbrook, Oxfordshire**
Erected in 1613 to the memory of Sir Edmund Fettiplace, his father and grandfather, this monument is a fine example of the short-lived vogue for semi-reclining, slightly uncomfortable-looking effigies.

OVERLEAF LEFT **Hambledon, Buckinghamshire**
The tomb of Sir Cope D'Oyley, who died in 1633, shows Sir Cope, his wife and numerous children. Those of his offspring who predeceased him are depicted holding skulls.

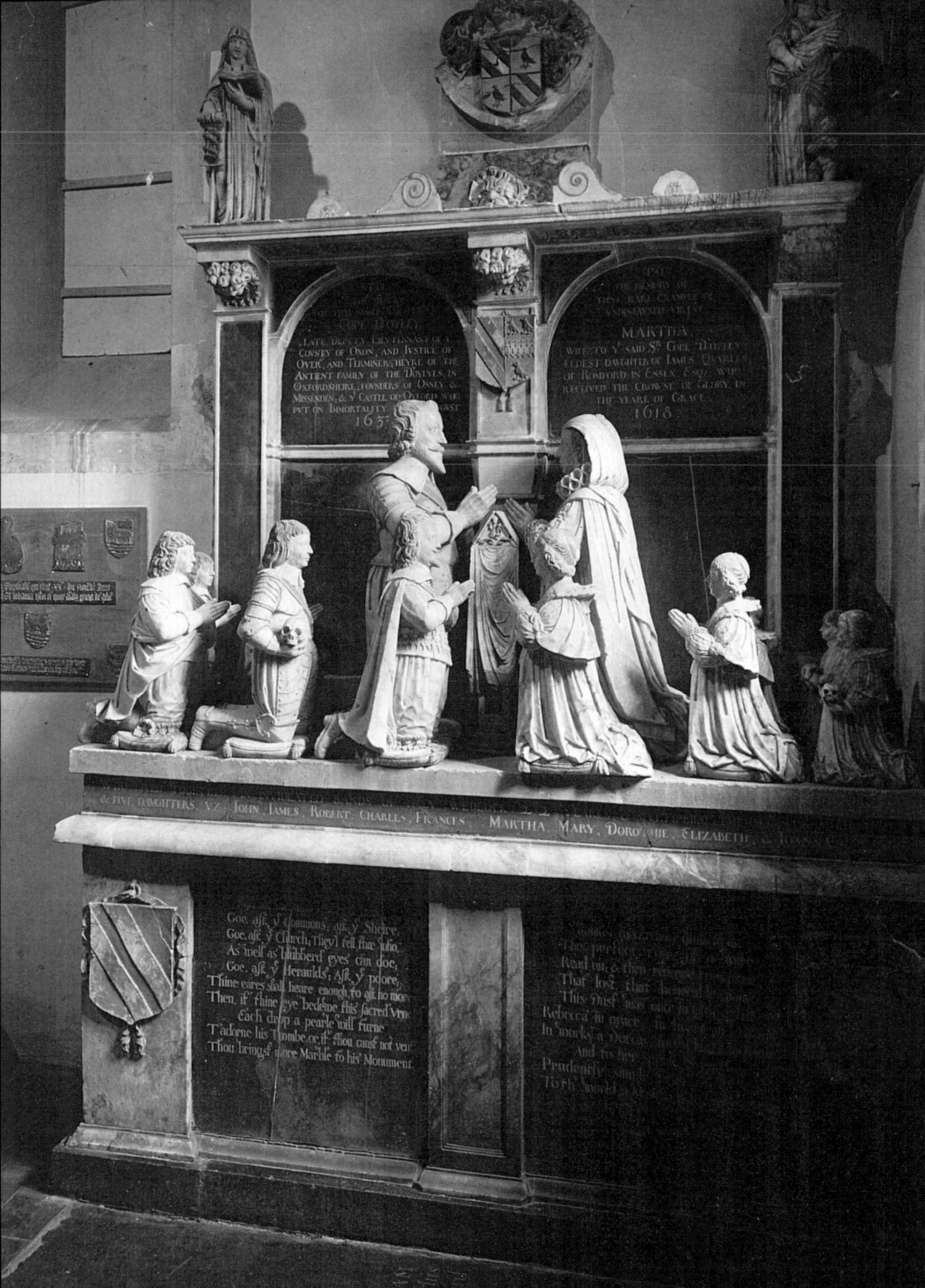

MARTHA
1618
& FIVE DAUGHTERS, VZ: JOHN, JAMES, ROBERT, CHARLES, FRANCES, MARTHA, MARY, DOROTHIE, ELIZABETH
Goe, ask ye Commons, ask ye Sheire,
Goe, ask ye Church, They'l tell thee who,
As well as blubberd eyes can doe,
Goe, ask ye Heraulds; Ask ye poore,
Thine eares shall heare enough to ask no more
Then, if thine eye bedewe this sacred Vrne
Each drop a pearle will turne
T'adorne his Tombe, or, if thou canst not vent
Thou bringst more Marble to his Monument.

HERE LIETH THE
BODY OF Sr EDMVND
FETIPLACE KNIGHT
SONNE AND HEYRE
TO WILLIAM FETT
PLACE ESQVIER
HE ESPOVSED ANNE
DAVGHTER OF ROGER
ALFORDE ESQVIER
NVLLOVE
VNE
HEARELIETH THE BODY OF WILLIAM
OF ALEXANDER FETIPLACE ESQVIER
HEYR OF Sr EDMVND ASHFIELD KNIGHT
FETIPLACE ESQVIER SONNE AND HEYR
POWSED ELIZABETH ASHFIELD DAVGHTER AND
SVE 3 SONNS HE DECEASD THE 1 DAY OF MAY 1562
HEARE LYETH THE BODY OF ALEXANDER
FETIPLACE SONNE AND HEYRE OF ANTHO
NYE FETIPLACE ESQVIER HE WAS FIRST ESPO
WSED TO AME DAVGHTER AND HEYR OF WILLIAM
ESQVIER
NNS AND 7 DAVGHTERS HE DISCESED THE 20 OF SEPTEMBER

Norfolk, for example, the monument to Meriall Coke, who died in 1626, includes the kneeling figures of herself, her husband, her fifteen children, and also her parents and grand-parents.

The increase in the size of tombs was as striking as the changes in their form. The masons exaggerated the figures portrayed by the development of increasingly massive archi-tectural surrounds. Many eighteenth-century archiepiscopal visitations commented on the way these tombs crowded the churches, and complained about their tendency to block out light from the windows.

During the troubled years of the Com-monwealth in the mid seventeenth century, there was a considerable decline in the construction of large tombs. Only in the more stable conditions following the Restoration of the monarchy did the wealthy classes begin

The Lytton Chapel, Knebworth, Hertfordshire
Like so many churches isolated within landscaped parks, the church of St Mary and St Thomas is full of the memorials of the owners of Knebworth House. The Lytton chapel is dominated by the lavish early eighteenth-century monuments to the Lytton family, surmounted by their monstrous and elegantly clad funerary statues.

once again to demonstrate their status in elaborate funeral monuments, and these were in styles rather different to those of the pre-revolutionary years. Kneeling or recumbent figures were no longer in fashion. Instead the deceased landowners were portrayed standing, sitting, or reclining in effigies that were life size or even larger. These often gross and bewigged figures, sprawling across their monuments, convey an air of dominance, but also of complacent security. In the chapel at Knebworth in Hertfordshire, for example, the eighteenth-century monuments to the Strode and Lytton families are topped with huge and elaborately dressed figures. Another feature of these monuments is that children are rarely represented, although they often depict spouses, and sometimes allegorical figures such as Time, Death or Justice. This may reflect the development of greater security of tenure amongst the landed classes in the years after the Glorious Revolution. The landowners may have felt less threatened and therefore less concerned about reinforcing their lineage.

The eighteenth century also saw a proliferation of smaller funerary monuments, wall tablets and ledger slabs, erected to the memory of the lesser gentry, minor members of aristocratic families, or members of the professions. Such monuments are often very telling about the social structure of the village and the local pattern of landholding, indicating whether the community was dominated by one or two great local landowners, or whether there were a number of lesser local gentry. Those churches which were isolated within eighteenth-century landscape parks almost invariably betray the influence of a single landed family in their monuments. The parish church of Lydiard Tregoze in Wiltshire, for example, is situated in the grounds of Lydiard Park, for generations the seat of the St John family. Within the church a fine collection of funerary monuments commemorate departed St Johns from the sixteenth to the nineteenth century.

In the course of the nineteenth century the average size of funerary monuments diminished, and even the most important corpses began to be commemorated by a relatively discreet plaque. In large measure this seems to have been a response to changes in religious thinking, and in particular in the organization of the established Church. The Oxford Movement and the Tractarians became very influential within the Church of England in the nineteenth century, and these groups were both opposed to excessive secular display. Indeed, in a number of places they even sought to remove some of the larger sixteenth- and seventeenth-century tombs. They were also anxious to revive some of the medieval ritual in the religious service, and to make church interiors resemble their medieval form more closely.

As a result of the changes instigated in the nineteenth century, it is now very difficult to get a clear picture of what post Reformation churches must originally have looked like. Only rarely, in some out-of-the-way village or hamlet, is it possible to find a church forgotten by the Victorians which gives some idea of what they destroyed. Good examples can be found at Midhopestones in Yorkshire, Warminghurst in West Sussex, and Clodock in Herefordshire, but such survivals are extremely rare. Of around 8000 pre Victorian churches, perhaps as few as 150 retain substantially untouched interiors.[7]

A particularly unfortunate loss is the seating that characterized the reformed church. This had been introduced here and there in the late Middle Ages, but it was the Reformation that really served to encourage its spread. The active participatory ritual of the medieval service was replaced at this time by an emphasis on passive attendance to the minister's word. The church was also increasingly regarded as a special and sacred building, and was no longer used for general get-togethers, such as church ales, so that it was no longer necessary for the church to be a great open space. The early seating was almost invariably removed in the nineteenth century and replaced by the rather boring pitch-pine pews so often seen today. Where it is still possible to see pre Victorian church seats, these give a striking insight into the nature of the communities which sat on them.

The wealthiest were generally seated in private pews, known as 'closed seats'. These first appeared towards the end of the medieval period, often by simply adapting chantry chapels, and were relatively common by the seventeenth century. They consisted of a number of seats enclosed within a large and often elaborately decorated box, open at the front and sometimes surmounted by an ornately decorated canopy. Many of these 'closed seats' were constructed in aisles which were specially built for the purpose, and which also served as burial places for the families who sat in them. Others stood in galleries, often at the western end of the church. One such gallery was erected in the church of Chaddleworth in Berkshire, and the motives for its construction were expressed in a resolution passed by the vestry (a group of parishioners who settled the affairs of the parish and temporal matters relating to the church) of Chaddleworth on 3 May 1724:

> Whereas our parish church of Chaddleworth is Strait and hardly Capable of affording Roome for the parishioners to attend divine Service And whereas Bartholomew Tipping Esqr one of our principall Inhabitants is destitute of Convenient Roome or pew for his Tennant and family the said Bartholomew Tipping . . . [is] willing and desirous at his owne proper Coste and Charge to Erect a Gallery at the west of our said Churche for the use of such of this Tennant and ffamily on the one side and the other side for the use of such person as the parish shall think proper.[8]

Within such pews the local squire and his family could sit in comfort. Indeed, in some places, such as Stapleford in Leicestershire or Ogwell in Devon, the pews were provided with fireplaces. Often, as at Chaddleworth, the status of the occupants was further enhanced by the physical elevation of the pew. Surviving examples include the Hastings Pew in the church of Melton Constable in Norfolk, and the Milbanke Pew in the church at Croft in North Yorkshire. Just as the construction of the landscape park removed the country house from the rest of the village, so the seating in the village church set the inhabitants of that house apart from the rest of the community.

The seating in the church as a whole could demonstrate the social organization of the village more generally. Much of the seating in the seventeenth- and eighteenth-century church consisted of box pews, with high backs and doors. In some areas it was usual for farm labourers to be seated in such pews with the farmer's family, and in some cases individual pews were labelled with the names of local farms. Such an arrangement served to underline the importance of the farm within the community, and the subservient position of labourers on the farm.

Sometimes pews were of varying sizes, symbolizing the range of wealth and status within the community. The principal landowners and wealthy farmers would sit in the largest box pews, towards the front of the nave, near the chancel arch. The smaller farmers and tradesmen sat further back, near the western end, and in rather smaller pews. The labourers did not have enclosed pews, but had to sit on open benches at the back of the church. It is still possible to see rigidly stratified seating of this kind in the parish church at Wilby in Norfolk.

In the sixteenth and early seventeenth century pews were usually attached to certain dwellings, like common rights, and passed with them when they were sold or inherited. But in the late seventeenth and eighteenth centuries it became usual for seats to be allotted by churchwardens and the vestry. Such men were very conscious of the fact that the organization of the seating needed to be an accurate reflection of the village hierarchy. When replacing the seating of their church at Frieston in Lincolnshire in 1786, the vestry declared that it would have to, 'place the landowners, Parishioners and Inh[ab]it[ant]s of the S[ai]d Parish in such new Seats or pews to their respective Degrees, state, quality and Interests' [punctuation added]. But this task was not always easy, and frequently produced quarrels within the community. Indeed on some occasions, as at Packington in Leicestershire in 1773, the disputes led to litigation.

Although seating arrangements only rarely survived the attentions of the Victorians, many parish churches contain some early fittings which, like the tombs and monuments, could sometimes serve to display local power and patronage. Bishopsbourne in Kent and Sywell in Northamptonshire, for example, still have stained-glass windows displaying the coats of arms of the local gentry. Churches today more commonly contain 'hatchments' — lozenge-shaped wooden boards bearing coats of arms. These were made for wealthy families, particularly in the seventeenth and eighteenth centuries, and were placed outside a house when one of its members died. After about a year, hatchments were transferred to the local church.

Wilby, Norfolk
Few churches today contain furnishings dating from before the nineteenth century, as in most places earlier seating was ripped out by Victorian 'restorers'. In the quiet Norfolk village of Wilby, however, the church has an interior which has remained almost unchanged since the seventeenth century, and still has the rigidly stratified seating which was once to be found in many churches. The enclosed box pews in the foreground were occupied by the more prosperous members of the village community: the benches behind them were for the labourers and the poor.

Elsewhere texts remind the congregation of the benevolence and patronage of the local landowner. Many churches contain large painted boards which give details of past charitable bequests. These were often erected in the eighteenth century, possibly to prevent such money being absorbed into the general parish funds administered by the overseers of the poor. They certainly left the poor of the parish in no doubt about what they were owed and by whom it was given. Other inscriptions not only reveal the benevolence of the donor, but also instructed the poor to behave obediently and correctly. For example, below a clock inside the church of Lower Winchendon in Buckinghamshire is written:

This CLOCK was given by the will of Jane Beresford, widow Lady of this Manor; that it may Remind all who hear it, to spend the Time in an honest Discharge of their Calling, and in the Worship of God; that Repentence may not come too late. MDCCLXXII.

The puritan sentiment expressed in this inscription well illustrates the attitude of the landed classes to the poor in the eighteenth and nineteenth centuries. The continual exhortations to labour, and the stress on punctuality, demonstrate the widespread belief that the poor were fundamentally lazy, and needed to be forced to work.

Thus in a multitude of ways the internal organization and fittings of post medieval churches reflected the social organization of the communities which they served. The whole principle of the 'congregation', of the gathering together of the parish, provided an image of social unity, but the organization of the church interior was a continual reminder of the social divisions which lay within each community. Extravagant churches like Ayot St Lawrence or Nuneham Courtenay, however, did something more. They were designed to be appreciated for their external appearance, and to be understood in terms of the principles of aristocratic taste. Like other such features of the élite landscape they were intended to be viewed from a certain standpoint, the standpoint of the aristocratic observer.

In the nineteenth century landowners stopped adapting churches in this way, and began to look on them not so much as features within an élite landscape, but as meeting places for the rural population. At a time when social revolution and working-class radicalism were beginning to be widely feared, many landlords attempted to stimulate a sense of community which would serve to forestall dissent. The maintenance of the parish church became very important, for the church was the only place where the whole village community could come together. Within this communal space landlords could display their paternalism and benevolence, and justify their position as the 'natural leaders' of society. Moreover, the congregation could be taken to symbolize the interdependence of different social classes, and could foster a sense of community overriding class divisions and factional interests.

The growth of alternatives to Anglicanism in the nineteenth century was inevitably seen by the landed class as a threat to the stability of society. The increasing popularity of nonconformity, and in particular of Methodism, represented a challenge to the traditional institutions of patriarchal authority, and thereby to the social status quo. The connection between radicalism and nonconformity which obsessed the landed classes in the nineteenth century was not entirely imaginary. George Loveless, leader of the Tolpuddle Martyrs, and Joseph Arch, founder of the National Agricultural Labourers' Union, were both Methodist lay preachers. The growth of religious diversity seemed to symbolize social divisions, and the fragmentation of the population that was seen by the landed classes as a feature of the development of an advanced capitalist society.

The Victorian landed élite exerted all its power to prevent the proliferation of chapels and meeting houses which were believed to threaten the position of the established Church.

Such buildings were prohibited in villages where local landowners were a dominating influence. As a result, the distinctive Victorian nonconformist chapels are rarely to be seen in closed villages, but are a feature of open parishes. Few are found in those arable areas where communities were traditionally weak, but they are numerous in places like the fens, and in the pasture farming areas of the country.

Dissenting chapels generally contain few secular or religious symbols and this reflects their disavowal of the hierarchical and patriarchal structure of Anglicanism, as well as their 'low' Christian doctrines. They therefore have a cultural importance and interest equal to that of medieval parish churches, and although they tend to be off the beaten track which leads to our more orthodox heritage, many of them are

Keach's Meeting House, Winslow, Buckinghamshire
The simple interior of this baptist chapel epitomizes the quiet austerity of early nonconformist architecture. The building may date from as early as 1675, although the fittings are of eighteenth-century date.

Cholesbury, Burkinghamshire
The new parish churches built during the nineteenth century are not entirely lacking in interesting details: here the head of a Victorian soldier adorns the porch of a church constructed in 1845.

well worth a visit. One such building is Keach's Meeting House, a tiny late seventeenth-century Baptist chapel, tucked down a back alley in the market town of Winslow in Buckinghamshire. The lack of ostentation in this simply furnished building forms a striking contrast to the grandeur of our parish churches.

The landowners' antipathy to the growth of nonconformity also had a positive side, as it encouraged considerable government and private investment in church-building and restoration. Many landowners displayed their benevolent paternalism by constructing new churches or refurbishing the old, and in 1818 Parliament allocated one million pounds towards a massive programme of church construction. Many of these new churches were located in big new cities such as Manchester, Bolton and Oldham, where the population had grown rapidly since the seventeenth century, but some were also built in rural areas. In particular, they sprang up in areas like the Chiltern Hills and the Yorkshire Dales which had been poorly provided with churches in the medieval period.

These new nineteenth-century churches were almost invariably constructed in the gothic style, consciously harking back to a supposedly more harmonious medieval past. In some areas, such as the Chiltern Hills, they blend surprisingly well with the general landscape and earlier churches. They are small, and are built of the flint that is so characteristic of the region. Although they lack the complex construction of gradually evolved medieval structures, they often have distinctive and interesting decorative features. At Cholesbury in Buckinghamshire, for example, the church porch is adorned with the carved head of a dashing Victorian soldier.

As we have seen, the furnishings of churches and their funerary monuments often contain clues to the social and tenurial history of the villages that they serve. The parish church is much more than just a traditional feature within the English rural landscape, or an architectural relic: it is a communal space which has been used by the rural community for centuries, and it has been shaped by the way this community ordered itself.

TEN

The Private Landscape

BY THE NINETEENTH CENTURY most of the land of England was firmly under the control of a very small minority of the population. The landscape was no longer a patchwork of smallholdings, its exploitation no longer governed by the long established traditions of local communities. It was now largely enclosed into private fields, and exploited by standardized and efficient agricultural methods. Not only the houses, cottages and country parks, but the whole fabric of the English landscape embodied the tenurial hegemony of the landed élite. It was shaped by their aesthetic preferences, their economic interests and their leisure pursuits.

The influence of great landowners was perhaps revealed above all in what can be described as the 'great replanting'. From the seventeenth to the nineteenth century the English landed élite planted literally millions of trees, stimulated by a combination of aesthetic, economic and patriotic motives.[1] The result was a transformation of the face of the landscape. While many woodland areas had always been quite well wooded, in the eighteenth century much of the upland and champion regions was almost bare of trees. The vast majority of the many trees that are now to be seen in these areas are the consequence of the replanting that took place from the late seventeenth century.

There had been government attempts to stimulate tree-planting as early as the middle of the sixteenth century, because of concern about the scarcity of timber for shipbuilding. The most important was a statute of 1543, which required that woods contained a minimum of twelve standard (or uncoppiced) trees per acre; that they should be fenced after their timber was felled to prevent their degeneration into open pasture, and that they should not be grubbed out. None the less, it was only with the spread of enclosure and the rise of the great estates that the great replanting really got under way.

As we have already indicated, woods could only be created in landscapes that were enclosed. Their growth depended on the progressive eradication of common rights and communal agriculture, but it was also encouraged by the concomitant decline in the importance of the small landowner. Growing timber was a very long-term investment. It might be many decades before a plantation of oaks could be cropped and so this sort of land use was obviously not suitable for the farmer with only thirty or forty acres.

In the post-revolutionary decades, tree-planting was represented as a patriotic duty by the great landowners. During the course of the Commonwealth the country's stock of timber had been severely depleted. The government had felled vast quantities of trees in the royal parks and forests and on sequestrated estates, and many convicted royalists had indulged in an orgy of felling to pay their fines.

Despite the landlords' rhetoric, however, it

was not pure patriotism which led them to replant their estates in the post-revolutionary period. Some planted for profit, some for sport, and some for aesthetic reasons and it was a combination of these factors which led to the majority of eighteenth- and nineteenth-century plantings.

As many contemporary writers observed, it was ridiculous to divorce the artistic shaping of the land entirely from the concept of utility. William Marshall expressed the aristocratic ethos when he wrote in 1803 that:

> In matters of planting it was difficult to separate entirely the idea of ornament from that of use. Trees, in general, are capable of producing an ornamental effect; and there is no tree which may not be said to be more or less useful. But their difference in point of value, when arrived at maturity, is incomparable; and it would be the height of folly to plant a tree whose characteristic is principally ornamental, when another, which is more useful and equally ornamental, may be planted in its stead.[2]

Even where plantations were primarily intended to beautify the landscape, profit could be reaped from the repeated thinnings such decorative woodlands required. The nation's timber needs were therefore in part supplied by the ornamental woodlands that were created in the eighteenth and nineteenth centuries. These can still be seen, and are still producing valuable timber today. Particularly distinctive are the clumps and plantations of beech which are a feature of the downland areas of southern England, and which sometimes crown ancient archaeological features, such as Bronze Age round barrows or Iron Age hillforts. At Danebury in Hampshire, for example, or at Wandlebury Ring on the Gog Magog hills in south Cambridgeshire, the beech woods flourish within the ramparts of the Iron Age earthworks.

Not all plantations established in the eighteenth century were as obviously landscaped as these. 'Distance decay' ensured that the further a wood was sited from the centre of a great estate, the more it would be managed on primarily economic rather than aesthetic principles. Those estates that were formed from the enclosure of high moorland or light sandy soils were planted extensively, because commercial plantations made good use of this marginal land. On the Brocklesby estate in north Lincolnshire, the earls of Yarborough planted 17½ million trees between 1787 and 1889; by the end of the nineteenth century the estate contained 8000 acres of ornamental and commercial woodland.[3]

A great many of the trees planted at this time were conifers and exotics rather than traditional English hardwoods such as the oak and the elm. Scots pine trees were particularly popular. Thomas Coke got the nickname 'King Pine' from the thousands of trees which he planted in the area around Holkham in Norfolk, and William Howitt wrote in *The Rural Life in England* in 1844 that the 'sandy heaths of Surrey are covered in many places with miles of Scots Fir'.

The Scots pine was not an exotic, but it had virtually died out in England (as opposed to Scotland) by the end of the Roman period. The innumerable Scots pine trees that now grace the

OVERLEAF LEFT **Chanctonbury Ring, West Sussex**
Like many of the plantations and tree clumps in downland areas of southern England, these beech trees — sited within the Iron Age hillfort of Chanctonbury Ring — seem to have stood in the landscape from time immemorial. But they are far from ancient: like many similar groups of trees, they are a consequence of the 'great replanting' of the eighteenth and nineteenth centuries. These particular examples were planted in 1760.

OVERLEAF RIGHT **Brocklesby, Lincolnshire**
The great replanting of the eighteenth and nineteenth centuries transformed the landscape in many areas of England. On the Yarborough estate near Brocklesby 17½ million trees were planted between 1787 and 1889.

landscape of England are almost all the products of the great replanting of 1660 to 1860. The European larch and the Norway spruce, staples of modern forestry, were also introduced and widely disseminated at this time. They were brought into England during the seventeenth century, and soon became popular both in landscape parks and in the commercial plantations of the great estates. In part this was a consequence of their convenient ability to thrive on poor soils. As Howitt noted, 'even the cold hills of the Peak of Derbyshire have been planted in some parts extensively'.[4] Many thousands of acres of larch and spruce were established in Sherwood Forest after its enclosure, on the estates of Earl Manvers, Lord Scarborough, the Duke of Portland and the Duke of Newcastle.

Yet almost from their first introduction there were mixed reactions to the serried ranks of conifers. Wordsworth articulated a commonly felt objection to the planting of these softwoods on formerly productive land:

> To those who plant for profit, and are thrusting every tree out of the way to make room for their favourite, the Larch, I would utter . . . a regret, that they should have selected these lovely vales for their vegetable manufactory, when there is so much barren and irreclaimable land in the neighbouring moors, and in other parts of these islands.[5]

Nowadays many people would endorse Wordsworth's dislike of a 'vegetable manufactory', but perhaps not his suggestion that it should be confined to barren and irreclaimable land. Today vast areas of moorland have disappeared under coniferous plantations and the remaining open country is a much valued part of the environment.

Humphry Repton was also an early opponent of the pine. He used conifers sparingly in his landscape designs, but he became increasingly hostile to the spread of these non-indigenous trees. Like many of his contemporaries he associated the slow-growing hardwoods, and, in particular, the sturdy English oak, with long-established landed families, traditional values and landed wealth. Investment in indigenous timber was an investment for the distant future, and represented faith in the stability of society and the system of property ownership. There would be no point planting a group of oaklings if you did not think your descendants would be able to reap the great profits that could be made from the full-grown trees. In contrast, the fast-growing softwoods symbolized the philosophy of small profits and quick returns. They were associated with parvenues and the upwardly mobile elements of society that were pushing their way into the landed élite from the world of commerce and industry. These people were accused of having brought their commercial instincts into the realm of agricultural production, and it was thought that they had neither the patience of the old landowners nor their faith in the status quo.

The use of trees and the imagery of trees had important political connotations in the eighteenth and nineteenth centuries, and revealed society's ambiguous attitudes to change and economic growth. The decision whether to create deciduous or coniferous plantations was based on a combination of practical economic considerations, such as the rate at which the landlord would require a return on his investment, and personal preferences that were both political and aesthetic. Some landlords regarded conifers as symbols of the new society, some clung to the hardwoods as relics of the old. In this way, the élite landscape shows clearly the interdependence of economic, political and aesthetic ideas.

Not all landlords chose to create plantations. On many estates the standing timber was scattered about the agricultural landscape, beautifying the fields and hedgerows, but also providing the landowner with profit. This form of planting became particularly popular in the late eighteenth and nineteenth century, but it developed from an early eighteenth-century feature of the landscape known as the *ferme ornée*.

The *ferme ornée* was initially devised for those who had insufficient means to create parks in the grand manner. Ornamental features were created amidst what was basically a working farm. A grassy walk would lead the visitor past the beauties of the place, past trees, ruins, gothic buildings, bridges or alcoves, and there would be seats situated in strategic positions which would provide prospects over the landscape.

The most famous example of the *ferme ornée* was that created by William Shenstone in the 1740s at The Leasowes in Hagley near Birmingham. This was widely copied and many eighteenth-century landowners attempted some limited degree of landscape ornamentation. As time passed, however, the *ferme ornée* became progressively less *ornée*, as the style simplified into more general attempts to combine beauty with utility. Landowners began to concentrate less on the picturesque ruins and gothic garden features, and more on the planting of trees and the beautification of practical agricultural buildings.

The kind of general landscaping which descended from the *ferme ornée* and the pleasure farm seems to have been far more widespread and to have had a far greater influence on the appearance of the landscape than is generally recognized. It was a feature of the home farms of the great estates, and of other agricultural land which bordered on the estate centre, as well as of the estates of small landowners. Although only minor alterations were made to the landscape, which were insignificant in themselves, they had a considerable impact on the agricultural environment. This 'picturesque farming' epitomized the incorporation of aesthetic and economic considerations, as Thomas Ruggles indicated in his articles on the subject in the *Annals of Agriculture*.[6]

One type of tree planting which Ruggles describes as characteristic of the picturesque style was the extension of hedgerows to round the corners and blur the edges of geometrically-shaped arable fields. This often involved the establishment of small patches of standing trees, and these tended to be conifers such as the Scots pine, the larch, the silver fir and the Weymouth pine. These species were thought to have an intrinsic beauty, they were profitable, and they could serve as 'nurses' for the more slow-growing deciduous trees. As well as the planting of small patches of trees, Ruggles recommended the various species which he believed would best beautify the agricultural landscape. He suggested that brooks and meadow lands should be planted with planes and with white and Lombardy poplar, and that bare pools should be ornamented with the weeping willow.

Picturesque planting of this kind can cause confusion in the interpretation of the landscape of today. In the Weald of Kent and Sussex, for example, and in parts of Hertfordshire and Essex, features often known as shaws are dispersed amongst the fields. These consist of long strips of woodland up to fifty feet in width. They have an air of immense antiquity, seeming to be residual survivors from the great primeval wildwood, and indeed many of them are very old. But some originated in the tree-planting schemes of the late eighteenth and nineteenth centuries.[7] Similarly, the fashion for planting and replanting hedges with the wide range of indigenous shrubs recommended by Ruggles can cause problems for those who believe it is possible to date a hedgerow by counting the number of species it contains.

On many occasions, however, the landscaping of an area involved the removal rather than the addition of hedgerows, as well as the destruction of many hedgerow trees. Ruggles was on the whole opposed to the presence of trees in hedgerows, and believed that where such trees existed they should not be 'in regular order and distance as cabbages are planted; they should rather crowd into clumps, leaving here and there, one of particular beauty by itself'. In his view, as the new plantations on the farm grew to maturity, the hedgerow trees would become redundant and could therefore be cut down.

The countryside around country houses shows that this aspect of Ruggles' advice was not widely accepted. The hedges in these areas usually contain large numbers of evenly-spaced trees which were clearly planted in the late eighteenth and nineteenth centuries. But the form of these trees indicates that Ruggles' strongly felt antipathy to pollarded trees was more widely shared. This prejudice was partly based on economic considerations. Ruggles believed that the dense shade produced by pollarding would harm growing crops and that the spreading branches would harbour hungry birds. In addition the repeated pollarding of trees was believed to damage the quality of the standing timber, and the landlords of the eighteenth and nineteenth century generally had no need for the poles, apart from in Kent where they were used for growing hops. Although pollards were a valuable source of firewood for the poor, the rich were able to use coal and were not dependent on wood for fuel.

Above all, Ruggles objected to pollarded trees on the basis that they were ugly. 'Let the axe fall', he exclaimed, 'with undistinguished severity on all these mutilated trees.' This was not an abstract aesthetic judgement. The upper classes seem to have regarded pollards as unattractive because by the eighteenth century they were a particular feature of common land. Unlike the new plantations, they symbolized the traditional systems of communal control over the exploitation of land.

Discreet landscaping involving the planting of certain types of tree and the shaping of woods and hedgerows went on to a certain extent all over the country. It was especially popular in the immediate vicinity of country houses, and with those whose educated aesthetic sense and taste for landscape design were not matched by their resources in either cash or land. Clergymen in particular were enthusiastic advocates of picturesque farming, and the hedges of many glebelands betray their attempts at aesthetic planting.

Picturesque farming had the greatest impact, however, on the landscape in the south and east, and in particular in the home counties of Hertfordshire, Buckinghamshire, Surrey, Sussex and Kent. Here there were large numbers of resident gentry, who frequently occupied relatively small estates. These areas had traditionally carried a woodland landscape of ancient hedges and long-established trees. Unlike the newly-enclosed landscapes of the champion regions, they were ripe for the subtle adornments of the picturesque treatment. They did not require total reconstruction or complete landscaping, but merely a few sympathetic alterations, to ensure that their natural beauty and character were brought out.

The landscape of the eighteenth and nineteenth centuries was therefore transformed by the great replanting, as the landed élite responded to a variety of political, social and aesthetic stimuli. At the same time the countryside was undergoing considerable alterations as a result of a much more specific cause — the landed élite's obsession with ritual slaughter.

The countryside has been used for recreational purposes as far back as we can trace. As well as the deer-hunting of the élite, it has traditionally been the scene of a whole host of rural sports. In the early eighteenth century, for example, John Bridges recorded that 198 of the 290 parishes he visited in Northamptonshire had annual feasts which involved such activities as wrestling, boxing, cock-fighting, bull-baiting, dancing and the chasing of a greased pig.[8] It was customary for many villages to hold violent football matches involving up to a hundred players with goals several miles apart. With the spread of enclosure, however, and in particular with the demise of many village greens, rural communities were increasingly deprived of the space in which to hold such activities, and rural sports became the preserve of the landed rich.

In the medieval period game laws had

restricted the right to hunt to those whose property was worth 40 shillings per annum. In 1671, following a series of further laws, this was set at £100 for freeholders and £150 for tenants. In an unenclosed landscape, however, the poaching of small game was both difficult to detect and difficult to stop. It appears that villagers frequently hunted on their local wastes and commons and that there was a certain amount of toleration for these regular infringements of the law. By the eighteenth and nineteenth centuries, however, the situation was very different. The spread of enclosure denied the poor access to those areas which they had been accustomed to poach, but also made it

Castle Acre, Norfolk
These circular beech plantations were established on an outlying part of the Holkham estate in the early nineteenth century.

possible for hunting to be organized on a much more serious basis. Covers could be created within an enclosed landscape in which game (in particular pheasants) could be reared and sheltered. At the same time, with the development of the flintlock gun, shooting became ever more popular among the élite.

The large numbers of plump, hand-reared pheasants which roosted in the coverts provided a considerable temptation to the less fortunate, particularly after enclosure had contributed to widespread rural poverty. Draconian laws against poaching were introduced in the eighteenth and nineteenth centuries, and coverts began to be protected by man-traps and spring-guns. Laws of 1828 and 1831 served to temper the severity of these Game Laws a little, but none the less hunting was almost exclusively the preserve of the rich throughout the nineteenth century. This caused considerable hardship not only to the poor, but also to tenant farmers. They were not usually allowed to destroy the pheasants, partridges, hares and rabbits which fattened themselves on their fields, although the more enlightened estates sometimes compensated them for the losses that they sustained, or allowed a certain amount of controlled culling. It was not until the passing of the Ground Game Act of 1881 that tenants were able to destroy hares and rabbits without their landlord's permission.

The immense enthusiasm for hunting which swept the landed classes in the eighteenth and nineteenth centuries had a considerable and often little recognized impact on the appearance and organization of the landscape. In the nineteenth century large areas of the great estates, particularly those on light sandy soils, were used for the intensive production of pheasants, hares, partridges and rabbits and were planted up with belts and coverts in which these creatures could live. Mrs Cresswell, a tenant of the Sandringham estate, described the county of Norfolk in the 1860s as 'almost entirely a game-preserve'. In her book *Eighteen Years on the Sandringham Estate* she gives a detailed account of the alterations that were made to the estate in order to improve the shooting when it was taken over by the Prince of Wales (later Edward VII) in 1863:

> Strips were cut across my fields like a gridiron, and planted for game shelters, and until the trees were sufficiently grown to smother them a mass of noxious weeds grew . . . no one being allowed to cut them for fear of disturbing the nesting.

As a result of these changes Mrs Cresswell's crops were spoilt, but the Prince of Wales raised the annual 'bag' of the shoot from 7000 to 30,000 creatures.[9]

Dead pheasants at Studley Royal, North Yorkshire
The game wagon is being loaded after a two-day shoot for six guns organized by the second Marquis of Ripon in 1901.

The majority of the coverts were planted with coniferous trees. These provided better shelter for the game than deciduous hardwoods, because they did not shed their leaves in winter. Beneath the standing timber and around the edges of the covert shrubs were planted, such as holly, privet, elder, snowberry, rhododendron and cotoneaster, providing the dense, low growth that pheasants in particular required.

There were various disputes over the form which coverts should take, and the shape which would maximize the number of creatures that presented themselves to the waiting guns. Long, thin coverts like those which were planted in many parts of Norfolk tended to be unsatisfactory. Once the hand-rearing of pheasants became customary, the plump birds were often afflicted with an understandable aversion to flight, so that when beaters went into the covert the pheasants kept out of the line of fire by walking down the length of the wood. As a result, many estates experimented with smaller, more compact blocks of woodland, separated with wide glades, across which the pheasants could be driven into flight.

In many places, the quality of shooting was improved by the adaptation of old woods rather than the creation of new ones. Additional trees, and in particular pines, were planted together with shrubs for ground-cover such as the rhododendron. Alleys or rides were cut through the woods and many of these can still be seen today, sometimes being mistaken for medieval features where they run through ancient woods.

During the nineteenth century the shooting of rabbits also became fashionable and many estates created artificial warrens in order to encourage them to breed. These consisted of mounds or banks of earth, and were sometimes very elaborate. Some included ditches to facilitate drainage, and even bridges so that the rabbits could cross the ditches easily.[10]

But it is the story of the rise of fox-hunting that most clearly dramatizes the themes at the centre of this book: the progressive privatization of the landscape, the gradual spread of enclosure, the disappearance of the small owner-occupier, and the increasing dominance of the landholding system by a small, élite group of people. These developments both encouraged and are revealed in the changes that took place in fox-hunting from the medieval period to the nineteenth century.[11]

In the Middle Ages fox-hunting did not have the élite connotations it has now. It was primarily seen as a means of pest-control, and often involved the whole village community, who would descend on the fox, armed with sticks. When the gentry held recreational fox hunts the idea was to keep the fox within the covert, rather than to chase it across the fields. The sport was based on the exhumation of the fox from its earth, and most of the thrill seems to have come from lying on the ground and listening to an underground battle between the fox and the terriers that had been sent down after it.

In the course of the eighteenth century, however, fox-hunting began to resemble its modern form, with the fox being chased over long distances and prevented from going to ground. Various theories have been advanced as to why this change in the basis of the sport should have taken place at this time. It has been suggested that the development of faster horses, and of dogs that were both fast and good at scenting, made possible the evolution of the chase. Although these factors were clearly important, they seem to have been dependent on a more fundamental change — in the structure of the ownership of land. The fox-hunt as an extended chase would have been difficult to institute if England, like France, had been owned by large numbers of small freeholders. But the existence of many very sizeable estates meant that long interrupted runs need only involve the property of a few rich individuals who were in sympathy with the sport.

The new form of hunting was first developed and extensively practised in the 'shire' counties of Leicestershire, Northamptonshire, Lincoln-

ABOVE **The Meet**
This print by Henry Alken gives some idea of how the East Midlands landscape must have looked immediately after enclosure. The countryside was still very open, and as a result early fox hunts involved riding very fast across the flat. Leaping fences was not considered a proper part of the sport.

shire and the old county of Rutland. Here there were very few freeholders and the landholding structure was dominated by wealthy squires and great estates. Furthermore much of the land in these areas was put down to grass in the eighteenth century, and grassland was particularly good country for hunting. Horses could be ridden fast on turf and dogs could pick up the fox's scent fairly easily. It was thus in a eulogistic vein that the great fox-hunting writer and enthusiast Surtees described the East Midland shire counties as 'grass, grass, grass, nothing but grass for miles and miles'.[12]

The evolution of the fox-hunt seems to have been partly encouraged by changes in the landscape, and it is possible to link developments in the form of the hunt with alterations in the countryside. In the late eighteenth century, many of the shire counties still had a very open appearance, for although large areas had been enclosed, they were often not immediately subdivided into small fields. In some places there were hundreds of acres of former common or open field, which were simply surrounded by a ring fence and put down to grass. The eighteenth-century fox-hunt therefore consisted of a very fast chase across open country, with hardly any jumps. As Surtees commented at the time, 'real sportsmen take no pleasure in leaping'.

From the eighteenth century to the nineteenth century the landscape was progressively subdivided, and hedges and ditches became common features. Ditches not only served as obstacles, but also resulted in drier, firmer turf.

Horses could now gallop faster than before, but their riders had to negotiate the hazards of hedge and ditch. Jumping these natural obstacles and trying to follow a straight course across a subdivided landscape therefore came to be seen as very much part of the thrill of hunting. At the same time the growing importance of the idea of the English village as an organic community meant that fox-hunting was seen as a recreational activity in which the whole community could participate. Tenant farmers were usually able to take part in the sport, and the poor were often permitted to follow on foot.

BELOW **Snob is Beat**
Another of Alken's prints indicates how the nature of the fox hunt changed as the landscape was gradually enclosed. As the number of hedges in the countryside increased, the ability to negotiate these obstacles began to be valued.

It seems likely that the lack of standard trees in the hedgerows of Leicestershire and the old county of Rutland is in part a consequence of the importance of fox-hunting in these areas.[13] Landowners were probably reluctant to encourage such trees in any substantial numbers, because they would tend to interfere with the chase. Furthermore, the landscape of these counties is dotted with small patches of woodland, created as covers in the nineteenth century to stimulate an increase in the fox population after its dramatic decline in the eighteenth century.[14] The enclosure of open heathland had deprived the fox of much of its natural habitat, at the same time as it was being pressurized by fox-hunts and also by the gamekeepers of pheasant shoots. In some places the lack of indigenous foxes was made up for by the use of 'bagmen'. These were foxes that were brought into an area and released for the chase, although in many circles this practice was thought to be unsporting.

Covers therefore fulfilled an important function in providing foxes with a much-needed haven where they could breed undisturbed, and they also provided the huntsmen with a place where they were almost sure of finding a fox. In the areas where woods were abundant the hunts often rented patches of woodland, which could be used as covers, but in areas like the East Midlands where woods were scarce in the eighteenth century most of the covers had to be planted from scratch. Nowadays they tend to consist of fairly dense woodland, but they were originally made up of low scrub and, in particular, gorse, with only a few trees planted for ornamental purposes. This provided the foxes with excellent cover, and discouraged those who might be tempted to steal the cubs for bagmen.

Of course, covers harboured not only foxes, but all kinds of other creatures, many of which fed on the crops of local tenant farmers. On Abbeycroft Down near Wimbourne in Dorset, for example, about seventy acres of land were set aside for a fox cover in the mid nineteenth century. Within a few years it was said to be home to 50,000 rabbits.[15]

Elsewhere the hunts went so far as to construct artificial earths for foxes to live in. These were sometimes elaborate constructions, with brick-lined dens and passages, often topped with a circular mound, and are occasionally mistaken for prehistoric burial mounds. One on Stanmore Common in Greater London, for example, has caused considerable archaeological speculation, but its name, 'The Fox Earth', indicates that it was built to shelter foxes by the local Old Berkely Hunt.

Kennel blocks were added to many country houses in the eighteenth and nineteenth centuries to house the local pack of hounds. Like many estate buildings, these were often designed to blend in with the status landscape and were constructed in extravagant gothic or picturesque styles. At Milton Park, at Castor in Cambridgeshire, for example, the kennels were built in 1767 in the form of a medieval gatehouse. This curious edifice has a great round tower of undressed stone, castellations, low lattice windows and buttresses.

Nevertheless, the most aristocratic form of hunting remained the 'sport of kings', the slaughter of deer, an occupation which caused considerable social upheaval in the eighteenth century.[16] The special measures which protected royal deer, and the restrictions on the exploitation of the forest lands in which they lived, frequently conflicted with the customary rights of the inhabitants of these areas. There were numerous disputes over whether villagers should have the right to gather turf or wood within the forests, and the damage done to crops by the roaming deer — particularly the large and voracious red deer — was a regular source of contention. As a result, forest law was frequently flouted in the eighteenth century, and, in the 1720s in particular, various acts of violence were committed against the timber, deer and keepers of the royal forests. As E.P. Thompson has indicated in his fascinating study *Whigs and Hunters*, a number of the offenders were not from the ranks of the poor and dispossessed but were lesser gentry, artisans and yeomen. They resented being deprived of what they regarded as their traditional rights by the corrupt officials of the forest authorities, who were often themselves notorious for embezzling the king's deer and timber.

The resistance of the villagers was savagely answered in 1723 by the passing of the bloodthirsty 'Black Act'. This created around fifty new capital offences, including the hunting, poaching or wounding of deer; the wearing of disguise or carrying of arms 'in any forest, chase, park, paddock, or grounds inclosed with any wall, pale or other fence, wherein any deer have been or shall be usually kept, or in any warren or place where hares or conies have been or shall be usually kept, or in any high road, open heath, common or down'; the cutting down of trees 'planted in any avenue, or growing in any garden or plantation for ornament, shelter or profit'; the burning of any house, barn or haystack; and the sending of anonymous letters demanding 'money, venison, or other valuable thing'. As an eminent legal historian has noted, 'It is very doubtful whether any other country possessed a criminal code with anything like so many capital provisions as there were in this single statute.'[17]

Following the passing of the Black Act, numerous people were executed or transported, but the royal forests continued to be gradually eaten away, as courtiers and members of the forest authorities sold the trees and cleared the wastes to make way for arable. Moreover, despite the legal penalties in many areas the village communities continued to exert what they believed to be their rights to the forest, cutting turf, fern and heath, and taking gravel and sand. Little by little, the great forests in areas such as Windsor and Hampshire shrank, and lost much of their tree cover. Most forests which survived into the nineteenth century were finally removed as a result parliamentary enclosure, so that only vestiges now remain of most of these former arenas of royal sport.

Whatever we may feel about the morality of killing animals for pleasure and about the psychology of the people who do it, hunting has clearly had a considerable impact on the landscape of rural England. Fox covers, pheasant coverts, deer parks, rides, forests and warrens were introduced for the specific purpose of fostering rural sports and many of these features are still extremely common. Indeed, the continued importance of shooting is directly responsible for the survival of vast quantities of woodland in southern England and of moorland in the north. These areas provide telling evidence of the way in which the landscape has been dominated and shaped by a wealthy landed élite, and by considerations which were not purely economic or environmental. It was only once the land was firmly in the hands of the rich that it could be exploited for pleasure or shaped to meet aesthetic preferences. Enclosure and the rise of the great estates not only brought about changes in the appearance of the landscape, but altered the whole conceptual framework governing the use of land.

The increasing importance of rural sports for both gentry and aristocracy was part of a more general tendency to demonstrate status by an association with the agricultural landscape. Fox covers, picturesque villages and farm buildings were all products of the same social phenomenon, stimulated by changes in the pattern of land ownership. The aesthetic taste of the landed élite created the whimsical rural world of the model village. But it also operated to protect this world from the realities of a commercial and increasingly industrial England. In particular, many landowners sought to prevent the disruption of their estate landscape by the corruptive incursions of the railway.

The transport improvements of the seventeenth and eighteenth centuries brought by the Turnpike Trusts and the canals had been both passively and actively supported by a great many of the most important landowners. The Duke of Bridgewater commissioned James Brindley's canal from the coal mines of Worsley to Manchester in 1760, and it has been estimated that the gentry made up just under a third of the shareholders in eighteenth-century canal schemes.[18] Many members of the landed classes also invested in the railway construction programmes of the nineteenth century, especially in industrializing areas like the Black Country, but in general they were unsympathetic to this new mode of transport. Even the investors were anxious to prevent the lines from traversing their own estates.

In 1844 George Hudson, the 'railway king', planned a railway line that would run from York to Bridlington. The most convenient route passed near Boynton, where the wealthy landowner Sir George Strickland had his seat. Strickland wrote to Hudson that the railway line:

> would be totally destructive of that place which has been the residence of my ancestors and family

for five hundred years. I should, therefore, feel it to be my duty to my family and to myself to make every exertion in my power, and to spend all the money I could afford, in opposition to a plan so injurious to myself and, as I believe, uncalled for by the general public.[19]

Many landowners believed that the railways would damage their economic interests, as well as the peace and the landscape of their parks. A great many estates ran a monopoly over the supply of goods such as coal or building materials to their tenants, and it was thought that the railways would open up these lucrative markets. Moreover, it was widely feared that the railways would alter the water levels in the countryside and disrupt the pattern of farming.

Opposition to the railways was, however, less rooted in practical economic considerations than in a general distrust of the new, commercial society. Railways were seen as the tentacles of progress, reaching out from corrupt and dirty cities to the supposedly harmonious communities of the countryside. Or they were arteries, along which ran not only the spirit of industrialism, but also radicalism and that particularly pernicious form of corruption, democracy. 'I rejoice in it', remarked Dr Arnold, as he watched a train draw out of Rugby, 'and think that feudality is gone for ever.' Others thought the same but were less enthusiastic about it. They believed that the railways would spread dissatisfaction among the rural poor, by widening their horizons and bringing disruptive elements (and in particular navvies) into formerly peaceful areas.

The landed élite were rarely able to prevent railways from being constructed, but their influence over the land is revealed by the many instances where they prevented lines from running within sight of their parks. Some of the greatest feats of the nineteenth-century railway engineers were necessitated not by geological or geographical factors, but by the aesthetic predispositions of the landed classes. Thus the mile long tunnel with ornamental portals to the north of Watford, on the London to Birmingham line, had to be built because the Earl of Essex and Lord Clarendon refused to allow the railway to follow the valley of the River Gade. Had it done so it would have cut through their parks. Many workmen lost their lives in the construction of the tunnel.

One landowner who was particularly vigorous in his opposition to the construction of railways was Lord Harborough. When the Midland Railway decided to construct a line from Leicester to Peterborough which would run through his seat Stapleford Park, Harborough mounted an armed guard to prevent the surveyors from entering his land. Thus the line that was finally approved by parliament included a great diversion around Harborough's estate, which came to be known as 'Lord Harborough's Curve'.

Ordnance Survey maps reveal many such exertions of power in the land. A railway line will be following the course of a river valley, and then will suddenly veer off into the hills on one side, only returning to the relatively level ground of the valley after a distance of a couple of miles. Such meanderings are usually explained by the proximity of a country house and park. Elsewhere lines pass through cuttings or tunnels so as not to disrupt the view from a park. In south Cambridgeshire and northwest Essex the Cambridge to Liverpool Street railway line runs along the valley of the River Cam, but just to the north of the village of Littlebury the line leaves the valley and passes through a series of substantial cuttings and embankments and two tunnels before it returns to the valley near Audley End station. This diversion seems to have been created to ensure that the railway would avoid the vicinity of Audley End House, the seat of the Braybrooke family, which stands in the valley of the Cam. Where the landowner did not have the money or influence to force a railway company to construct a detour round his estate, he had to rest content with planting a line of trees, behind which passing trains could be at least partially concealed.

Landowners were usually not too proud to take advantage of a railway, even though they wanted it out of sight, and in many cases they persuaded the railway company to build a station within a short distance of their house. Furthermore, a number of stations were built in a style that would blend in with the architecture of the surrounding estate. At Waverton in Cheshire, for example, the station is an attractive single-storey building with a steeply-pitched roof, tall twisting chimneys and spiked finials, to harmonize with the buildings on the Duke of Westminster's estate of Eaton Hall. Somerleyton in Suffolk, Alton Towers in Staffordshire and Brocklesby Park in Humberside have similarly elaborate stations, and these curious buildings are striking symbols of the durability of landed power in the industrial age.[20] The development of new forms of wealth, and the absorption of new types of landowners into the landholding structure, seems only to have stimulated new forms of landscape manipulation, rather than to have challenged the influence of the great estates over the land.

Brocklesby, Humberside
The architecture of Brocklesby station was designed to accord with the style of building on the Yarborough estate.

ELEVEN

The Modern Landscape: Destruction and Decline

FROM THE END OF the nineteenth century to the present day the landscape has continued to change. With rising population and increasing industrialization large areas of the countryside have disappeared under roads, housing and industry. These new developments have caused a considerable contraction in the rural landscape, but they have not been instrumental in altering its essence. The primary influence over its appearance is the same process which has been shaping the environment for the last 5000 years. Farming created the countryside and gave it its fascinating diversity, and now farming is destroying it. Although many of the features within the landscape — the churches, chapels, country houses and cottages — have survived, much of the basic fabric has disappeared over recent years. Fields, woods, hedges and footpaths have fallen victim to the intensification of agriculture, and in this last sad chapter of our narrative as much as in our first, the patterns of landscape change are connected with the patterns of power in the land.

For most of the nineteenth century farmers in England were generally successful. Some came unstuck after the Napoleonic Wars, having borrowed too heavily in the boom years of the height of the conflict, but from the 1830s both arable and livestock producers flourished. This was the era of Victorian high farming, but during the 1870s the halcyon days of prosperity came to a halt, and agriculture moved into depression.[1]

The decline in farming profits was at first attributed to the weather, which had resulted in a series of bad harvests. But it was not long before it became apparent that rather more complex and serious causes were at work. In particular, agricultural decline was connected with the inability of English farmers to compete with cheap imports from Argentina, Australia, New Zealand and the American prairies. These countries were able to export vast quantities of agricultural goods because of improvements in the technology of transport and the decline in the cost of freightage. As a result the sale price of cattle and sheep dropped by between 25 and 35 per cent between 1875 and 1895, and the prices of wool and wheat were halved. Moreover, as the profits of agriculture dwindled, investment was diverted from farming into manufacturing industry. Many tenant farmers went to the wall as the price of their products plummeted. As a result, agricultural rents declined and farms became increasingly hard to let.

However, while arable farmers were failing, particularly in the big grain-producing areas of the south and east, their fellows in the dairying areas of the country were managing to do fairly well. They were not so drastically affected by foreign competition because of the perishable nature of their produce, and they were also able to cash in on the rising demand for dairy products from the growing population of the towns and cities. Moreover, they now had access to low-priced grain with which to feed their stock. Indeed, there was a considerable expansion in the amount of land that was under both permanent and temporary grass in the late nineteenth century.[2]

But the threat that was posed to the landed élite at the end of the nineteenth century was more than just economic. Not only were their ruined tenants failing to pay their rents, but there was some diminution in the extent of their political power. This was partly because the nineteenth-century Reform acts had brought about the gradual extension of the franchise, while reforms in the organization of local government had limited their local authority. Such political changes were part and parcel of a gradual alteration in attitudes to both landowners and the land. As the urban and commercial middle classes became increasingly numerous and vociferous in the nineteenth century, they began to question the privileged position of the agricultural interest. They dismissed the idea that great landowners were the natural legislators of the country, and scorned the theory that agriculture was the basis of national wealth.

In many ways, the repeal of the Corn Laws in 1845 was the writing on the wall for landowners and farmers. The Corn Laws had restricted the importation of grain until domestic prices reached a certain level, and were thus intended to safeguard the profits of farmers and landlords at the expense of the rest of the population. Their repeal represented a shift in the balance of political power away from the agricultural sector, and by the 1870s the results of this shift were coming home to roost.

Just as great landowners were beginning to feel the first effects of the economic squeeze, an increasing number of people were questioning their right to own so much of the country's land. In the newly-reformed Parliament of the 1870s the 'land question' became a hot political issue. Reformists complained that the land of Britain was under the control of an élite of only 30,000 people. It was in order to refute such claims that Lord Derby instituted what came to be known as the 'New Domesday', a complete survey of property ownership. The results of this survey came as a surprise to everyone, and not least to Lord Derby himself, for it revealed that more than 80 per cent of the land in Britain was under the control, not of 30,000, but of a mere 7000 landowners.[3]

Of course this survey strengthened the case of the liberal complainants, who continued to clamour for some measure of land reform. The first direct measures came in Lloyd George's famous budget of 1908, in which he introduced various new taxes on land. These were designed to loosen the stranglehold of the élite on the landholding system and they seem to have contributed to the change in property ownership that followed. Land sales increased considerably between 1910 and 1914; and from 1918 to 1922, in the wake of World War I, the land market reached a level of activity unequalled since the Dissolution. In these four years many great estates were broken up, and as much as 25 per cent of the land of England changed hands.

Most of this land was bought by the tenant farmers by whom it had formerly been worked. As a result, while only 10 per cent of the farmland in England and Wales was in owner-occupation before World War I, by 1927 this proportion had risen to over 35 per cent. Even so, the majority of farmland was still in the hands of tenants.

World War I and its immediate aftermath brought a brief flurry of prosperity to English agriculture, but by 1922 farming had returned to a state of slump. In many parts of the country the land was undercultivated and unkempt. Hedges grew high and wide in unmanaged abandon, and wild flowers (i.e. weeds) proliferated in the fields. Some pieces of land went out of cultivation altogether, and many former arable fields were put down to grass.

Soldiers clearing scrub in 1917
World War I provided a short interlude in the agricultural depression of the late nineteenth and early twentieth centuries. This photograph shows soldiers clearing bushes from disused farmland, as part of a campaign to expand domestic food production during the war.

The current view of changes that have taken place in the modern landscape has been coloured by memories of the countryside in the interwar years. Many people hark back to a time when great tracts of the country were grassland, and contrast accounts or memories of the landscape of the 1920s with the arable expanses of today. Yet this is a slightly misleading comparison in view of the fact that the farmland of England was abnormally under-used in the 1920s.

In the 1930s agriculture became more profitable, following the government's intervention in 1932 to support the price of wheat. This action was motivated by fears of impending war, but it was only after the war had actually started that the fortunes of farmers really began to improve. While hostilities lasted the State was directly involved in many aspects of the organization of agriculture. Moreover, the food shortages which afflicted Europe in the post-war period persuaded the government that it was necessary to maintain an effective agricultural industry and that the production of food was too important to be left to market forces.

This concern led to the 1947 Agriculture Act, which guaranteed certain prices to be paid to farmers. The State made up the difference between a pre-arranged price and that which agricultural products were fetching in the market-place. This ensured that farmers were kept in business, but also that the price of food was kept down by inexpensive imports. The scheme benefited arable more than pastoral agriculture, and brought about an increase in the amount of land that was put to the plough.

In 1973, when Britain joined the EEC, this

method of price support was changed. Under the European system, agricultural products also have a target price, but the policy is not to make up the difference to farmers when market values fall below this. Instead intervention agencies buy up all the surplus at the target price, until demand forces prices to rise again. This scheme can only work with considerable import controls, and as well as driving up the price of goods it is ruinously expensive. The European Community has to buy quantities of produce which it cannot use, and also has to pay exorbitant costs for storage.

The maintenance of agriculture is, however, one of the major aims, perhaps *the* major aim, of EEC policy. The price support system in fact consumes over 65 per cent of the total EEC budget, and on top of this member governments give their own farmers various forms of additional aid. In Britain, for example, agricultural land is exempt from the payment of rates.

After World War II, therefore, farming moved into the black, and by the 1970s it was positively booming. This has had various consequences for the pattern of landholding. The new stability and profitability stimulated technological improvements, and in particular the spread of the tractor and the combine harvester. Modern machinery and equipment involves considerable capital investment and is also geared towards use over substantial acreages, so the area of land which can be economically worked as a farm has inevitably increased. This trend has also been actively encouraged by the EEC and the government, with the provision of grants towards the amalgamation of holdings, and with a system of subsidies heavily biased towards the largest and most productive farms.

None the less, this general picture masks considerable regional variations. In predominantly arable areas farms are generally large, often several thousand acres in size, whereas those farms devoted to dairying or livestock production are usually very much smaller. The tenurial system has also influenced the amount of amalgamation which has taken place. Farms in areas which have long contained large numbers of small owner-occupiers were not consolidated as easily or as quickly as those in regions where tenant farmers predominated.

The changes that have taken place in agriculture over the last seventy years have brought about considerable alterations in the nature of land ownership. In particular there has been an increase in the number of farms that are in owner-occupation, so that at present around 70 per cent of the land in England is farmed by its owner. This is only in part the result of tenant farmers buying their farms, for the great estates have not continued to fragment at the rate that they did in the 1920s. An important reason why this figure is so high is that many of the great landowners have taken very large quantities of land under their direct control. Far from being confined to the home farms of the nineteenth century, many estate farm companies now work lands that were formerly divided between a multiplicity of small tenants. Despite the upheavals in agriculture over the last century, many of the great estates are therefore alive and well, and our landholding system continues to be dominated by a few very powerful individuals. Even today around 60 per cent of the land in Britain is owned by less than 0.5 per cent of the population.

On the other hand the middling landowners, the gentry, have gone into decline since the 1920s and recent years have seen a rise in the amount of land in the hands of institutions. In the last decades land has provided one of the safest investments available and city institutions, pension funds and trade unions have been investing heavily in it. Land is particularly attractive to institutions because, unlike individuals, they cannot die, and so are not subject to the burden of capital transfer tax.

One of the consequences of the artificial profitability and increased commercialization of agriculture is that investment has been directed away from manufacturing industry and the inner cities. These factors have also tended to encourage the emergence of purely commercial concepts of both landholding and the land. Institutional landholders and large agribusiness farmers have a very different attitude to property from that of the eighteenth- and nineteenth-century landed magnates. The average pension fund sees land only as a financial asset and has not the slightest interest in using the landscape to display wealth and status. Many institutions have therefore taken control of the farmland of earlier estates, without the more elegant appendages of the parkland and country house. The same is also true of many members of the landed élite, who still exploit ancestral acres, but have disposed of the ancestral home. Some country houses have been demolished or allowed to fall into disrepair, while others are supported by the heritage industry or have been turned into public schools, research establishments, hotels, health farms, religious retreats, adult education centres, art centres, luxury flats or homes for hi-tech industries.[4] Many of the parks designed by Brown and Repton have been found to make excellent golf courses, such as those at Ashridge and Moor Park in Hertfordshire, but many more have been ploughed up in the past fifty years.

The tie between élite landscapes and the source of wealth which maintained them has been gradually severed. The automatic assumption that the owner of a country house will be a substantial landowner no longer holds. In the increasingly specialized modern economy the integrated landed estate has lost its social and economic rationale. It no longer embodies the involvement of its owner in all aspects of rural life and is no longer used to display status or the taste and wealth of its possessor. Land is merely an economic resource which conveys no obligations and responsibilities. Individual and institutional farmers, as well as national and European powers, have propagated the idea that the only function of land is to produce food. Moreover, since there is an artificially unlimited market for the products of agriculture, there is no incentive to consider ways in which land could be used to satisfy a wide range of needs.

The destruction of the landscape which has been so widely and so justifiably lamented is therefore a consequence of a combination of economic factors, developments in farming technology and new attitudes to land. In the absence of normal market conditions agricultural production has escalated, with farmers encouraged to introduce all kinds of new methods to increase their own returns. Almost all the innovations have tended to result in further despoilation of the countryside.[5]

Hedgerows have suffered particularly badly. Large machines, and in particular combine harvesters, can only be effective in very large fields, so the use of increasingly large machinery has necessitated the removal of thousands of miles of these formerly characteristic features of our landscape. Furthermore, as agriculture has become highly mechanized, there has been a decline in mixed farming. Farmers cannot afford to invest in the plant that is appropriate for carrying on both arable and pastoral enterprises, while the availability of all sorts of artificial fertilizers means that arable farmers are no longer dependent on dung. They do not need to keep animals and so they have no need for hedges — no barrier is necessary to prevent the barley from getting into the wheat. Hedges have become not only redundant but a nuisance, and until fairly recently financial inducements were offered to farmers to destroy them.

While the mixed farming and predominantly arable areas have been becoming increasingly monocultural, large acreages of formerly pastoral land have been converted to arable agriculture. This process started before World War II, but intensified considerably in the 1960s and 1970s. The grass shires of the Midlands, and in particular Northamptonshire and Leicestershire, are being increasingly used for the production of cereals, and large tracts of chalk downland have fallen under the plough, in many cases for the first time since the prehistoric period. The heathlands of southern England are being eaten away, and some farmers have even tried to plough the North York Moors. Many ponds and extensive areas of water meadow have been drained, and numerous woods and small copses have been destroyed. A range of valuable and individual habitats are being reduced to a wholly homogeneous arable plain.

Even in areas where pastoral farming is still predominant, the agricultural environment has been substantially damaged. Even here hedges have been removed, as farmers have rationalized their fields, or moved over to barriers of barbed wire or electric fencing. The increasing use of chemical sprays has destroyed wild flowers in pasture, hedgerows and verges, while much grassland has lost its ecological variety. Fields which had formerly contained a multiplicity of grasses and plants have been ploughed up and reseeded with a monoculture of extremely boring rye grass.

Elsewhere the countryside has disappeared beneath the barren environment of coniferous plantations. Since the establishment of the Forestry Commission in 1919, these serried rows of trees have revolutionized the appearance of the landscape in many parts of the country. The sandy wastes of the East Anglian Breckland have almost all been lost, converted to a vast coniferous forest, and many ancient woodlands in southern England have been

Coniferous plantation
Beneath the coniferous trees that now cover much of upland England, there is little sign of wildlife. Few flowers can grow in the dark and acidic conditions beneath the pines, and the absence of birdsong gives the plantations a strange silence. Thousands of acres of moorland have been destroyed during the twentieth century in order to make way for scenes such as this.

heavily coniferized. The most widespread opposition to the spread of the pine has been in the moorlands of the north and west. These areas are famous for their scenic beauty and ecological interest, and many people resent the conversion of wild romantic moors to sterile and uninteresting forests.

In answer to criticisms of modern agriculture the farming lobby often argues that the English countryside is always changing. The present depredations are therefore seen as merely the latest of a never-ending series of alterations. Yet although it is true that the landscape is the product of the activities of the farmers of the past, this does not mean that modern farming methods must be embraced as the inevitable perpetuation of this process of change.

No one would deny that some change is essential in response to new technology. As large machinery replaced horses it was inevitable that fields would get bigger, and hedges would be removed. Indeed hedge removal is by no means a wholly recent phenomenon, for it has been going on in some areas on a small scale since the last century. Moreover, those who lament the introduction of new technology, and look back nostalgically to the days of true horse power, should remember the back-breaking physical labour that the old system required. In the early twentieth century, as in the days of Victorian high farming, agricultural profits were made from the toil of underprivileged and poorly paid rural labourers. In some ways, therefore, farming has changed for the better over the past twenty years, but there is still much to be condemned in the scale of its destructiveness.

The farming of the past created the fabric of the landscape, by adding new features while others were taken away. In contrast the farming of the present is almost exclusively destructive. It has done little or nothing to enrich the environment, it has added few new habitats to replace those which have been lost, and both ecologically and aesthetically its consequences have been almost entirely negative.

In particular, the nineteenth- and twentieth-century agricultural developments have done much to suppress the diversity of the countryside. The innumerable local variations in landscape, as well as more regional contrasts such as that between woodland and champion areas, have been gradually blurred by the emergence of a number of very broad agricultural regions. A basic distinction between an arable east and a pastoral west has gradually replaced the complex pattern of specialized farming regions which characterized earlier centuries.[6]

The landscape has been least affected by the changes of recent years in the western parts of the country, in a zone running from Cornwall and Devon through Somerset, west Gloucestershire, Shropshire, Herefordshire and Staffordshire up to Cheshire and Lancashire. This is livestock country and many of the fields are fairly small and still bounded by hedges. These are often ancient and sinuous, interspersed with numerous deciduous trees.

To the east of this region there is a kind of intermediate zone, consisting of the central and western Midlands — western Northamptonshire, north Oxfordshire, north Buckinghamshire, Warwickshire and Nottinghamshire. This area contains a large number of arable eyesores, but substantial tracts of grassland survive. Much of this is still covered in the earthworks of ridge and furrow, monuments to the last arable expansion which took place in these former champion areas. Moreover, although many hedges have been removed in this region over the past forty years, the basic field pattern has been simplified rather than destroyed. In recent years, new trees have been planted in some of the hedges, as well as in the patches of woodland that are scattered across the countryside, although such efforts have not reversed the overall decline in the quality of the environment.

This Midland region forms a striking contrast with the landscape of many parts of the south and east. In East Anglia, Essex,

ABOVE **View near Hembury, Devon**
The Iron Age hillfort of Hembury is in the wood on the skyline. The western areas of England have been far less affected by the depredations of modern agriculture than the flatter, drier eastern counties, where arable agriculture has been most intensive.

RIGHT **Mursley, Buckinghamshire**
This north Buckinghamshire landscape is typical of the modern Midland countryside. The field pattern has been considerably simplified, but many trees and hedges remain, particularly in areas where livestock farming is still important. The pasture fields in the foreground are much smaller than the arable fields beyond.

Hertfordshire, Bedfordshire, Cambridgeshire, and in a zone from Lincolnshire to Northumberland, as well as in southern counties such as Berkshire, Wiltshire and Dorset, much of the countryside is under intensive arable cultivation, and much has been extensively spoilt. Some parts of the south and east, such as the Weald of Kent, contain substantial areas of grassland, but on the whole it is this part of the country which has been worst affected by the expansion of arable farming which has taken place over the last fifty years. Thousands and thousands of miles of hedges have been uprooted, and acres upon acres of ancient grassland have gone under the plough. The typical landscape of many parts of this region is now a bare and windswept arable plain.

Many hedgerows, trees and woods have been lost through deliberate destruction, but others are suffering as a result of lack of management and neglect. They are sprayed with pesticides and assailed by fire, and old trees are not replaced with young ones. The degeneration of these environments is therefore likely to continue, even if no further planned depredation takes place.

These regional pictures are, of course, generalizations, and there are still considerable local variations in the appearance of the landscape. Individual farmers have not all

Arable fields near Bury St Edmunds, Suffolk
The agricultural changes of the past forty years have led to the removal of many of the features which formerly gave the English countryside its interest and variety. Deterioration has been particularly marked in the eastern counties, where arable farming has been most intensive. The trees in the middle distance used to stand in hedgerows, and although they have been allowed to survive after the hedges themselves were grubbed out, it is most unlikely that they will be replaced when they die. They are simply an inconvenience to the farmer.

adopted modern techniques, even in intensive arable areas. Some practise the new American-style cultivation avidly, whereas others have maintained many of their hedges and woods. To some extent these variations are purely the result of personal circumstances, but even on this individual level certain patterns emerge. Some types of landowner are very likely to alter the landscape, while others are more inclined to maintain traditional features.

In the pastoral west there are still many fairly small family farms, and here the landscape seems to have escaped the worst ravages of modern agriculture. It is often suggested that these small farmers have preserved the traditional countryside because they have a natural affinity with the land on which they work, but this romantic model of the small eco-farmer is not necessary to explain the general survival of the landscape in the west. The features that make up the traditional rural landscape, the ponds, grasslands and hedgerows, are far less redundant in a pastoral economy than in one which specializes in arable production. Moreover, small farmers tend to practise more traditional methods and utilize well-established machinery, simply because they lack the capital to invest in the latest improvements and mechanization.

Outside the regions where the landholding structure is based around small farmers, the landscape is often least changed in areas still held by the great landed families. Although many of the estate farm companies have adopted the new utilitarian attitudes to land, some maintain much of the traditional fabric of the countryside. Trees are still planted, and the woods and hedges not only survive but are often carefully managed. Such conservation policies are either carried out by the landowners directly, on the land which they farm themselves, or are instituted by tenant farmers whose leases oblige them to maintain and protect hedges and trees. Once again these practices need not be entirely explained by a fondness for the traditional landscape. The existence of farming dynasties on these inherited estates gives a particular dimension to the economic as well as the emotional attitude to the land. Very long-term but ultimately high-yield forms of investment can be justified if the son will be able to harvest the profits of his father's or grandfather's actions. With so much of our landscape now devoted to coniferous forests, the planting of deciduous trees is becoming just such a profitable investment, for over the next hundred years substantial specimens of deciduous timber will become rarer and increasingly valuable.

Those who run farms on the lines of manufacturing industry, with the aim of maximizing short-term returns, have less incentive to engage in long-term planning than those who still see themselves to some extent as tenants-for-life of their estates. Furthermore, in those areas dominated by the great landed families, the hedges, copses and woods are still used to provide cover for pheasants, foxes and even sometimes deer, which are now a source of income as well as grisly pleasure for the landed élite.

Hunting, and in particular shooting, are now big business, and it is an unfortunate irony that in many areas the survival of numerous habitats and their wildlife is almost entirely dependent on the fact that certain privileged members of our society get pleasure from the slaughter of animals. Without blood sports further miles of hedgerow would disappear, and many woods and copses would be rooted out. Any attempt to control hunting and shooting should therefore be preceded by measures to safeguard the landscapes that these sports currently protect.

Not all the great estates are pillars of ecological virtue, and as in the nineteenth century many manifest a certain amount of distance decay. Hedges and trees often survive far better near the owner's home than on more distant parts of his land. None the less, it is generally true that the destruction of the landscape has been far less dramatic on traditional estates than on those of the new industrial farmers. This has added a regional dimension to the broader pattern of variations in landscape decline. In areas like the Chiltern Hills or parts of north and west Norfolk, where there are still numerous great estates, the survival of these traditional landholding units has been a major factor in preserving the landscape.

As a landowning class, the wealthy grain barons have one of the worst records for conservation. They practise very profitable arable agriculture, employ very little labour, and the size of their landholding units enables them to gain maximum benefits from the subsidy system. Many of these farmers tend to regard farming as just another industry, and therefore they tend to look for very rapid returns. Although there is considerable variation in the degree to which even these industrial farmers have wrecked the land, the high degree of mechanization and the capital-intensive methods they employ have inevitably led to extensive disruption of the rural fabric in many parts, and in particular in the south and east of England.

The depredations of this new landowning class are only exceeded by those of farmers who represent financial institutions. As things stand, these institutions hold only a small proportion of agricultural land, and this must be counted as a blessing. Since they are only accountable to their investors, the impact of these farmers on the appearance of the landscape is almost invariably disastrous.

Yet in making these criticisms and comparisons it would not be right to hold individual farmers entirely responsible. The government and the EEC have encouraged farmers to produce as much food as possible, irrespective of national and international demand. Our complaint is not against those who have put these policies into effect, but against the thinking behind them, those who drew them up, and to some extent the agricultural pressure groups which have seen that they are maintained.

The National Farmers' Union has campaigned very successfully for the perpetuation of the system of agricultural subsidies, even though this has not always been to the benefit of the whole farming community. The great grain barons have flourished on the profits of arable subsidies, but smaller farms, and in particular the mixed and pastoral enterprises, have tended to go to the wall. This undoubtedly reflects the fact that farming pressure groups have been dominated by the largest and wealthiest farmers who have been most in favour of adopting new destructive techniques.

Furthermore, conservation should not be merely the responsibility of the farmers. The landscape is the shared heritage of us all, and must be recognized as an important part of our culture. It is ridiculous that it should be at the mercy of farmers, for we cannot expect them to preserve it while they are paid to plough it up.

It seems strange that this situation should have come about, for it is not as though the conservation movement or interest in the landscape is a new development in England. Concern about the countryside has a long history, and it is perhaps surprising that conservationists have been in many respects so spectacularly unsuccessful.

Interest in the countryside began in the nineteenth century as the population became progressively urban. The traditional contrast between the harmonious countryside and the corrupt and pestilential city was given a new force in the Victorian novel, with the portrayal of an urban proletariat who had no choice about where they were to live. Elizabeth Gaskell and Charles Dickens both represent workers trapped in the city who dream of a rural life of fresh air and liberty.

Yet while the countryside was being invested with nostalgia, the last surviving expanses of open land were rapidly being enclosed and from the mid nineteenth century there was considerable pressure to protect access to the remaining open spaces. In 1865 the Commons, Open Spaces and Footpath Preservation

Society was set up, to be followed by a number of other groups devoted to protecting the environment and its wildlife. In 1889 the Royal Society for the Protection of Birds was founded, and in 1895 The National Trust grew out of the Open Spaces Society. The Society for the Preservation of Nature Reserves was established in 1912, and the Ramblers Association was set up in 1935. These organizations did not all originate as the purely middle-class pressure groups which they often appear to be today. Many working people, particularly in the north of England, were dedicated to hill-walking and other forms of rural recreation, and fought to protect their right to enjoy these pleasures. The strength of this popular enthusiasm for the countryside was demonstrated in 1955, when the right of ordinary people to enjoy access to the Peak District was won by the mass trespass on Kinder Scout.

None the less, despite the long history of popular interest in the landscape, there was no state intervention in its conservation until after World War II. The Town and Country Planning Act of 1947 was followed by numerous other measures, including the National Parks and Access to the Countryside Act of 1949, and the Countryside Act of 1968. The main effect of these new laws was to establish certain areas which were subject to special controls, categorized as nature reserves, National Parks, Areas of Outstanding Natural Beauty (AONBs) and Sites of Special Scientific Interest (SSSIs).

It has been estimated that as much as 20 per cent of the land of England is in one or other of these various specially protected regions. This sounds like a high proportion, but in fact there are serious limitations on the extent to which agriculture can be controlled in even these designated areas. The land within National Parks and AONBs is rather like the regions denominated forest in the medieval period — these areas are still in the hands of private individuals, but their use is circumscribed by certain national laws. Just as there were ways of getting round the rigours of the forest restrictions in the medieval period, so the controls on the exploitation of National Parks and AONBs contain a great many loop holes.

The National Parks, AONBs, SSSIs and nature reserves were originally conceived to counter the threat to the landscape from urban and industrial expansion rather than from the intensification of agriculture. So although the urbanization or industrialization of all these protected areas is controlled, when they were first established the legislation did not provide for restrictions on agricultural exploitation. For many years, therefore, these areas suffered from the same sort of changes as those found in other parts of the country, with hedges being removed, marshes drained, and heaths and downlands ploughed. In 1981, however, the situation was clarified, even if it could not be said to have been improved, with the passing of the now notorious Wildlife and Countryside Act. This decreed that any farmer wishing to change the use of, or otherwise alter, any land within a national park or SSSI should consult the National Park Authority, Nature Conservancy Council or Countryside Commission. If a grant for the 'improvement', or permission to carry out the work, was refused on the grounds of conservation, then the farmer was entitled to compensation for the profits that he would have made if the work had been done. Not only was this compensation based on the artificially high prices resulting from EEC support, but it had to be paid by the underfunded conservation bodies themselves (the NPAs, the NCC and the CC).

Twentieth-century conservation legislation has thus been characterized by lack of teeth. Even within the supposedly specially protected areas, it has tended to be dependent on the voluntary co-operation of the owners of the land. As a result, conservation authorities have been unable to halt the gradual degeneration of even those areas under their particular care. The legislation has also had consequences for the landscape as a whole, outside the areas which it has particularly tried to preserve.

The designation of certain areas of peculiar beauty or interest has tended to encourage the idea that the rest of the countryside is fair game. Many farmers now feel that they need not worry about the destruction of their own lands since the outstanding areas are safe. The general perception of the landscape has also been affected, for people are prepared to tolerate the overall degeneration of the environment, in the knowledge that numerous isolated beauty spots still exist. These attitudes are peculiarly destructive because the interest of our landscape lies in its variety. This can only be preserved by a conservationist agricultural policy, and by the imposition of certain controls over the use of the land. As things stand there are almost no limitations on the exploitation of farmland that has not been granted any special status, apart from a few minor and often toothless controls, such as tree preservation orders.

The widespread failure of the attempts that have been made to protect the traditional form of the working landscape are in marked contrast to the success of attempts to preserve the appearance of traditional rural settlements. Villages have experienced a certain amount of destruction, but old cottages, barns and other buildings have generally survived far better than the rural environment which used to support village communities.

The quaint and neat cottages to be seen in most villages, and the schools and nonconformist chapels which have been converted into architect-designed homes, represent the preservation of at least one aspect of a wider rural environment. But in other ways these villages embody changes that have taken place in the countryside in general. Labourers' cottages still survive, but in most villages the labourers no longer live in them, and they do not reflect the existence of a viable local community rooted in the land. They are no longer part of an organic unit, including shops and local businesses as

well as houses. The decline of the local community is evident in house names such as 'The Old School House', 'The Old Rectory' and 'The Old Post Office', and is a result of changes that have taken place over the past fifty years.

The movement towards increasingly large and more mechanized and efficient farms from the 1930s has brought about a progressive reduction in the number of people employed on the land. At first this change was fairly slow. As late as 1948 573,000 people still worked full-

time on the land, but in the post-war years the rate of decrease began to accelerate, particularly after the introduction of the labour-saving combine-harvester. By 1973 there were only 184,000 people employed in agriculture, and today the number is probably less than 150,000.[7]

In the post-war years this drop in the number of farm workers brought about a decline in the rural population as a whole, as villagers moved to the cities in order to search for work. In more remote parts of the country, away from the

Hay-making at Lockinge, Oxfordshire, in 1905
One of the greatest changes in the appearance of the countryside during the twentieth century has been the gradual decline in the number of people working on the land. The mechanization of agriculture, and in particular the introduction of the tractor, has ensured that even the largest farms require only a handful of workers. This crowded photograph provides a striking contrast to the empty fields of the modern landscape, but the work was hard and pay and conditions extremely poor.

population centres, this decline has continued to the present day. But in most places it began to be reversed from the early 1960s. In some areas, such as the West Country and Norfolk, country cottages began to be bought up as retirement homes by exiles from the cities. In the more picturesque parts of England, such as the Cornish coast or the Cumbrian lakes, some became holiday cottages, but in most areas the majority of villages have become dormitories for people working in nearby towns and cities.

These new villagers usually have very different attitudes to rural life from the previous inhabitants. For them cottages have a picturesque charm; they are not associated with the poverty and deprivation of old-fashioned country life. Moreover, the affluent middle classes have enough money to make comfortable what would otherwise be rather damp and squalid homes. There is therefore a powerful middle-class lobby to preserve the olde-worlde atmosphere of villages from change and many buildings have been protected by legislation. One in forty of the buildings in England is 'listed' and there are strenuous controls on new developments of housing and industry.

While we would not (and are in no position to) criticize the desire of these people to live in and enjoy the countryside, their protectionist attitudes to the landscape have badly affected the indigenous inhabitants. Many houses that could have once been rented to local people have been sold off at prices way beyond their means. At the same time new housing developments have been strictly controlled, and the existence of these controls has forced up the price of cottages even further. Moreover, the prevention of light or small-scale industrial development has led to a shortage of jobs and the perpetuation of very low wages, while the fact that many new villagers have cars has brought about a dramatic decline in the availability of public transport and local services.

All these changes have made it increasingly difficult for the original inhabitants to stay in the villages of their birth, and many have been forced to move away because of lack of housing and jobs. Yet the construction of cheap homes and rural factories would have nothing like the deleterious effects on the landscape that have been caused by agriculture over the last thirty years. With proper controls they would only affect a small area of the landscape, whereas agriculture has been destroying the countryside as a whole.

The middle-class invasion of the countryside is not new. It began in the late nineteenth century with the creation of good rail connections to the major towns and cities. This led to the emergence of landscapes of suburban development, and most strikingly to the 'metroland' to the west of London. As a result these areas very soon ceased to be rural, as the newcomers destroyed the very environment for which they had left town.

This suburban settlement was in itself an extension down the social scale of the eighteenth- and nineteenth-century tradition of living in the country and carrying on business in the town. Yet it was only from the middle of the twentieth century, as car ownership spread, that people began to move *en masse* into cottages located at some distance from towns, cities or railway stations. This latest phase of bourgeois settlement has produced a considerable realignment of the pattern of power in the land, but in some respects it also reveals a degree of continuity.

Those villages which have been most extensively settled, where new developments have been outlawed and planning controls most rigidly enforced, are often those which were once 'closed villages'. Here the authority of the owners in the nineteenth and early twentieth centuries prevented any radical developments. The villages therefore survived in an unaltered picturesque form to the time when middle-class settlement and planning controls began. Nowadays, many of these closed villages have become what is known as 'conservation areas', in other words their development is even more rigidly controlled than that of other settlements.

These villages epitomize the modern image of a traditional English village. Their houses are beautifully maintained and preserved and they are unsullied by signs of labour or employment. Yet despite the success of the new villagers in preserving their immediate environment, the landscape in which the village lies is often witness to the absence of controls over farming, especially in the arable areas of the south and east. Much agricultural vandalism obviously took place before the arrival of many of the newcomers, but, despite their apparent interest in conservation, they have been unable to put a check upon its progress.

The contrast between the 'preserved' village and the devastated countryside beyond is a clear reflection of the present distribution of power in the land. As tied cottages have been sold into private ownership, the middle classes have come to own and rule the villages, but they have little influence over the rest of the landscape. The new villagers are anxious to preserve the villages because it makes economic sense for them to do so. The prevention of new housing and industrial development will increase the value of their properties. But there is little incentive for the farmers to indulge in the conservation of the rest of the landscape and in some cases, as we have seen, they are given economic inducements to destroy the historic countryside.

The overall failure of the conservation movement is therefore in part the result of the way in which the countryside is owned. The vast majority of farmland is in private hands, and its exploitation is virtually unconstrained by communal controls. The landowner is to a large extent free to do what he likes, even though the rest of the local community have to face the consequences of his depredations.

There are some signs, however, that attitudes at all levels are beginning to change. The rate of destruction has certainly slowed down in many areas, and the presence of plastic grow-tubes all over the countryside, in hedges, on roadsides, and in inconvenient corners of fields, testifies to a new wave of tree-planting. Some is the work of the county councils, but much has been done by the farmers themselves, supported by the Countryside Commission. Farmers seem at last to have recognized that, since much of their income comes from the tax-payer, it is in their interests to keep the public happy. It is also true that the hedgerow destruction of the 1960s and 1970s was to some extent spurred by agricultural fashion. Farmers were eager to display efficiency and modernity and turned their backs on old methods and old landscapes. Nowadays, they are beginning to share the nostalgia for the past which has afflicted most of British society, and in the countryside as in the cities an ethos of destructiveness is beginning to be replaced by a new respect for the old.

This change in the attitudes of farmers has been accompanied by some alteration in the position of the government, and in the policies of the EEC. Over the last few years milk quotas have been imposed, and limitations on arable production will soon follow. The British government is pressing the EEC to pay farmers for setting land aside from production; an expansion of forestry has been proposed, and planning controls are to be relaxed to encourage the use of agricultural land for housing and for leisure facilities such as golf courses. Although measures such as these may do something to ease the financial burdens of the EEC, they are unlikely to do a great deal either for the environment or for the problems of rural poverty. The spread of executive housing across the farmland of southeast England will not halt the rise in rural house prices, nor assuage the chronic shortage of rented accommodation, and the proposed expansion of forestry poses a further threat to our dwindling resources of heath and moorland.

Although the recent institution of 'Environmentally Sensitive Areas' has made it possible for farmers in a few special areas, such as the Norfolk Broads, to be paid for the maintenance of farming practices which preserve the distinctive landscape, this scheme is both voluntary and limited. Most farmers are still being paid to destroy the countryside, and in order to halt the damage to the rural environment it will be necessary to take much more drastic measures. These must involve more than extending planning controls or pulling the plug on EEC subsidies. In fact, cutting off direct support could merely accelerate the destructiveness of agriculture, as farmers try to make up for their loss by increasingly intensive production. All the traditional elements in the landscape, the hedges, woods, trees and grasslands, need to be managed and maintained rather than just preserved. As our narrative has demonstrated, the landscape is largely man-made. It is the product of the activities of man, and depends upon agriculture for its survival. Downland must be grazed, meadows must be mowed, hedges must be laid or trimmed, and woodland must be managed or coppiced.

Conservation can thus only really succeed with the help of, rather than in spite of, the farmers. We need a strategy for the countryside which embraces the needs of the whole community. The rural landscape should not be seen as a place solely used for the production of food, but as a recreational resource to be used and enjoyed by a whole variety of people. The countryside is appreciated by walkers, naturalists, artists, sportsmen, landscape historians and even those who just like a drive in the country. But the pleasure of all these groups is being lessened by the destruction of the landscape's historic fabric.

If an agricultural strategy were to recognize these activities as legitimate uses of the countryside, the system of subsidies could be redirected to encourage conservation. This would not necessarily mean the introduction of inefficient or unprofessional agriculture, but merely a return to some of the traditional patterns of specialization. Upland areas, for example, should be used for the rearing of livestock; downland farmers should be encouraged to return to the production of sheep;

Agricultural prairie with fertilizer bag, near Harlton, Cambridgeshire
This photograph captures the final stage in the destruction of the English countryside. The bleak scene is enlivened only by the empty fertilizer bag blowing across the field. There are no hedges, and the nearest trees are well over a mile away. Without a radical change in agricultural policy, this could be the shape of things to come.

and in wetland areas there should be economic incentives to encourage farmers to practise traditional livestock grazing and dairying.

These changes would represent an increase rather than a decrease in the true efficiency of agriculture. Most of these areas are patently unsuitable for the production of arable crops and can only be cultivated under the present, heavily subsidized system, with the injection of vast quantities of capital in fertilizers and irrigation. Since we are paying our farmers large sums of money, it would make sense to finance them to maintain or restore a landscape which we can all enjoy. If we encourage the maintenance of hedges, ponds and woodland, and the reconstruction of those areas that have been most devastated, the countryside could serve not only a social and cultural function, but also a more diverse economic function than merely the production of food.

As the conservation of the landscape is far more labour-intensive than its destruction,

numerous other benefits would follow from a policy of this kind. Agricultural innovations, combined with the expansion of tourism, could help to counteract the chronic shortage of jobs and the appalling wage levels currently found in rural areas, especially if the conservation of the countryside were to be combined with a controlled programme of rural development. In a rich and varied landscape, where the interests of nature are recognized, there must be a role for industry and housing. These are essential parts of a multi-use landscape, which would fulfil a wide range of needs and functions. In a society based around democratic restrictions, and in which agriculture is subsidized by the state, there must be scope for increasing the power of the majority over the land. The land is now in the hands of a very small minority of the population, but it has been shaped by the activities of rural communities over the centuries. The land is the common heritage of the people, and it should be for everyone to enjoy.

Notes

Introduction

1 Cowper, *The Task*, line 749.

2 M.Turner, 'The Landscape of Parliamentary Enclosure', in M.Reed, *Discovering Past Landscapes* (London, 1984), p. 132.

1 An Old Country

1 G.C.Homans, *English Villagers of the Thirteenth Century* (Cambridge, Mass., 1941). A.R.H.Baker and R.A.Butlin, *Studies of Field Systems in the British Isles* (Cambridge, 1973).

2 Homans, ibid., p. 21.

3 O.Rackham, *Trees and Woodland in the British Landscape* (London, 1976), p. 17.

4 C.C.Taylor, *Village and Farmstead* (London, 1983).

5 T.M.Williamson, 'The Roman Countryside: Settlement and Agriculture in North West Essex', *Britannia* 15 (1984), pp. 225–30. T.M.Williamson, 'The Development of Settlement in North West Essex: The Results of a Recent Field Survey', *Essex Archaeology and History* 17 (1986).

6 W.Rodwell, 'Relict Landscapes in Essex', in C.Bowen and P.J.Fowler, *Early Land Allotment* (Oxford, 1978), pp. 89–98. P.Drury and W.Rodwell, 'Settlement in the Later Iron Age and Roman Periods', in D.G.Buckley, *The Archaeology of Essex to A.D. 1500* (London, 1980), pp. 59–75. T.M.Williamson, 'Parish Boundaries and Early Fields: Continuity and Discontinuity', *Journal of Historical Geography* 12 (1986), pp. 241–8.

7 G.Foard, 'Systematic Fieldwalking and the Investigation of Saxon Settlement in Northamptonshire', *World Archaeology* 9 (1978), pp. 357–74. J.G.Hurst, 'The Wharram Research Project: Results to 1983', *Medieval Archaeology* 28 (1984), pp. 77–111.

8 D.Hall, *Medieval Fields* (Aylesbury, 1980).

9 M.Harvey, 'Planned Field Systems in East Yorkshire — Some Thoughts on their Origins', *Agricultural History Review* 31 (1983), pp. 91–103.

10 H.S.A.Fox, 'Approaches to the Adoption of the Midland System', in T.Rowley, *The Origins of Open Field Agriculture* (London, 1981), pp. 64–111. J.Thirsk, 'The Common Fields' and 'The Origins of the Common Fields' in R.H.Hilton, *Peasants, Knights and Heretics* (Cambridge, 1976), pp. 10–32, 51–6.

11 For a good introduction to this subject see M.Aston, *Interpreting the Landscape* (London, 1983), chap. 3. See also P.H.Sawyer, 'Medieval English Settlement: New Interpretations', in P.H.Sawyer, *English Medieval Settlement* (London, 1976), pp. 1–8. G.R.S.Jones, 'Multiple Estates and Early Settlement', in Sawyer, *ibid.*, pp. 9–34.

12 M.Gelling, *Signposts to the Past: Place-names and the History of England* (London, 1978), pp. 61–86.

2 The Early Middle Ages — A Customary Landscape

1 This account draws on E.Miller and J.Hatcher, *Medieval England: Rural Society and Economic Change 1086–1348* (London, 1978).

2 S.Harvey, 'The Knight and the Knight's Fee in England', in R.H.Hilton, *Peasants, Knights and Heretics* (Cambridge, 1976), p. 138.
3 G.E.Mingay, *The Gentry: The Rise and Fall of a Class* (London, 1976), p. 27.
4 Hatcher and Miller, *op. cit.*, pp. 20–1.
5 R.A.Dodgshon, *The Origins of British Field Systems; An Interpretation* (London, 1980). Homans, *English Villagers*, pp. 83–106. M.Reed, *The Buckinghamshire Landscape* (London, 1979), p. 92.
6 Homans, *ibid.*, p. 98.
7 B.K.Roberts, *Rural Settlement in Britain* (Folkestone, 1977), pp. 99–100.
8 Quoted in Fox, *op. cit.*, p. 96.
9 B.Roberts, 'The Study of Village Plans', *Local Historian* 9, 5 (1971), pp. 233–41. J.Sheppard, 'Medieval Village Planning in Northern England: Some Evidence from Yorkshire', *Journal of Historical Geography* 2 (1976), pp. 3–20.
10 J.Sheppard, 'Metrological Analysis of Regular Village Plans in Yorkshire', *Agricultural History Review* 22 (1974), pp. 118–35.
11 F.M.Stenton, *The First Century of English Feudalism, 1066–1166* (Oxford, 1961), p. 65.
12 R.H.Hilton, 'Agrarian Class Structure and Economic Development in Pre-Industrial Europe: A Crisis of Feudalism', *Past and Present* 80 (1978), pp. 3–19.
13 M.Mate, 'Medieval Agriculture: the determining factors?', *Agricultural History Review* 33 (1985), pp. 22–31.
14 R.H.Hilton, *Bond Men Made Free* (London, 1973), p. 11.
15 Homans, *op. cit.*, p. 262.
16 Homans, *op. cit.*, p. 281.
17 J.Hatcher, 'English Serfdom and Villeinage: Towards a Reassessment', *Past and Present* 90 (1981), pp. 3–39.
18 Quoted in A.MacFarlane, *The Origins of English Individualism* (Oxford, 1978), p. 106.
19 R.J.Faith, 'Peasant Families and Inheritance Customs in Medieval England', *Agricultural History Review* 14 (1966), pp. 85–93.
20 Homans, *op. cit.*, pp. 109–20.
21 C.Howell, 'Stability and Change 1300–1700', *Journal of Peasant Studies* 2, 4 (1975), pp. 468–81.
22 W.O.Ault, *Open Field Farming in Medieval England* (London, 1972), p. 33.
23 *Ibid.*, p. 119.
24 D.Knowles, *The Religious Orders in England* (Cambridge, 1956–61). C.Platt, *The Abbeys and Priories of Medieval England* (London, 1984).
25 C.Platt, *ibid.*, p. 200.
26 Quoted in Platt, *ibid.*, p. 94.
27 Platt, *ibid.*, p. 94.
28 Quoted in H.C.Darby, *The Medieval Fenland* (Cambridge, 1940), p. 52.

3 Power in the Land

1 R.Allen Brown, *English Castles* (London, 1954). L.Cantor, 'Castles, Fortified Houses, Moated Homesteads and Monastic Settlements', in L.Cantor, *The English Medieval Landscape* (London, 1982), pp. 126–53.
2 R.Allen Brown, 'A List of Castles 1154–1216', *English Historical Review* 74 (1954), pp. 249–80.
3 M.Girouard, *Life in the English Country House* (London, 1980), p. 23.
4 Homans, *op. cit.*, p. 357–9.
5 R.Harris, *Timber Framed Buildings* (Aylesbury, 1978), pp. 49–50.
6 D.Wilson, *Moated Sites* (Aylesbury, 1985), p. 30.
7 For more information about medieval parish churches see W.Rodwell and J.Bentley, *Our Christian Heritage* (London, 1984), and C.Platt, *The Parish Churches of Medieval England* (London, 1981).
8 D.Dymond, *The Norfolk Landscape* (London, 1985), p. 132.
9 C.Trice Martin, 'Clerical life in the fifteenth century, as illustrated by proceedings of the court of chancery', *Archaeologia* 60 (1907), p. 369.
10 W.O.Ault, 'Manor Court and Parish Church in Fifteenth-Century England: A Study of Village By-laws', in *Speculum* 42 (1967), p. 65.
11 See O.Rackham, *Trees and Woodlands in the British Landscape* (London, 1976), and *Ancient Woodland* (London, 1980). L.Cantor, *Forests, Chases, Parks and Warrens* in Cantor, *The English Medieval Landscape* (London, 1982), pp. 56–85.
12 O.Rackham, *ibid.*
13 M.Beresford, *History on the Ground* (Gloucester, 1984), p. 218.

4 Crisis in the Countryside

1 A.MacFarlane, *The Origins of English Individualism* (Oxford,

1978).

2 P.R.Hyams, 'The Origins of a Peasant Land Market in England', *Economic History Review* 23 (1970), pp. 18–31. R.Smith, 'Kin and Neighbours in a Thirteenth Century Suffolk Community', *Journal of Family History* 4 (1979), pp. 219–56.

3 C.Howell, 'Stability and Change 1300–1700', *Journal of Peasant Studies* 2, 4 (1975), pp. 468–81.

4 R.H.Hilton, *The Decline of Serfdom in Medieval England* (London, 1969), pp. 17–26.

5 Quoted in Hatcher and Miller, *op. cit.*, p. 119.

6 W.G.Hoskins and L.D.Stamp, *The Common Lands of England and Wales* (London, 1963). Michael Williams, 'Marshland and Waste', in L.Cantor, *op. cit.*, pp. 86–125.

7 Hoskins and Stamp, *op. cit.*, p. 37.

8 D.Dymond, *The Norfolk Landscape* (London, 1985), p. 107.

9 J.Sheppard, 'The Field Systems of Yorkshire', in A.R.H.Baker and R.A.Butlin, *Studies of Field Systems in the British Isles*, (Cambridge, 1972), pp. 176–80.

10 Homans, *op. cit.*, p. 84.

11 D.Dymond, *The Norfolk Landscape*, p. 108.

12 O.Rackham, *Trees and Woodlands in the British Landscape*, (London, 1976).

13 Hoskins and Stamp, *op. cit.*, p. 48.

14 Rackham, *op. cit.*, p. 80.

15 B.K.Roberts, 'A Study of Medieval Colonisation in the Forest of Arden, Warwickshire', *Agricultural History Review* 16 (1968), pp. 101–13.

16 P.Wade Martins, 'Village Sites in the Launditch Hundred', *East Anglian Archaeology* 10 (1980).

17 P.Warner, 'Origins: The Example of Green-Side Settlement in East Suffolk', *Medieval Village Research Group Report* 31 (1983), pp. 42–4.

18 P.F.Brandon, 'Demesne Arable Farming in Coastal Sussex During the Late Middle Ages', *Agricultural History Review* 19 (1971). B.Campbell, 'Agricultural Progress in Medieval England: Some Evidence from Eastern Norfolk', *Economic History Review* 36 (1983), pp. 24–46. A.Smith, 'Regional Differences in Crop Production in Medieval Kent', *Archaeologica Cantiana* 78 (1963), pp. 147–60.

19 A.E.Levett, *Studies in Manorial History* (London, 1938), pp. 248–50.

20 R.H.Hilton, *Bond Men Made Free* (London, 1973).

21 M.W.Beresford and J.G.Hurst, *Deserted Medieval Villages* (London, 1971). C.Dyer, 'Deserted Medieval Villages in the West Midlands', *Economic History Review* 35 (1980), pp. 19–34.

22 H.S.A.Fox, 'Contraction: Desertion and Dwindling of Dispersed Settlement in a Devon Parish', *Medieval Village Research Group Report* 31 (1983), pp. 40–2.

23 J.E.Martin, *Feudalism to Capitalism: Peasant and Landlord in English Agrarian Development* (London, 1983), p. 125. C.Dyer, 'Population and Agriculture on a Warwickshire Manor', *University of Birmingham Historical Journal* 11 (1968).

24 C.Howell, 'Stability and Change 1300–1700', *Journal of Peasant Studies* 2, 4 (1975), pp. 468–81. E.Kerridge, *Agrarian Problems in the Sixteenth Century and After* (London, 1969).

25 M.W.Beresford, *The Lost Villages of England* (London, 1954), p. 105.

26 M.W.Beresford and J.K.St Joseph, *Medieval England: An Aerial Survey*, 2nd edn. (Cambridge, 1979), p. 123.

27 Beresford, *Lost Villages*, p. 207.

28 *Ibid.*, p. 208.

5 After the Middle Ages: The Progress of Enclosure

1 E.Kerridge, *The Agricultural Revolution* (London, 1967), and *The Farmers of Old England* (London, 1973).

2 J.Thirsk, 'Seventeenth Century Agriculture and Social Change', in *Land, Church and People*, supplement to *Agricultural History Review* 18 (1970), pp. 148–77.

3 G.E.Mingay, 'The East Midlands', in J.Thirsk, *The Agricultural History of England and Wales* vol. 5, I (1649–1750) (Cambridge, 1984), p. 124.

4 Quoted in C.Hill, *The World Turned Upside Down* (London, 1972), p. 42.

5 C.Hill, *Reformation to Industrial Revolution* (London, 1967), p. 63.

6 C.Hill, *The World Turned Upside Down*, p. 41.

7 J.A.Yelling, *Common Field and Enclosure in England 1450–1850* (London, 1977), p. 6.
8 L.Munby, *The Making of the Hertfordshire Landscape* (London, 1977), p. 165.
9 J.R.Wordie, 'The Chronology of English Enclosure 1500–1914', *Economic History Review* 36 (1983), pp. 483–505. R.A.Butlin, 'The Enclosure of Open Fields and the Extinction of Common Rights in England, *circa* 1600–1750: a review', in H.S.A.Fox and R.A.Butlin, *Change in the Countryside: Essays on Rural England, 1500 to 1900* (London, 1979), pp. 65–82.
10 M.E.Turner, *English Parliamentary Enclosure* (Folkestone, 1980).
11 M.Reed, *The Buckinghamshire Landscape*, p. 177–9.
12 M.Reed, 'Pre-Parliamentary Enclosure in the East Midlands, 1550 to 1750, and its Impact on the Landscape', *Landscape History* 3 (1981), pp. 60–8.
13 M.Turner, 'The Landscape of Parliamentary Enclosure', in Michael Reed *Discovering Past Landscapes* (London, 1984), pp. 132–66.
14 Yelling, *op. cit.*, p. 8.
15 J.Broad, 'Alternate Husbandry and Permanent Pasture in the Midlands, 1650–1800', *Agricultural History Review* 28 (1980), pp. 77–89.
16 G.E.Mingay, 'The East Midlands', in J.Thirsk, *The Agricultural History of England and Wales*, vol. V, part I (Cambridge, 1984), p. 95.
17 Broad, *op. cit.*, p. 83.
18 Mingay, 'The East Midlands', p. 116.
19 Ibid, p. 117.
20 D.Dymond, *The Norfolk Landscape*, p. 216. Reed, 'Pre-Parliamentary Enclosure', p. 65.
21 Cobbett, *Political Register* 3, 16 Oct. 1824, p. 146; and 39, 26 May, 1821, pp. 518–20.
22 K.D.M.Snell, *Annals of the Labouring Poor: Social Change and Agrarian England 1660–1900* (Cambridge, 1985).
23 Cobbett, *Political Register* 39, pp. 520–1.

6 The Rise of the Great Estates

1 This account draws extensively on H.A.Clemenson, *English Country Houses and Landed Estates* (London, 1982) and J.P.Cooper, 'The Social Distribution of Land and Men in England, 1436–1700', *Economic History Review* 20 (1967), pp. 419–40.
2 N.Pevsner, *The Architecture of Oxfordshire* (London, 1974), pp. 809–11.
3 C.Hill, *Reformation to Industrial Revolution*, p. 66.
4 *Ibid.*, p. 61.
5 J.V.Beckett, 'English Landownership in the Later Seventeenth and Eighteenth Centuries', *Economic History Review*, 30 (1977), pp. 567–81.
6 G.E.Mingay, *English Landed Society in the Eighteenth Century* (London, 1963), p. 74.
7 Clemenson, *op. cit.*, p. 12–13; p. 74.
8 J.T.Ward, *East Yorkshire Landed Estates in the Nineteenth Century* (York, 1967), p. 13.
9 R.W.Ketton-Cremer, *Felbrigg: the Story of a House* (London, 1962), p. 201.
10 *Ibid.*, p. 202.
11 E.Burke, *Reflections on the Revolution in France* Penguin edn., pp. 194–5.
12 J.B.Burke, *The Rise of the Great Families* (London, 1873), quoted in H.Clemenson, *op. cit.*, p. 41.
13 Quoted in J.R.Lander, *Crown and Nobility 1450–1509* (London, 1976), p. 127.
14 E.P.Shirley, *The Noble and Gentle Men of England* (Westminster, 1859).
15 See J.G.A.Pocock, *The Machiavellian Moment: Florentine Political Thought and the Atlantic Republican Tradition* (Princeton, NJ, 1975) and J.Barrell, *An Equal Wide Survey* (London, 1984).
16 *The Spectator*, no. 1, vol. 1.
17 G.E.Mingay, *The Gentry: The Rise and Fall of a Class* (London, 1976), pp. 88–90.
18 J.V.Beckett, 'The Decline of the Small Landowner in Eighteenth and Nineteenth Century England: Some Regional Considerations', *Agricultural History Review* 30 (1982), pp. 97–111. Clemenson, *op. cit.*, pp. 20–8. Bateman, *The Great Landowners of Great Britain and Ireland*, 1883, rpt. (Leicester, 1971).
19 R.Newton, *The Northumberland Landscape* (London, 1972), p. 120.
20 R.Millward and A.Robinson, *North Devon and North Cornwall* (London, 1971), pp. 68–72.

21 H. Fuller, 'Landownership and the Lindsey Landscape', *Annals of the Association of American Geographers* 66 (1976), pp. 45–64.

7 A Place in the Country

1 W. Goldsmith, *The Traveller*, lines 405–10.
2 A. Pope, *Epistle to Burlington*.
3 This account draws on M. Girouard's excellent *Life in the English Country House: a social and architectural history* (London, 1980).
4 H. Fielding, *Tom Jones*, Book 13, ch. 7. With thanks to Adam Barker for drawing our attention to this quotation.
5 This chapter draws extensively on: H. Prince, *Parks in England* (Isle of Wight, 1967); H. Clemenson, *op. cit.*; M. Hadfield, *A History of English Gardening* (London, 1960); E. Hyams, *Capability Brown and Humphry Repton* (New York, 1971); C. Hussey, *English Gardens and Landscapes 1700–1750* (London, 1967); and D. Jarrett, *The English Landscape Garden* (London, 1978).
6 C. C. Taylor, *Village and Farmstead* (London, 1983), pp. 201–2.
7 Royal Commission on Historical Monuments: Dorset, vol. 3, part 1.
8 C. C. Taylor, *Fieldwork in Medieval Archaeology* (London, 1974), p. 139.
9 C. C. Taylor, *Village and Farmstead* (London, 1983), p. 170.
10 H. Repton, *An inquiry into the Changes of Taste in Landscape Gardening* (London, 1806), 35.
11 C. C. Taylor, *The Archaeology of Gardens* (Aylesbury, 1983).
12 J. Harris, *The Artist and the English Country House* (London, 1978).
13 Quoted in Hussey, *op. cit.*, p. 43.
14 Jarrett, *op. cit.*, pp. 7–9.
15 A. Ashley Cooper, 3rd Earl of Shaftesbury, 'The Moralists' (1705), in *Characteristics of Men, Manners, Opinions, Times* (London, 1711), ed. J. M. Robertson (New York, 1964), treatise 5, part 3, section 2, p. 125.
16 O. Rackham, *Trees and Woodland in the English Landscape* (London, 1976), pp. 148–9.
17 A. Ashley Cooper, *op. cit.*
18 Prince, *op. cit.*, pp. 13–14.
19 H. Colvin, *Calke Abbey: a Hidden House Revealed* (London, 1985), p. 121.
20 See in particular, H. Repton, *op. cit.*
21 This account of Repton draws heavily on the fascinating work of S. Daniels, 'Humphry Repton and the Politics of Landscape', in J. R. Gould and J. Burgess, *Valued Environments* (London, 1982), pp. 124–44; and 'The Political Landscape' in G. Carter, P. Goode and K. Laurie, *Humphry Repton, Landscape Gardener, 1752–1818* (Norwich, 1982), pp. 110–21.
22 H. Repton, *An Inquiry into the Changes of Taste in Landscape Gardening*, 1806, p. 31.
23 *Letters of Anna Seward, 1784–1807*, 6 vols. (Edinburgh, 1811), iv, pp. 10–11.
24 B. Coates, 'Park Landscapes of the East and West Ridings in the Time of Humphry Repton', *Yorkshire Archaeological Journal* (1965), pp. 465–80.
25 U. Price, *Essay on the Picturesque* (1798), vol. 2, p. 352.

8 Village Architecture and Village Life

1 This section owes a great deal to R. H. Machin, 'The Great Rebuilding: A Reassessment', *Past and Present* 77 (1977), pp. 33–56.
2 E. Mercer, *The English Vernacular House: A Study of Traditional Farmhouses and Cottages* (London, 1979).
3 Mercer, *op. cit.*, pp. 50–9.
4 B. A. Holderness, '"Open" and "Close" Parishes in England in the Eighteenth Century and Nineteenth Century', *Agricultural History Review* 20 (1972), pp. 126–39. D. R. Mills, *Lord and Peasant in Nineteenth Century Britain* (London, 1980).
5 Quoted in B. A. Holderness, *op. cit.*, p. 126.
6 F. Emery, *The Oxfordshire Landscape* (London, 1974), pp. 173–6.
7 E. Marshall, *An Account of the Parish of Sandford* (1866), p. 51.
8 D. Dymond, *The Norfolk Landscape*, p. 245.
9 For a full account of the history of the model village, see G. Darley, *Villages of Vision* (London, 1975). For a more general work on working-class housing see E. Gauldie, *Cruel Habitations: A History of Working Class Housing 1780–1918* (London, 1974).

10 See J.Barrell, *The Dark Side of the Landscape: The Rural Poor in English Painting* (Cambridge, 1980).
11 C.Waistell, *Designs for Agricultural Buildings* (London, 1827), p. 9.
12 Clemenson, *op. cit.*
13 J.M.Robinson, *Georgian Model Farms: A Study of Decorative and Model Farm Buildings in the Age of Improvement 1700–1846* (Oxford, 1983), p. 40.
14 *Ibid.*, p. 31.
15 See *The Gentleman and Farmer's Architect* (London, 1762), plates 24 and 25.

9 Churches and Tombs

1 L.Munby, *The Hertfordshire Landscape*, p. 161.
2 N.Pevsner, *The Buildings of Buckinghamshire* (London, 1960), pp. 287–9.
3 A.Pope, *Epistle to Burlington*, lines 141–50.
4 F.Burgess, *English Churchyard Memorials* (London, 1963).
5 For a detailed discussion of monumental sculpture see K.A.Esdaille, *English Church Monuments 1510–1840* (London, 1946) and B.Kemp, *English Church Monuments* (London, 1980).
6 J.Webster, *The Duchess of Malfi*, act IV, scene 2, lines 155–8.
7 M.Chatfield, *Churches the Victorians Forgot* (Ashbourne, 1979).
8 B.Clarke, *The Building of the Eighteenth Century Church* (London, 1963), p. 28.

10 The Private Landscape

1 M.Hadfield, *Landscape with Trees* (London, 1967), pp. 79–174.
2 W.Marshall, *On Planting and Rural Ornament, A Practical Treatise* (London, 1803), vol. I, p. 47.
3 H.Clemenson, *op. cit.*, p. 76.
4 W.Howitt, *The Rural Life of England* (London, 1844), p. 60.
5 W.Wordsworth, *Guide to the Lakes of Westmoreland and Cumberland* (1810).
6 *Annals of Agriculture* 6 (1786), pp. 175–84; 7 (1786), pp. 20–8; 8 (1787), pp. 89–97, and 9 (1788), pp. 1–15.
7 P.F.Brandon, 'The Diffusion of Designed Landscapes in South East England', in H.S.A.Fox and R.A.Butlin, *Change in the Countryside: Essays on Rural England 1500–1900* (London, 1979), pp. 165–87.
8 M.Reed, *The Georgian Triumph 1700–1830* (London, 1983), p. 192.
9 L.Cresswell, *Eighteen Years on the Sandringham Estate* (London, 1899), p. 64.
10 J.Sheial, *Rabbits and their History* (Newton Abbot, 1971).
11 R.Carr, *English Fox Hunting: A History* (London, 1976).
12 *Ibid.*, p. 70.
13 W.G.Hoskins, *The Making of the English Landscape* (London, 1956), p. 196.
14 J.Patten, 'Fox Coverts for the Squirearchy', *Country Life*, 23 Sept., 1971, pp. 726–40.
15 Sheial, *op. cit.*, p. 142.
16 For further information on this subject see E.P.Thompson, *Whigs and Hunters: The Origins of the Black Acts* (London, 1975).
17 L.Radzinowicz, *Cambridge Law Journal* ix (1945), p. 72.
18 G.E.Mingay, *The Gentry: The Rise and Fall of a Class* (London, 1976), p. 103.
19 Quoted in J.T.Ward, *East Yorkshire Landed Estates in the Nineteenth Century* (York, 1967), p. 7.
20 M.Binney and D.Pearce (eds.), *Railway Architecture* (London, 1979), p. 115.

11 The Modern Landscape: Destruction and Decline

1 J.Blunden and N.Curry, *The Changing Countryside* (London, 1985).
2 For more information on the condition of agriculture and the rural community in the present day, see H.Newby, *Green and Pleasant Land* (London, 1980).
3 J. Bateman, *The Great Landowners of Great Britain and Ireland* (London, 1883; rpt. Leicester, 1971).
4 Clemenson, *op. cit.*, pp. 151–78.
5 M.Shoard, *The Theft of the Countryside* (London, 1980). R.Mabey, *The Common Ground* (London, 1980).
6 N.Fairbrother, *New Lives, New Landscapes* (London, 1872). R.Westmacott and T.Worthington, *New Agricultural Landscapes* (HMSO, 1974).
7 Newby, *op. cit.*, p. 122.

Index

References to illustrations appear in italics.